OpenGL Data Visualization Cookbook

Over 35 hands-on recipes to create impressive, stunning visuals for a wide range of real-time, interactive applications using OpenGL

Raymond C. H. Lo

William C. Y. Lo

BIRMINGHAM - MUMBAI

OpenGL Data Visualization Cookbook

First published: August 2015

Production reference: 1210815

Published by Packt Publishing Ltd.
Livery Place
35 Livery Street
Birmingham B3 2PB, UK.

ISBN 978-1-78216-972-7

www.packtpub.com

Credits

Authors
Raymond C. H. Lo
William C. Y. Lo

Reviewers
Samar Agrawal
Sebastian Eichelbaum
Oscar Ripolles
Qing Zhang

Commissioning Editor
Erol Staveley

Acquisition Editors
Subho Gupta
James Jones

Content Development Editor
Adrian Raposo

Technical Editor
Mohita Vyas

Copy Editor
Stuti Srivastava

Project Coordinator
Kinjal Bari

Proofreader
Safis Editing

Indexer
Tejal Daruwale Soni

Graphics
Sheetal Aute
Jason Monteiro

Production Coordinator
Shantanu N. Zagade

Cover Work
Shantanu N. Zagade

Cover Image
Raymond C. H. Lo
William C. Y. Lo

About the Authors

Raymond C. H. Lo is currently the CTO and cofounder of Meta (`http://www.getameta.com`), a company in Silicon Valley that is creating the world's first augmented reality eyeglasses with 3D gesture input and 3D stereoscopic display. This next-generation wearable computing technology, which is the result of his PhD research, has been featured extensively in news media, including CNN, MIT News, CNET, and *Forbes* magazine. During his PhD, Raymond worked with Professor Steve Mann, who is widely recognized as the *father of wearable computing*. Together, they published and presented papers at leading conferences, including the SIGGRAPH and IEEE conferences, on real-time high-dynamic-range (HDR) imaging, augmented reality, and digital eyeglasses, which involve high-performance computation using CUDA and visualization using OpenGL.

William C. Y. Lo is currently an MD-PhD candidate at Harvard Medical School. He is pursuing his PhD degree in the joint Harvard-MIT Medical Engineering and Medical Physics program under the guidance of Professor Brett Bouma (and co-advisor Professor Benjamin Vakoc) at Massachusetts General Hospital, who founded the NIH-funded Center for Biomedical OCT Research and Translation. He obtained his bachelor of applied science degree in computer engineering and his MSc degree in medical biophysics from the University of Toronto, where he worked with Professor Lothar Lilge and Professor Jonathan Rose on high-performance computing for photodynamic therapy planning using custom FPGA hardware and graphics processors with CUDA.

He, along with J. Rose and L. Lilge, worked on *Computational Acceleration for Medical Treatment Planning: Monte Carlo Simulation of Light Therapies Accelerated using GPUs and FPGAs, VDM Verlag*, 2010.

About the Reviewers

Samar Agrawal is a Python enthusiast with experience in developing large, scalable ERPs, SaaS systems, and other cloud-based live operational systems. In his current organization, he is responsible for the internal operational systems and automation systems. He loved computers from an early age of 6, much before Windows 95 debuted. He values clean code, admires new cutting-edge technologies, and likes taking on complex problems. In his free time, Samar can be found reading, trying new stuff, or exploring new places. He is currently based in Dubai. He holds a master's degree in advanced software engineering from the University of Sheffield, UK, and a bachelor's degree in computer science and engineering.

Sebastian Eichelbaum was born in 1983 in Leipzig, Germany. After school, he studied computer science and got his PhD in 2014. Since he got his first graphical calculator in school, he has enjoyed conducting the pixel's dance programmatically. During his PhD, Sebastian involved himself in the practical use of modern computer graphics (CG) in scientific visualization. He fortified his knowledge of visualization and modern CG technologies, both theoretically and practically. As he collaborated with users, developers, and scientists from different practical and scientific fields, he gained a broad insight into visualization and its tremendous application specificness. The enormous demand for usable and specific visualization tools made Sebastian start his own company. His visualization-centric software, technologies, and knowledge help others better understand and analyze data of all sorts and sources.

Oscar Ripolles received his degree in computer engineering in 2004 and his PhD in 2009 from Universitat Jaume I in Castellon, Spain. He was also a researcher at Université de Limoges, France, and Universidad Politecnica de Valencia, Spain. He is currently working in neuroimaging at Neuroelectrics in Barcelona, Spain. His research interests include multiresolution modeling, geometry optimization, hardware programming, and medical imaging. Some of the books he has worked on are *OpenGL Development Cookbook* and *GLSL Essentials*.

I would like to thank my other half, Anna, for her patience and support during the nights and weekends I spent reviewing this book.

Qing Zhang is currently a PhD candidate in the Department of Computer Science at the University of Kentucky, working with Professor Ruigang Yang. He obtained his bachelor of science degree in computer science from Tsinghua University in 2006 and his MS degree in mathematics from the University of Kentucky in 2010. His research interests span computer graphics and computer vision, in particular, human reconstruction and motion analysis. He was a research intern in the communication and collaboration systems group Microsoft Research (MSR) in 2008, and in the visual computing group Microsoft Research Asia (MSRA) in 2010. He is currently a reviewer on IEEE CVPR, ICCV, and TPAMI.

www.PacktPub.com

Support files, eBooks, discount offers, and more

For support files and downloads related to your book, please visit www.PacktPub.com.

Did you know that Packt offers eBook versions of every book published, with PDF and ePub files available? You can upgrade to the eBook version at www.PacktPub.com and as a print book customer, you are entitled to a discount on the eBook copy. Get in touch with us at service@packtpub.com for more details.

At www.PacktPub.com, you can also read a collection of free technical articles, sign up for a range of free newsletters and receive exclusive discounts and offers on Packt books and eBooks.

https://www2.packtpub.com/books/subscription/packtlib

Do you need instant solutions to your IT questions? PacktLib is Packt's online digital book library. Here, you can search, access, and read Packt's entire library of books.

Why Subscribe?

- Fully searchable across every book published by Packt
- Copy and paste, print, and bookmark content
- On demand and accessible via a web browser

Free Access for Packt account holders

If you have an account with Packt at www.PacktPub.com, you can use this to access PacktLib today and view 9 entirely free books. Simply use your login credentials for immediate access.

Table of Contents

Preface

OpenGL is a multiplatform, cross-language, and hardware-accelerated application programming interface for the high-performance rendering of 2D and 3D graphics. An emerging use of OpenGL is the development of real-time, high-performance data visualization applications in fields ranging from medical imaging, simulation or modeling in architecture and engineering, to cutting-edge mobile/wearable computing. Indeed, data visualization has become increasingly challenging using conventional approaches without graphics hardware acceleration as datasets become larger and more complex, especially with the evolution of big data. From a mobile device to a sophisticated high-performance computing cluster, the OpenGL libraries provide developers with an easy-to-use interface to create stunning visuals in 3D in real time for a wide range of interactive applications.

This book contains a series of hands-on recipes that are tailored to both beginners who have very little experience with OpenGL and more advanced users who would like to explore state-of-the-art techniques. We begin with a basic introduction to OpenGL in chapters 1 to 3 by demonstrating how to set up the environment in Windows, Mac OS X, and Linux and learning how to render basic 2D datasets with primitives, as well as more complex 3D volumetric datasets interactively. This part requires only OpenGL 2.0 or higher so that even readers with older graphics hardware can experiment with the code. In chapters 4 to 6, we transition to more advanced techniques (which requires OpenGL 3.2 or higher), such as texture mapping for image/video processing, point cloud rendering of depth sensor data from 3D range-sensing cameras, and stereoscopic 3D rendering. Finally, in chapters 7 to 9, we conclude this book by introducing the use of OpenGL ES 3.0 on the increasingly powerful mobile (Android-based) computing platform and the development of highly interactive, augmented reality applications on mobile devices.

Each recipe in this book gives readers a set of standard functions that can be imported to an existing project and can form the basis for the creation of a diverse array of real-time, interactive data visualization applications. This book also utilizes a set of popular open-source libraries, such as GLFW, GLM, Assimp, and OpenCV, to simplify application development and extend the capabilities of OpenGL by enabling OpenGL context management and 3D model loading, as well as image/video processing using state-of-the-art computer vision algorithms.

What this book covers

Chapter 1, Getting Started with OpenGL, introduces the essential development tools required to create OpenGL-based data visualization applications and provides a step-by-step tutorial on how to set up the environment for our first OpenGL demo application in Windows, Mac OS X, and Linux.

Chapter 2, OpenGL Primitives and 2D Data Visualization, focuses on the use of OpenGL 2.0 primitives, such as points, lines, and triangles, to enable the basic 2D visualization of data, including time series such as an electrocardiogram (ECG).

Chapter 3, Interactive 3D Data Visualization, builds upon the fundamental concepts discussed previously and extends the demos to incorporate more sophisticated OpenGL features for 3D rendering.

Chapter 4, Rendering 2D Images and Videos with Texture Mapping, introduces OpenGL techniques to visualize another important class of datasets—those involving images or vidcos. Such datasets are commonly encountered in many fields, including medical imaging applications.

Chapter 5, Rendering of Point Cloud Data for 3D Range-sensing Cameras, introduces the techniques used to visualize another interesting and emerging class of data—depth information from 3D range sensing cameras.

Chapter 6, Rendering Stereoscopic 3D Models using OpenGL, demonstrates how to visualize data with stunning stereoscopic 3D technology using OpenGL. OpenGL does not provide any mechanism to load, save, or manipulate 3D models. Thus, to support this, we will integrate a new library named Assimp into our code.

Chapter 7, An Introduction to Real-time Graphics Rendering on a Mobile Platform using OpenGL ES 3.0, transitions to an increasingly powerful and ubiquitous computing platform by demonstrating how to set up the Android development environment and create the first Android-based application on the latest mobile devices, from smartphones to tablets, using OpenGL for Embedded Systems (OpenGL ES).

Chapter 8, Interactive Real-time Data Visualization on Mobile Devices, demonstrates how to visualize data interactively by using built-in motion sensors called Inertial Measurement Units (IMUs) and the multitouch interface found on mobile devices.

Chapter 9, Augmented Reality-based Visualization on Mobile or Wearable Platforms, introduces the fundamental building blocks required to create your first AR-based application on a commodity Android-based mobile device: OpenCV for computer vision, OpenGL for graphics rendering, as well as Android's sensor framework for interaction.

What you need for this book

This book supports a wide range of platforms and open source libraries, ranging from Windows, Mac OS X, or Linux-based desktop applications to portable Android-based mobile applications. You will need a basic understanding of C/C++ programming and background in basic linear algebra for geometric models.

The following are the requirements for chapters 1 to 3:

- **OpenGL version**: 2.0 or higher (easy to test on legacy graphics hardware).
- **Platforms**: Windows, Mac OS X, or Linux.
- **Libraries**: GLFW for OpenGL Windows/context management and handling user inputs. No additional libraries are needed, which makes it very easy to integrate into existing projects.
- **Development tools**: Windows Visual Studio or Xcode, CMake, and gcc.

The following are the requirements for chapters 4 to 6:

- **OpenGL version**: 3.2 or higher.
- **Platforms**: Windows, Mac OS X, or Linux.
- **Libraries**: Assimp for 3D model loading, SOIL for image and texture loading, GLEW for runtime OpenGL extension support, GLM for matrix operations, and OpenCV for image processing
- **Development tools**: Windows Visual Studio or Xcode, CMake, and gcc.

The following are the requirements for chapters 7 to 9:

- **OpenGL version**: OpenGL ES 3.0
- **Platforms**: Linux or Mac OS X for development, and Android OS 4.3 and higher (API 18 and higher) for deployment
- **Libraries**: OpenCV for Android and GLM
- **Development tools**: Android SDK, Android NDK, and Apache Ant in Mac OS X or Linux

For more information, keep in mind that the code in this book was built and tested with the following libraries and development tools in all supported platforms:

- OpenCV 2.4.9 (`http://opencv.org/downloads.html`)
- OpenCV 3.0.0 for Android (`http://opencv.org/downloads.html`)
- SOIL (`http://www.lonesock.net/soil.html`)
- GLEW 1.12.0 (`http://glew.sourceforge.net/`)
- GLFW 3.0.4 (`http://www.glfw.org/download.html`)

- GLM 0.9.5.4 (`http://glm.g-truc.net/0.9.5/index.html`)
- Assimp 3.0 (`http://assimp.sourceforge.net/main_downloads.html`)
- Android SDK r24.3.3 (`https://developer.android.com/sdk/index.html`)
- Android NDK r10e (`https://developer.android.com/ndk/downloads/index.html`)
- Windows Visual Studio 2013 (`https://www.visualstudio.com/en-us/downloads/download-visual-studio-vs.aspx`)
- CMake 3.2.1 (`http://www.cmake.org/download/`)

Who this book is for

This book is aimed at anyone interested in creating impressive data visualization tools using modern graphics hardware. Whether you are a developer, engineer, or scientist, if you are interested in exploring the power of OpenGL for data visualization, this book is for you. While familiarity with C/C++ is recommended, no previous experience with OpenGL is assumed.

Sections

In this book, you will find several headings that appear frequently (Getting ready, How to do it, How it works, There's more, and See also).

To give clear instructions on how to complete a recipe, we use these sections as follows:

Getting ready

This section tells you what to expect in the recipe, and describes how to set up any software or any preliminary settings required for the recipe.

How to do it...

This section contains the steps required to follow the recipe.

How it works...

This section usually consists of a detailed explanation of what happened in the previous section.

There's more...

This section consists of additional information about the recipe in order to make the reader more knowledgeable about the recipe.

See also

This section provides helpful links to other useful information for the recipe.

Conventions

In this book, you will find a number of text styles that distinguish between different kinds of information. Here are some examples of these styles and an explanation of their meaning.

Code words in text, database table names, folder names, filenames, file extensions, pathnames, dummy URLs, user input, and Twitter handles are shown as follows: "We assume that all files are saved to a top-level directory called `code` and the `main.cpp` file is saved inside the `/code/Tutorial1` subdirectory."

A block of code is set as follows:

```
typedef struct
{
  GLfloat x, y, z;
} Data;
```

Any command-line input or output is written as follows:

```
sudo port install glfw
```

New terms and **important words** are shown in bold. Words that you see on the screen, for example, in menus or dialog boxes, appear in the text like this: "Check the **Empty project** option, and click on **Finish**."

Warnings or important notes appear in a box like this.

Tips and tricks appear like this.

Reader feedback

Feedback from our readers is always welcome. Let us know what you think about this book—what you liked or disliked. Reader feedback is important for us as it helps us develop titles that you will really get the most out of.

To send us general feedback, simply e-mail `feedback@packtpub.com`, and mention the book's title in the subject of your message.

If there is a topic that you have expertise in and you are interested in either writing or contributing to a book, see our author guide at `www.packtpub.com/authors`.

Customer support

Now that you are the proud owner of a Packt book, we have a number of things to help you to get the most from your purchase.

Downloading the example code

You can download the example code files from your account at `http://www.packtpub.com` for all the Packt Publishing books you have purchased. If you purchased this book elsewhere, you can visit `http://www.packtpub.com/support` and register to have the files e-mailed directly to you.

Downloading the color images of this book

We also provide you with a PDF file that has color images of the screenshots/diagrams used in this book. The color images will help you better understand the changes in the output. You can download this file from: `https://www.packtpub.com/sites/default/files/downloads/9727OS.pdf`.

Errata

Although we have taken every care to ensure the accuracy of our content, mistakes do happen. If you find a mistake in one of our books—maybe a mistake in the text or the code—we would be grateful if you could report this to us. By doing so, you can save other readers from frustration and help us improve subsequent versions of this book. If you find any errata, please report them by visiting `http://www.packtpub.com/submit-errata`, selecting your book, clicking on the **Errata Submission Form** link, and entering the details of your errata. Once your errata are verified, your submission will be accepted and the errata will be uploaded to our website or added to any list of existing errata under the Errata section of that title.

To view the previously submitted errata, go to `https://www.packtpub.com/books/content/support` and enter the name of the book in the search field. The required information will appear under the **Errata** section.

Piracy

Piracy of copyrighted material on the Internet is an ongoing problem across all media. At Packt, we take the protection of our copyright and licenses very seriously. If you come across any illegal copies of our works in any form on the Internet, please provide us with the location address or website name immediately so that we can pursue a remedy.

Please contact us at `copyright@packtpub.com` with a link to the suspected pirated material.

We appreciate your help in protecting our authors and our ability to bring you valuable content.

Questions

If you have a problem with any aspect of this book, you can contact us at `questions@packtpub.com`, and we will do our best to address the problem.

1
Getting Started with OpenGL

In this chapter, we will cover the following topics:

- Setting up a Windows-based development platform
- Setting up a Mac-based development platform
- Setting up a Linux-based development platform
- Installing the GLFW library in Windows
- Installing the GLFW library in Mac OS X and Linux
- Creating your first OpenGL application with GLFW
- Compiling and running your first OpenGL application in Windows
- Compiling and running your first OpenGL application in Mac OS X or Linux

Introduction

OpenGL is an ideal multiplatform, cross-language, and hardware-accelerated graphics rendering interface that is well suited to visualize large 2D and 3D datasets in many fields. In fact, OpenGL has become the industry standard to create stunning graphics, most notably in gaming applications and numerous professional tools for 3D modeling. As we collect more and more data in fields ranging from biomedical imaging to wearable computing (especially with the evolution of Big Data), a high-performance platform for data visualization is becoming an essential component of many future applications. Indeed, the visualization of massive datasets is becoming an increasingly challenging problem for developers, scientists, and engineers in many fields. Therefore, OpenGL can provide a unified solution for the creation of impressive, stunning visuals in many real-time applications.

The APIs of OpenGL encapsulate the complexity of hardware interactions while allowing users to have low-level control over the process. From a sophisticated multiserver setup to a mobile device, OpenGL libraries provide developers with an easy-to-use interface for high-performance graphics rendering. The increasing availability and capability of graphics hardware and mass storage devices, coupled with their decreasing cost, further motivate the development of interactive OpenGL-based data visualization tools.

Modern computers come with dedicated **Graphics Processing Units** (**GPUs**), highly customized pieces of hardware designed to accelerate graphics rendering. GPUs can also be used to accelerate general-purpose, highly parallelizable computational tasks. By leveraging hardware and OpenGL, we can produce highly interactive and aesthetically pleasing results.

This chapter introduces the essential tools to develop OpenGL-based data visualization applications and provides a step-by-step tutorial on how to set up the environment for our first demo application. In addition, this chapter outlines the steps to set up a popular tool called CMake, which is a cross-platform software that automates the process of generating standard build files (for example, makefiles in Linux that define the compilation parameters and commands) with simple configuration files. The CMake tool will be used to compile additional libraries in the future, including the GLFW (OpenGL FrameWork) library introduced later in this chapter. Briefly, the GLFW library is an open source, multiplatform library that allows users to create and manage windows with OpenGL contexts as well as handle inputs from peripheral devices such as the mouse and keyboard. By default, OpenGL itself does not support other peripherals; thus, the GLFW library is used to fill in the gap. We hope that this detailed tutorial will be especially useful for beginners who are interested in exploring OpenGL for data visualization but have little or no prior experience. However, we will assume that you are familiar with the C/C++ programming language.

Setting up a Windows-based development platform

There are various development tools available to create applications in the Windows environment. In this book, we will focus on creating OpenGL applications using Visual C++ from Microsoft Visual Studio 2013, given its extensive documentation and support.

Installing Visual Studio 2013

In this section, we outline the steps to install Visual Studio 2013.

Getting ready

We assume that you have already installed Windows 7.0 or higher. For optimal performance, we recommend that you get a dedicated graphics card, such as NVIDIA GeForce graphics cards, and have at least 10 GB of free disk space as well as 4 GB of RAM on your computer. Download and install the latest driver for your graphics card.

How to do it...

To install Microsoft Visual Studio 2013 for free, download the Express 2013 version for Windows Desktop from Microsoft's official website (refer to `https://www.visualstudio.com/en-us/downloads/`). Once you have downloaded the installer executable, we can start the process. By default, we will assume that programs are installed in the following path:

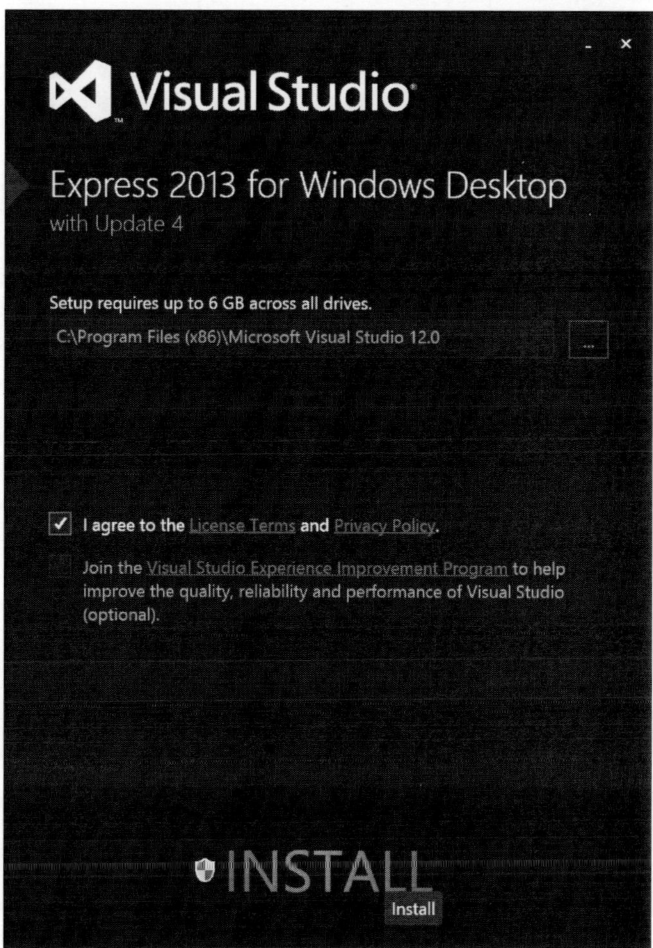

To verify the installation, click on the **Launch** button at the end of the installation, and it will execute the VS Express 2013 for Desktop application for the first time.

Installing CMake in Windows

In this section, we outline the steps to install CMake, which is a popular tool that automates the process of creating standard build files for Visual Studio (among other tools).

Getting ready

To obtain the CMake tool (CMake 3.2.1), you can download the executable (`cmake-3.2.1-win32-x86.exe`) from `http://www.cmake.org/download/`.

How to do it...

The installation wizard will guide you through the process (select **Add CMake to the system PATH for all users** when prompted for installation options). To verify the installation, run CMake(`cmake-gui`).

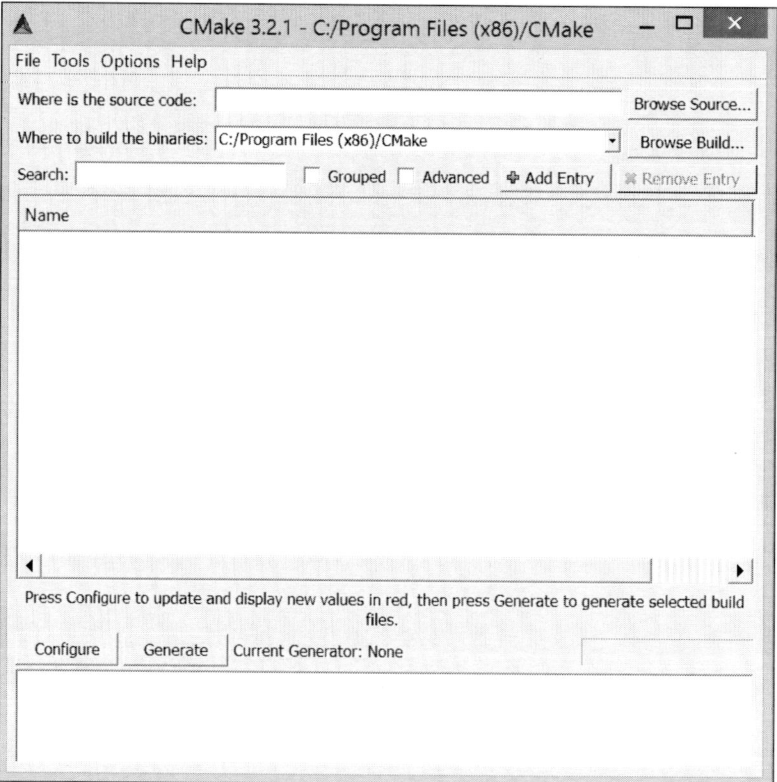

At this point, you should have both Visual Studio 2013 and CMake successfully installed on your machine and be ready to compile/install the GLFW library to create your first OpenGL application.

Setting up a Mac-based development platform

One important advantage of using OpenGL is the possibility of cross-compiling the same source code on different platforms. If you are planning to develop your application on a Mac platform, you can easily set up your machine for development using the upcoming steps. We assume that you have either Mac OS X 10.9 or higher installed. OpenGL updates are integrated into the system updates for Mac OS X through the graphics driver.

Installing Xcode and command-line tools

The Xcode development software from Apple provides developers with a comprehensive set of tools, which include an IDE, OpenGL headers, compilers, and debugging tools, to create native Mac applications. To simplify the process, we will compile our code using the command-line interface that shares most of the common features in Linux.

Getting ready

If you are using Mac OS X 10.9 or higher, you can download Xcode through the App Store shipped with Mac OS. Full installation support and instructions are available on the Apple Developer website (`https://developer.apple.com/xcode/`).

How to do it...

We can install the command-line tools in Xcode through the following steps:

1. Search for the keyword `Terminal` in **Spotlight** and run **Terminal**.

2. Execute the following command in the terminal:

```
xcode-select --install
```

   Note that if you have previously installed the command-line tools, an error stating "command-line are already installed" will appear. In this case, simply skip to step 4 to verify the installation.

3. Click on the **Install** button to directly install the command-line tools. This will install basic compiling tools such as **gcc** and **make** for application development purposes (note that CMake needs to be installed separately).
4. Finally, enter `gcc --version` to verify the installation.

```
Configured with: --prefix=/Applications/Xcode.app/Contents/Developer/usr --with-gxx
-include-dir=/usr/include/c++/4.2.1
Apple LLVM version 6.0 (clang-600.0.57) (based on LLVM 3.5svn)
Target: x86_64-apple-darwin14.1.0
Thread model: posix
```

See also

If you encounter the **command not found** error or other similar issues, make sure that the command-line tools are installed successfully. Apple provides an extensive set of documentation, and more information on installing Xcode can be found at `https://developer.apple.com/xcode`.

Installing MacPorts and CMake

In this section, we outline the steps to install MacPorts, which greatly simplifies the subsequent setup steps, and CMake for Mac.

Getting ready

Similar to the Windows installation, you can download the binary distribution of **CMake** from `http://www.cmake.org/cmake/resources/software.html` and manually configure the command-line options. However, to simplify the installation and automate the configuration process, we highly recommend that you use MacPorts.

How to do it...

To install MacPorts, follow these steps:

1. Download the MacPorts package installer for the corresponding version of Mac OS X (`https://guide.macports.org/#installing.macports`):
    - Mac OS X 10.10 Yosemite: `https://distfiles.macports.org/MacPorts/MacPorts-2.3.3-10.10-Yosemite.pkg`
    - Mac OS X 10.9 Mavericks: `https://distfiles.macports.org/MacPorts/MacPorts-2.3.3-10.9-Mavericks.pkg`
2. Double-click on the package installer and follow the onscreen instructions.

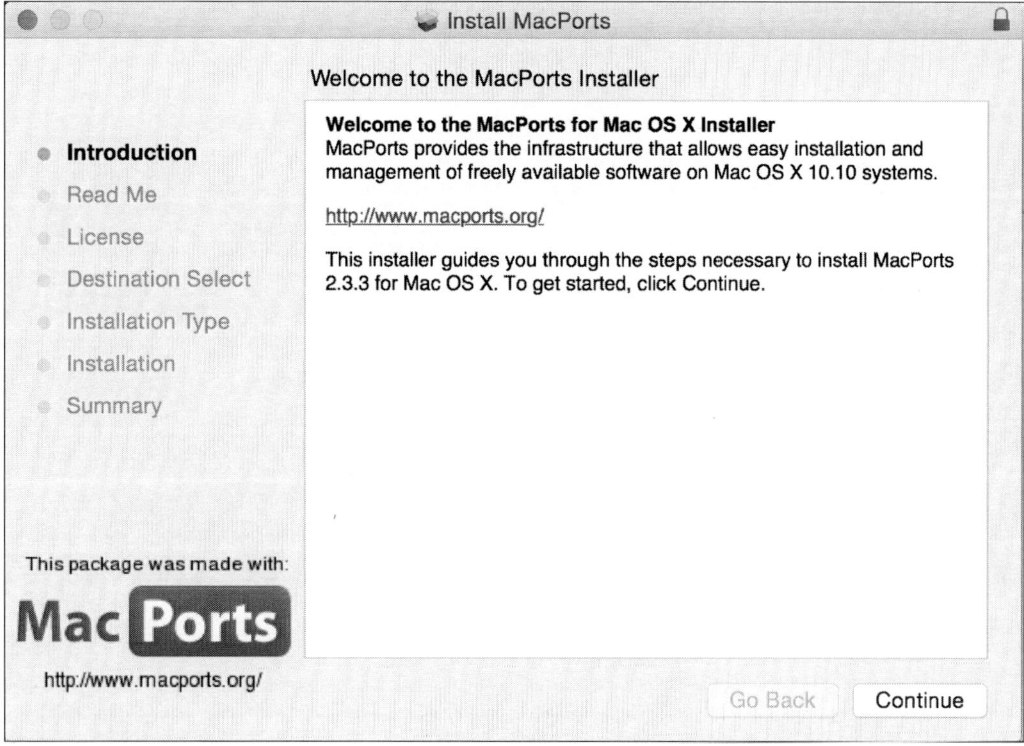

3. Verify the installation in the terminal by typing in `port version`, which returns the version of MacPorts currently installed (`Version: 2.3.3` in the preceding package).

To install **CMake** on Mac, follow these steps:

1. Open the **Terminal** application.
2. Execute the following command:

```
sudo port install cmake +gui
```

To verify the installation, enter `cmake -version` to show the current version installed and enter `cmake-gui` to explore the GUI.

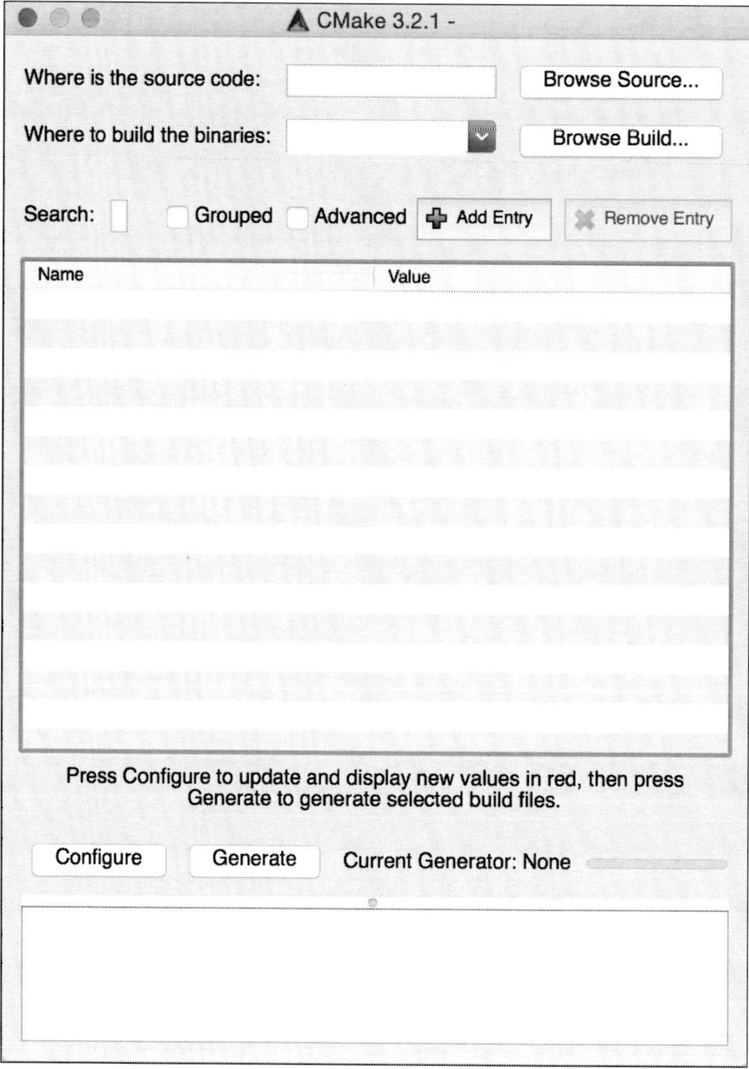

At this point, your Mac is configured for OpenGL development and is ready to compile your first OpenGL application. For those who have been more accustomed to GUIs, using the command-line interface in Mac can initially be an overwhelming experience. However, in the long run, it is a rewarding learning experience due to its overall simplicity. Command-line tools and interfaces are often more time-invariant compared to constantly evolving GUIs. At the end of the day, you can just copy and paste the same command lines, thereby saving precious time needed to consult new documentation every time a GUI changes.

Setting up a Linux-based development platform

To prepare your development environment on the Linux platform, we can utilize the powerful Debian Package Management system. The `apt-get` or `aptitude` program automatically retrieves the precompiled packages from the server and also resolves and installs all dependent packages that are required. If you are using non-Debian based platform, such as Fedora, you can find the equivalents by searching for the keywords of each packages listed in this recipe.

Getting ready

We assume that you have successfully installed all updates and latest graphics drivers associated with your graphics hardware. Ubuntu 12.04 or higher has support for third-party proprietary NVIDIA and AMD graphics drivers, and more information can be found at `https://help.ubuntu.com/community/BinaryDriverHowto`.

How to do it...

Use the following steps to install all development tools and the associated dependencies:

1. Open a terminal.
2. Enter the update command:
   ```
   sudo apt-get update
   ```
3. Enter the install command and enter `y` for all prompts:
   ```
   sudo apt-get install build-essential cmake-gui xorg-dev
   libglu1-mesa-dev mesa-utils
   ```
4. Verify the results:
   ```
   gcc --version
   ```
   If successful, this command should return the current version of `gcc` installed.

How it works...

In summary, the `apt-get update` command automatically updates the local database in the Debian Package Management system. This ensures that the latest packages are retrieved and installed in the process. The `apt-get` system also provides other package management features, such as package removal (uninstall), dependency retrieval, as well as package upgrades. These advanced functions are outside the scope of this book, but more information can be found at `https://wiki.debian.org/apt-get`.

The preceding commands install a number of packages to your machine. Here, we will briefly explain the purpose of each package.

The `build-essential` package, as the name itself suggests, encapsulates the essential packages, namely gcc and g++, that are required to compile C and C++ source code in Linux. Additionally, it will download header files and resolve all dependencies in the process.

The `cmake-gui` package is the CMake program described earlier in the chapter. Instead of downloading CMake directly from the website and compiling from the source, it retrieves the latest supported version that had been compiled, tested, and released by the Ubuntu community. One advantage of using the Debian Package Management system is the stability and ease of updating in the future. However, for users who are looking for the cutting-edge version, apt-get based systems would be a few versions behind.

The `xorg-dev` and `libglu1-mesa-dev` packages are the development files required to compile the GLFW library. These packages include header files and libraries required by other programs. If you choose to use the precompiled binary version of GLFW, you may be able to skip some of the packages. However, we highly recommend that you follow the steps for the purpose of this tutorial.

See also

For more information, most of the steps described are documented and explained in depth in this online documentation: `https://help.ubuntu.com/community/UsingTheTerminal`.

Installing the GLFW library in Windows

There are two ways to install the GLFW library in Windows, both of which will be discussed in this section. The first approach involves compiling the GLFW source code directly with CMake for full control. However, to simplify the process, we suggest that you download the precompiled binary distribution.

Getting ready

We assume that you have successfully installed both Visual Studio 2013 and CMake, as described in the earlier section. For completeness, we will demonstrate how to install GLFW using CMake.

How to do it...

To use the precompiled binary package for GLFW, follow these steps:

1. Create the `C:/Program Files (x86)/glfw-3.0.4` directory. Grant the necessary permissions when prompted.
2. Download the `glfw-3.0.4.bin.WIN32.zip` package from `http://sourceforge.net/projects/glfw/files/glfw/3.0.4/glfw-3.0.4.bin.WIN32.zip` and unzip the package.
3. Copy all the extracted content inside the `glfw-3.0.4.bin.WIN32` folder (for example, include `lib-msvc2012`) into the `C:/Program Files (x86)/glfw-3.0.4` directory. Grant permissions when prompted.
4. Rename the `lib-msvc2012` folder to `lib` inside the `C:/Program Files (x86)/glfw-3.0.4` directory. Grant permissions when prompted.

Alternatively, to compile the source files directly, follow these procedures:

1. Download the source package from `http://sourceforge.net/projects/glfw/files/glfw/3.0.4/glfw-3.0.4.zip` and unzip the package on the desktop. Create a new folder called `build` inside the extracted `glfw-3.0.4` folder to store the binaries.and open `cmake-gui`.
2. Select `glfw-3.0.4` (from the desktop) as the source directory and `glfw-3.0.4/build` as the build directory. The screenshot is shown as follows:

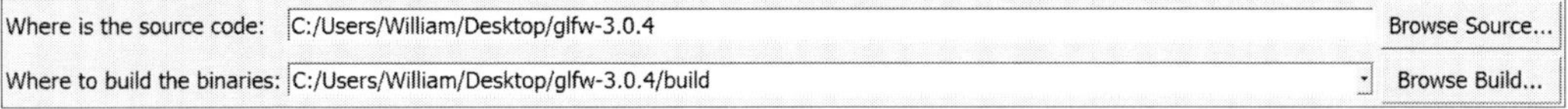

3. Click on **Generate** and select **Visual Studio 12 2013** in the prompt.

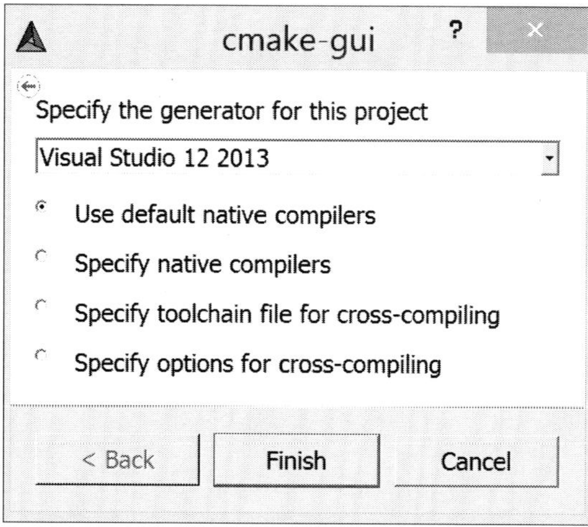

4. Click on **Generate** again.

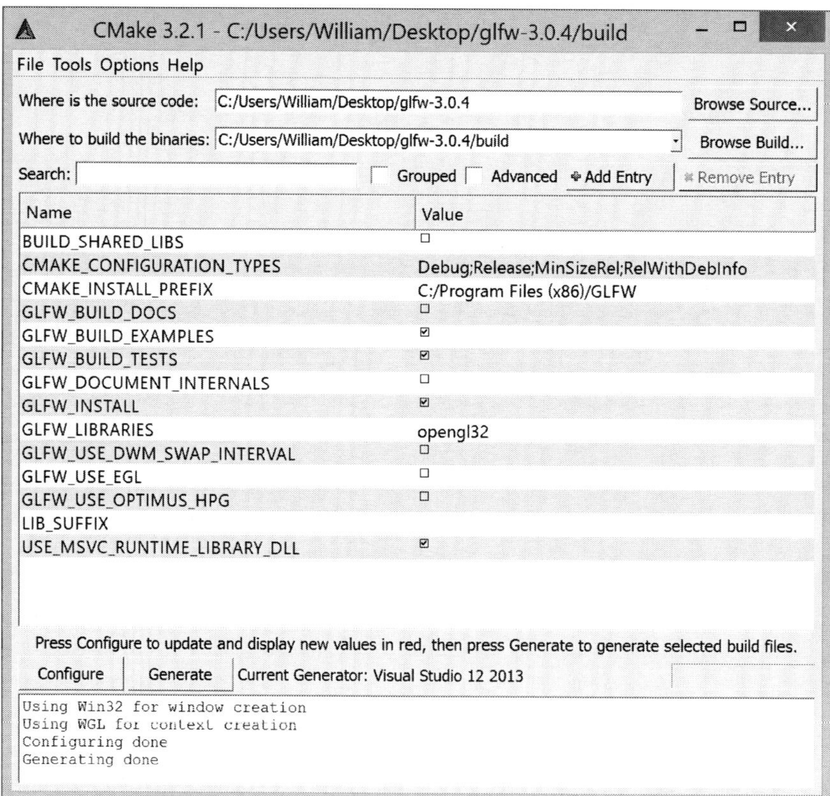

5. Open the `build` directory and double-click on **GLFW.sln** to open Visual Studio.
6. In Visual Studio, click Build Solution (press *F7*).
7. Copy **build/src/Debug/glfw3.lib** to **C:/Program Files (x86)/glfw-3.0.4/lib**.
8. Copy the `include` directory (inside `glfw-3.0.4/include`) to **C:/Program Files (x86)/glfw-3.0.4/**.

After this step, we should have the `include (glfw3.h)` and `library` (`glfw3.lib`) files inside the `C:/Program Files (x86)/glfw-3.0.4` directory, as shown in the setup procedure using precompiled binaries.

Installing the GLFW library in Mac OS X and Linux

The installation procedures for Mac and Linux are essentially identical using the command-line interface. To simplify the process, we recommend that you use MacPorts for Mac users.

Getting ready

We assume that you have successfully installed the basic development tools, including CMake, as described in the earlier section. For maximum flexibility, we can compile the library directly from the source code (refer to `http://www.glfw.org/docs/latest/compile.html` and `http://www.glfw.org/download.html`).

How to do it...

For Mac users, enter the following command in a terminal to install GLFW using MacPorts:

```
sudo port install glfw
```

For Linux users (or Mac users who would like to practice using the command-line tools), here are the steps to compile and install the GLFW source package directly with the command-line interface:

1. Create a new folder called `opengl_dev` and change the current directory to the new path:

   ```
   mkdir ~/opengl_dev
   cd ~/opengl_dev
   ```

2. Obtain a copy of the GLFW source package (`glfw-3.0.4`) from the official repository: `http://sourceforge.net/projects/glfw/files/glfw/3.0.4/glfw-3.0.4.tar.gz`.

3. Extract the package.

```
tar xzvf glfw-3.0.4.tar.gz
```

4. Perform the compilation and installation:

```
cd glfw-3.0.4
mkdir build
cd build
cmake ../
make && sudo make install
```

How it works...

The first set of commands create a new working directory to store the new files retrieved using the `wget` command, which downloads a copy of the GLFW library to the current directory. The `tar xzvf` command extracts the compressed packages and creates a new folder with all the contents.

Then, the `cmake` command automatically generates the necessary build files that are needed for the compilation process to the current `build` directory. This process also checks for missing dependencies and verifies the versioning of the applications.

The `make` command then takes all instructions from the Makefile script that is generated automatically and compiles the source code into libraries.

The `sudo make install` command installs the library header files as well as the static or shared libraries onto your machine. As this command requires writing to the root directory, the `sudo` command is needed to grant such permissions. By default, the files will be copied to the `/usr/local` directory. In the rest of the book, we will assume that the installations follow these default paths.

For advanced users, we can optimize the compilation by configuring the packages with the CMake GUI (`cmake-gui`).

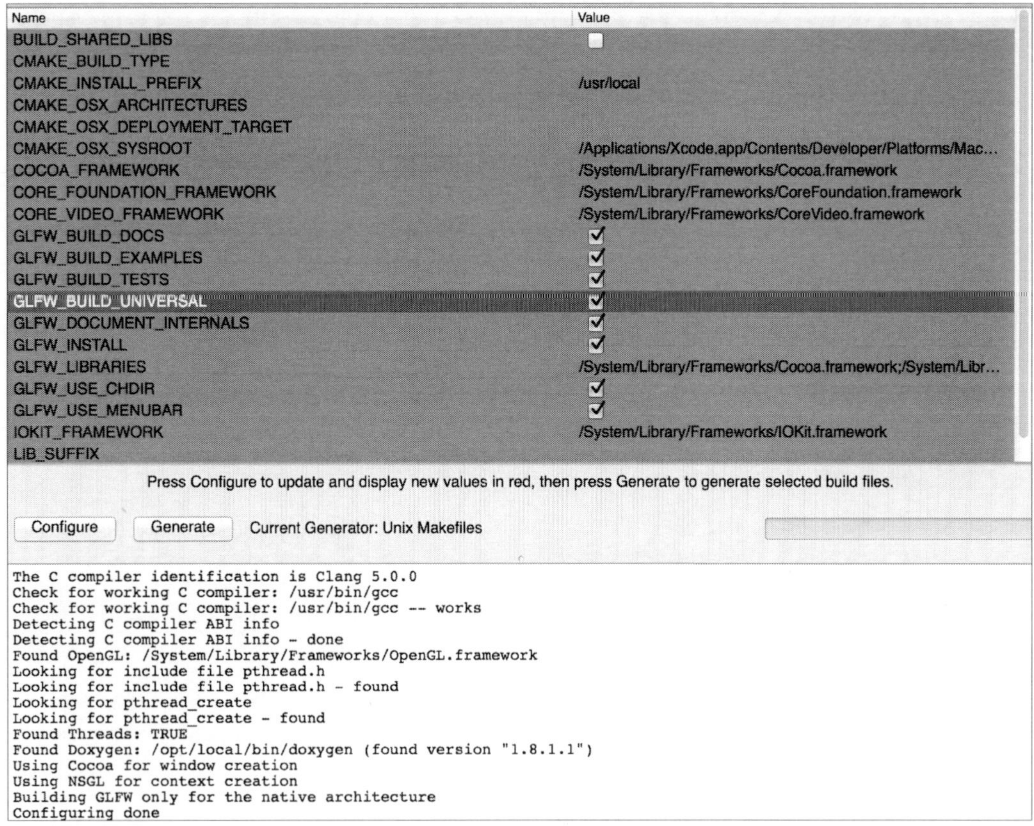

For example, you can enable the `BUILD_SHARED_LIBS` option if you are planning to compile the GLFW library as a shared library. In this book, we will not explore the full functionality of the GLFW library, but these options can be useful to developers who are looking for further customizations. Additionally, you can customize the installation prefix (`CMAKE_INSTALL_PREFIX`) if you would like to install the library files at a separate location.

Creating your first OpenGL application with GLFW

Now that you have successfully configured your development platform and installed the GLFW library, we will provide a tutorial on how to create your first OpenGL-based application.

Getting ready

At this point, you should already have all the pre requisite tools ready regardless of which operating system you may have, so we will immediately jump into building your first OpenGL application using these tools.

How to do it...

The following code outlines the basic steps to create a simple OpenGL program that utilizes the GLFW library and draws a rotating triangle:

1. Create an empty file, and then include the header file for the GLFW library and standard C++ libraries:

   ```
   #include <GLFW/glfw3.h>
   #include <stdlib.h>
   #include <stdio.h>
   ```

2. Initialize GLFW and create a GLFW window object (640 x 480):

   ```
   int main(void)
   {
     GLFWwindow* window;
     if (!glfwInit())
       exit(EXIT_FAILURE);
     window = glfwCreateWindow(640, 480, "Chapter 1: Simple
       GLFW Example", NULL, NULL);
     if (!window)
     {
       glfwTerminate();
       exit(EXIT_FAILURE);
     }
     glfwMakeContextCurrent(window);
   ```

3. Define a loop that terminates when the window is closed:

   ```
     while (!glfwWindowShouldClose(window))
     {
   ```

4. Set up the viewport (using the width and height of the window) and clear the screen color buffer:

```
float ratio;
int width, height;

glfwGetFramebufferSize(window, &width, &height);
ratio = (float) width / (float) height;

glViewport(0, 0, width, height);
glClear(GL_COLOR_BUFFER_BIT);
```

5. Set up the camera matrix. Note that further details on the camera model will be discussed in *Chapter 3, Interactive 3D Data Visualization*:

```
glMatrixMode(GL_PROJECTION);
glLoadIdentity();
glOrtho(-ratio, ratio, -1.f, 1.f, 1.f, -1.f);
glMatrixMode(GL_MODELVIEW);
glLoadIdentity();
```

6. Draw a rotating triangle and set a different color (red, green, and blue channels) for each vertex (*x*, *y*, and *z*) of the triangle. The first line rotates the triangle over time:

```
glRotatef((float)glfwGetTime() * 50.f, 0.f, 0.f, 1.f);
glBegin(GL_TRIANGLES);
glColor3f(1.f, 0.f, 0.f);
glVertex3f(-0.6f, -0.4f, 0.f);
glColor3f(0.f, 1.f, 0.f);
glVertex3f(0.6f, -0.4f, 0.f);
glColor3f(0.f, 0.f, 1.f);
glVertex3f(0.f, 0.6f, 0.f);
glEnd();
```

7. Swap the front and back buffers (GLFW uses double buffering) to update the screen and process all pending events:

```
    glfwSwapBuffers(window);
    glfwPollEvents();
  }
```

8. Release the memory and terminate the GLFW library. Then, exit the application:

```
  glfwDestroyWindow(window);
  glfwTerminate();
  exit(EXIT_SUCCESS);
}
```

9. Save the file as `main.cpp` using the text editor of your choice.

How it works...

By including the GLFW library header, `glfw3.h`, we automatically import all necessary files from the OpenGL library. Most importantly, GLFW automatically determines the platform and thus allows you to write portable source code seamlessly.

In the main function, we must first initialize the GLFW library with the **`glfwInit`** function in the main thread. This is required before any GLFW functions can be used. Before a program exits, GLFW should be terminated to release any allocated resources.

Then, the **`glfwCreateWindow`** function creates a window and its associated context, and it also returns a pointer to the `GLFWwindow` object. Here, we can define the width, height, title, and other properties for the window. After the window is created, we then call the **`glfwMakeContextCurrent`** function to switch the context and make sure that the context of the specified window is current on the calling thread.

At this point, we are ready to render our graphics element on the window. The **`while`** loop provides a mechanism to redraw our graphics as long as the window remains open. OpenGL requires an explicit setup on the camera parameters; further details will be discussed in the upcoming chapters. In the future, we can provide different parameters to simulate perspective and also handle more complicated issues (such as anti-aliasing). For now, we have set up a simple scene to render a basic primitive shape (namely a triangle) and fixed the color for the vertices. Users can modify the parameters in the **`glColor3f`** and **`glVertex3f`** functions to change the color as well as the position of the vertices.

This example demonstrates the basics required to create graphics using OpenGL. Despite the simplicity of the sample code, it provides a nice introductory framework on how you can create high-performance graphics rendering applications with graphics hardware using OpenGL and GLFW.

Compiling and running your first OpenGL application in Windows

There are several ways to set up an OpenGL project. Here, we create a sample project using Visual Studio 2013 or higher and provide a complete walkthrough for the first-time configuration of the OpenGL and GLFW libraries. These same steps can be incorporated into your own projects in the future.

Getting ready

Assuming that you have both Visual Studio 2013 and GLFW (version 3.0.4) installed successfully on your environment, we will start our project from scratch.

How to do it...

In Visual Studio 2013, use the following steps to create a new project and compile the source code:

1. Open Visual Studio 2013 (VS Express 2013 for desktop).
2. Create a new Win32 Console Application and name it as `Tutorial1`.

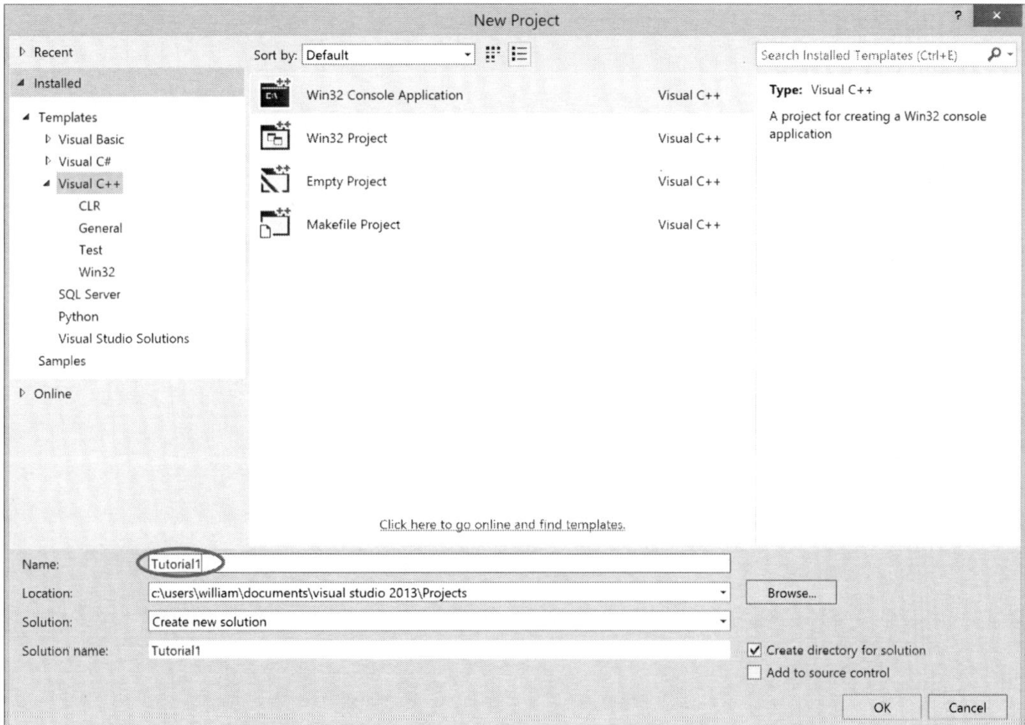

3. Check the **Empty project** option, and click on **Finish**.

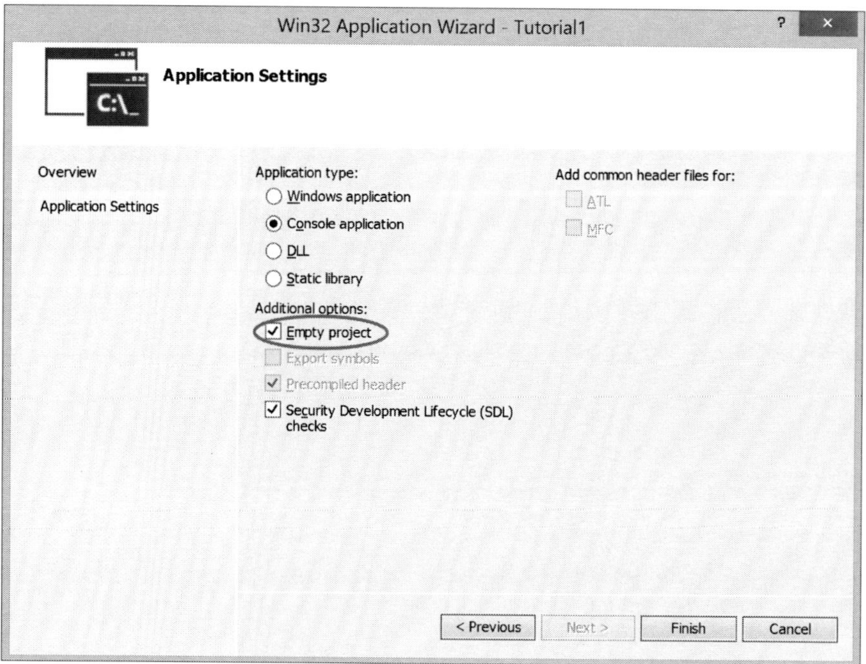

4. Right-click on **Source Files**, and add a new C++ source file (**Add** | **New Item**) called `main.cpp`.

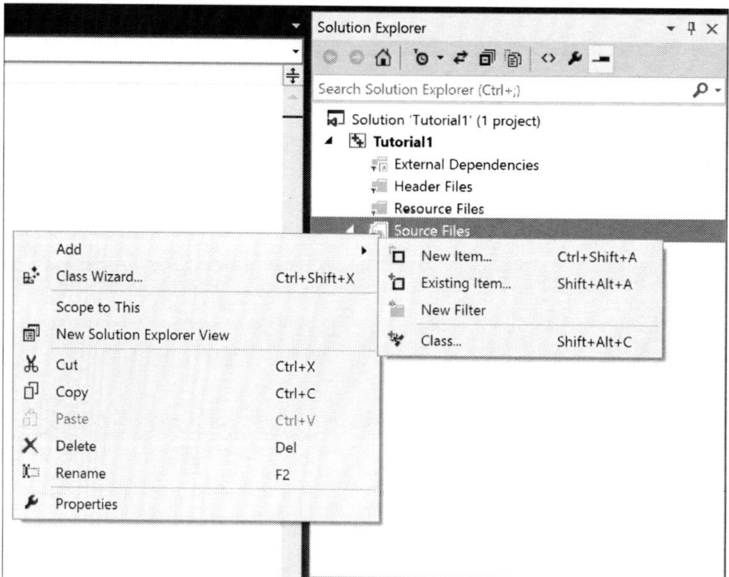

5. Copy and paste the source code from the previous section into the **`main.cpp`** and save it.
6. Open **Project Properties** (*Alt* + *F7*).
7. Add the `include` path of the GLFW library, **`C:\Program Files (x86)\glfw-3.0.4\include`**, by navigating to **Configuration Properties** | **C/C++** | **General** | **Additional Include Directories**.

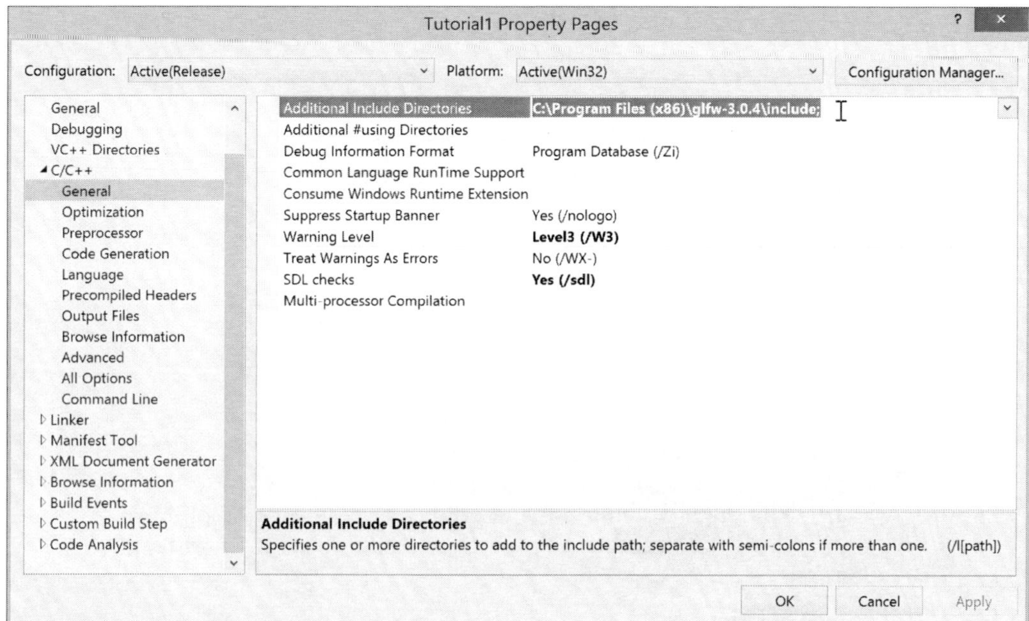

Downloading the example code

You can download the example code files from your account at `http://www.packtpub.com` for all the Packt Publishing books you have purchased. If you purchased this book elsewhere, you can visit `http://www.packtpub.com/support` and register to have the files e-mailed directly to you.

8. Add the GLFW library path, `C:\Program Files (x86)\glfw-3.0.4\lib`, by navigating to **Configuration Properties** | **Linker** | **General** | **Additional Library Directories**.

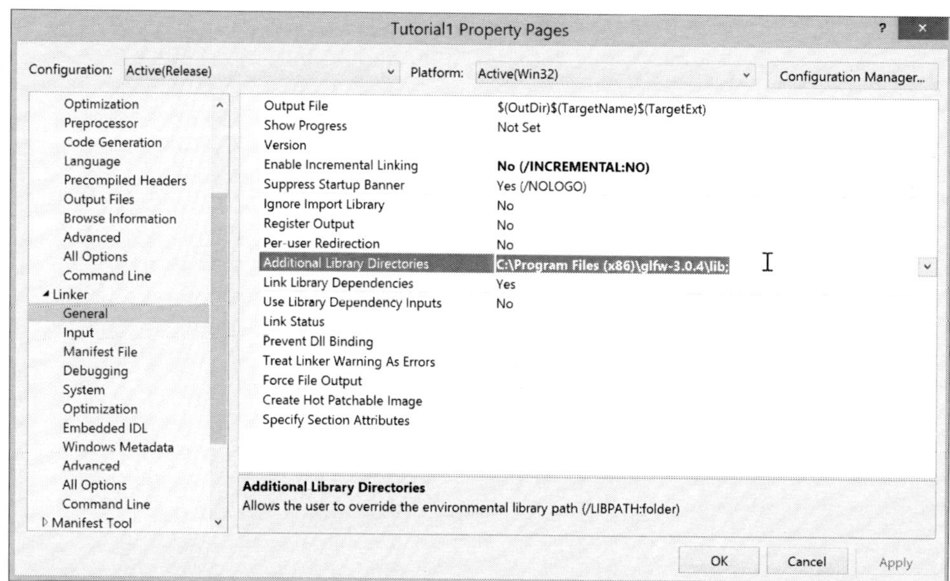

9. Add the GLFW and OpenGL libraries (`glu32.lib`, `glfw3.lib` and `opengl32.lib`) by navigating to **Configuration Properties** | **Linker** | **Input** | **Additional Dependencies**.

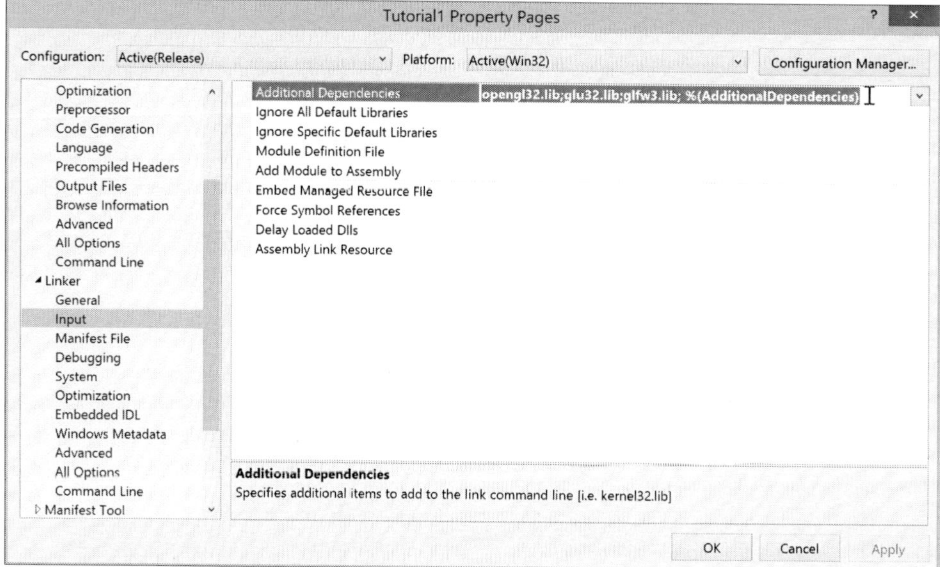

10. Build **Solution** (press *F7*).
11. Run the program (press *F5*).

Here is your first OpenGL application showing a rotating triangle that is running natively on your graphics hardware. Although we have only defined the color of the vertices to be red, green, and blue, the graphics engine interpolates the intermediate results and all calculations are performed using the graphics hardware. The screenshot is shown as follows:

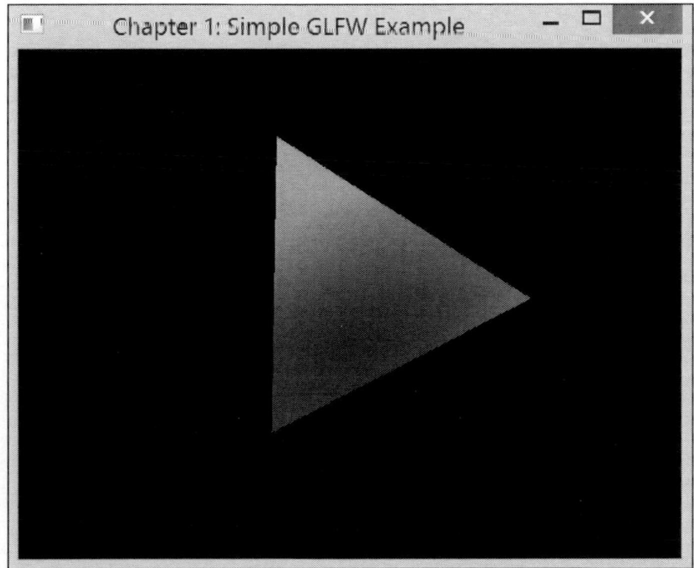

Compiling and running your first OpenGL application in Mac OS X or Linux

Setting up a Linux or Mac machine is made much simpler with the command-line interface. We assume that you have all the components that were discussed earlier ready, and all default paths are used as recommended.

Getting ready

We will start by compiling the sample code described previously. You can download the complete code package from the official website of Packt Publishing `https://www.packtpub.com`. We assume that all files are saved to a top-level directory called `code` and the `main.cpp` file is saved inside the `/code/Tutorial1` subdirectory.

How to do it...

1. Open a terminal or an equivalent command-line interface.
2. Change the current directory to the working directory:

```
cd ~/code
```

3. Enter the following command to compile the program:

```
gcc -Wall `pkg-config --cflags glfw3` -o main Tutorial1/main.cpp
`pkg-config --static --libs glfw3`
```

4. Run the program:

```
./main
```

Here is your first OpenGL application that runs natively on your graphics hardware and displays a rotating triangle. Although we have defined the color of only three vertices to be red, green, and blue, the graphics engine interpolates the intermediate results and all calculations are performed using the graphics hardware.

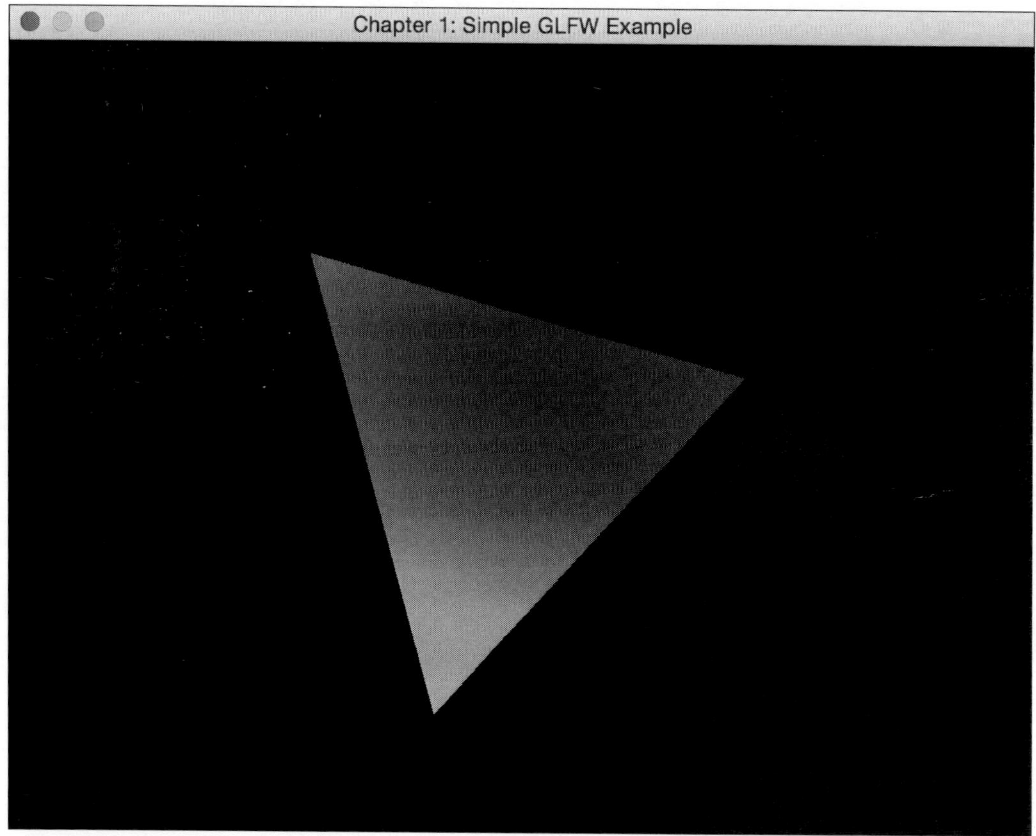

To further simplify the process, we have provided a compile script in the sample code. You can execute the script by simply typing the following commands in a terminal:

```
chmod  +x compile.sh
./compile.sh
```

You may notice that the OpenGL code is platform-independent. One of the most powerful features of the GLFW library is that it handles the windows management and other platform-dependent functions behind the scene. Therefore, the same source code (`main.cpp`) can be shared and compiled on multiple platforms without the need for any changes.

2
OpenGL Primitives and 2D Data Visualization

In this chapter, we will cover the following topics:

- OpenGL primitives
- Creating a 2D plot using primitives
- Real-time visualization of time series
- 2D visualization of 3D/4D datasets

Introduction

In the previous chapter, we provided a sample code to render a triangle on the screen using OpenGL and the GLFW library. In this chapter, we will focus on the use of OpenGL primitives, such as points, lines, and triangles, to enable the basic 2D visualization of data, including time series such as an **electrocardiogram** (**ECG**). We will begin with an introduction to each primitive, along with sample code to allow readers to experiment with the OpenGL primitives with a minimal learning curve.

One can think of primitives as the fundamental building blocks to create graphics using OpenGL. These building blocks can be easily reused in many applications and are highly portable among different platforms. Frequently, programmers struggle with displaying their results in a visually appealing manner, and an enormous amount of time may be spent on performing simple drawing tasks on screen. In this chapter, we will introduce a rapid prototyping approach to 2D data visualization using OpenGL so that impressive graphics can be created with minimal efforts. Most importantly, the proposed framework is highly intuitive and reusable, and it can be extended to be used in more sophisticated applications. Once you have mastered the basics of the OpenGL language, you will be equipped with the skills to create impressive applications that harness the true potential of OpenGL for data visualization using modern graphics hardware.

OpenGL primitives

In the simplest terms, primitives are just basic shapes that are drawn in OpenGL. In this section, we will provide a brief overview of the main geometric primitives that are supported by OpenGL and focus specifically on three commonly used primitives (which will also appear in our demo applications): points, lines, and triangles.

Drawing points

We begin with a simple, yet very useful, building block for many visualization problems: a point primitive. A point can be in the form of ordered pairs in 2D, or it can be visualized in the 3D space.

Getting ready

To simplify the workflow and improve the readability of the code, we first define a structure called `Vertex`, which encapsulates the fundamental elements such as the position and color of a vertex.

```
typedef struct
{
  GLfloat x, y, z; //position
  GLfloat r, g, b, a; //color and alpha channels
} Vertex;
```

Now, we can treat every object and shape in terms of a set of vertices (with a specific color) in space. In this chapter, as our focus is on 2D visualization, the *z* positions of vertices are often manually set to `0.0f`.

We can create a vertex at the center of the screen (0, 0, 0) with a white color as an example:

```
Vertex v = {0.0f, 0.0f, 0.0f, 1.0f, 1.0f, 1.0f, 1.0f};
```

Note that the color element consists of the red, green, blue, and alpha channels. These values range from 0.0 to 1.0. The alpha channel allows us to create transparency (0: fully transparent; 1: fully opaque) so that objects can be blended together.

How to do it...

We can first define a function called `drawPoint` to encapsulate the complexity of OpenGL primitive functions, illustrated as follows:

1. Create a function called `drawPoint` to draw points which takes in two parameters (the vertex and size of the point):

   ```
   void drawPoint(Vertex v1, GLfloat size){
   ```

2. Specify the size of the point:

   ```
   glPointSize(size);
   ```

3. Set the beginning of the list of vertices to be specified and indicate the primitive type associated with the vertices (`GL_POINTS` in this case):

   ```
   glBegin(GL_POINTS);
   ```

4. Set the color and the vertex position using the fields from the `Vertex` structure:

   ```
   glColor4f(v1.r, v1.g, v1.b, v1.a);
   glVertex3f(v1.x, v1.y, v1.z);
   ```

5. Set the end of the list:

   ```
     glEnd();
   }
   ```

6. In addition, we can define a function called `drawPointsDemo` to encapsulate the complexity further. This function draws a series of points with an increasing size:

   ```
   void drawPointsDemo(int width, int height){
     GLfloat size=5.0f;
     for(GLfloat x = 0.0f; x<=1.0f; x+=0.2f, size+=5)
     {
       Vertex v1 = {x, 0.0f, 0.0f, 1.0f, 1.0f, 1.0f, 1.0f};
       drawPoint(v1, size);
     }
   }
   ```

Finally, let's integrate these two functions into a complete OpenGL demo program (refer to identical steps in *Chapter 1, Getting Started withOpenGL*):

1. Create a source file called `main_point.cpp`, and then include the header file for the GLFW library and standard C++ libraries:

   ```
   #include <GLFW/glfw3.h>
   #include <stdlib.h>
   #include <stdio.h>
   ```

2. Define the size of the window for display:

   ```
   const int WINDOWS_WIDTH = 640*2;
   const int WINDOWS_HEIGHT = 480;
   ```

3. Define the `Vertex` structure and function prototypes:

   ```
   typedef struct
   {
     GLfloat x, y, z;
     GLfloat r, g, b, a;
   ```

```
} Vertex;
void drawPoint(Vertex v1, GLfloat size);
void drawPointsDemo(int width, int height);
```

4. Implement the `drawPoint` and `drawPointsDemo` functions, as shown previously.
5. Initialize GLFW and create a GLFW window object:

```
int main(void)
{
  GLFWwindow* window;
  if (!glfwInit())
    exit(EXIT_FAILURE);
  window = glfwCreateWindow(WINDOWS_WIDTH, WINDOWS_HEIGHT,
    "Chapter 2: Primitive drawings", NULL, NULL);
  if (!window){
    glfwTerminate();
    exit(EXIT_FAILURE);
  }
  glfwMakeContextCurrent(window);
```

6. Enable anti-aliasing and smoothing:

```
  glEnable(GL_POINT_SMOOTH);
  glHint(GL_POINT_SMOOTH_HINT, GL_NICEST);
  glEnable(GL_BLEND);
  glBlendFunc(GL_SRC_ALPHA, GL_ONE_MINUS_SRC_ALPHA);
```

7. Define a loop that terminates when the window is closed. Set up the viewport (using the size of the window) and clear the color buffer at the beginning of each iteration to update with new content:

```
  while (!glfwWindowShouldClose(window))
  {
    float ratio;
    int width, height;
    glfwGetFramebufferSize(window, &width, &height);
    ratio = (float) width / (float)height;
    glViewport(0, 0, width, height);
    glClear(GL_COLOR_BUFFER_BIT);
```

8. Set up the camera matrix for orthographic projection:

```
    glMatrixMode(GL_PROJECTION);
    glLoadIdentity();
    //Orthographic Projection
    glOrtho(-ratio, ratio, -1.f, 1.f, 1.f, -1.f);
    glMatrixMode(GL_MODELVIEW);
    glLoadIdentity();
    glClear(GL_COLOR_BUFFER_BIT | GL_DEPTH_BUFFER_BIT);
```

9. Call the `drawPointsDemo` function:

```
      drawPointsDemo(width, height);
```

10. Swap the front and back buffers of the window and process the event queue (such as keyboard inputs) to avoid lock-up:

```
      glfwSwapBuffers(window);
      glfwPollEvents();
    }
```

11. Release the memory and terminate the GLFW library. Then, exit the application:

```
    glfwDestroyWindow(window);
    glfwTerminate();
    exit(EXIT_SUCCESS);
  }
```

Here is the result (with anti-aliasing disabled) showing a series of points with an increasing size (that is, the diameter of each point as specified by `glPointSize`):

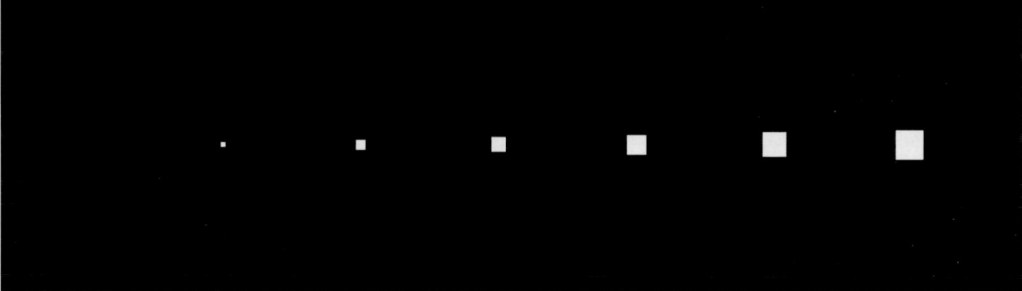

How it works...

The `glBegin` and `glEnd` functions delimit the list of vertices corresponding to a desired primitive (`GL_POINTS` in this demo). The `glBegin` function accepts a set of symbolic constants that represent different drawing methods, including `GL_POINTS`, `GL_LINES`, and `GL_TRIANGLES`, as discussed in this chapter.

There are several ways to control the process of drawing points. First, we can set the diameter of each point (in pixels) with the `glPointSize` function. By default, a point has a diameter of 1 without anti-aliasing (a method to smooth sampling artifacts) enabled. Also, we can define the color of each point as well as the alpha channel (transparency) using the `glColor4f` function. The alpha channel allows us to overlay points and blend graphics elements. This is a powerful, yet very simple, technique used in graphics design and user interface design. Lastly, we define the position of the point in space with the `glVertex3f` function.

In OpenGL, we can define the projection transformation in two different ways: orthographic projection or perspective projection. In 2D drawing, we often use orthographic projection which involves no perspective correction (for example, the object on screen will remain the same size regardless of its distance from the camera). In 3D drawing, we use perspective projection to create more realistic-looking scenes similar to how the human eye sees. In the code, we set up an orthographic projection with the `glOrtho` function. The `glOrtho` function takes these parameters: the coordinates of the vertical clipping plane, the coordinates of the horizontal clipping plane, and the distance of the nearer and farther depth clipping planes. These parameters determine the projection matrix, and the detailed documentation can be found in `https://developer.apple.com/library/mac/documentation/Darwin/Reference/ManPages/man3/glOrtho.3.html`.

Anti-aliasing and smoothing are necessary to produce the polished look seen in modern graphics. Most graphics cards support native smoothing and in OpenGL, it can be enabled as follows:

```
glEnable(GL_POINT_SMOOTH);
glEnable(GL_BLEND);
glBlendFunc(GL_SRC_ALPHA, GL_ONE_MINUS_SRC_ALPHA);
```

Here is the final result with anti-aliasing enabled, showing a series of circular points with an increasing size:

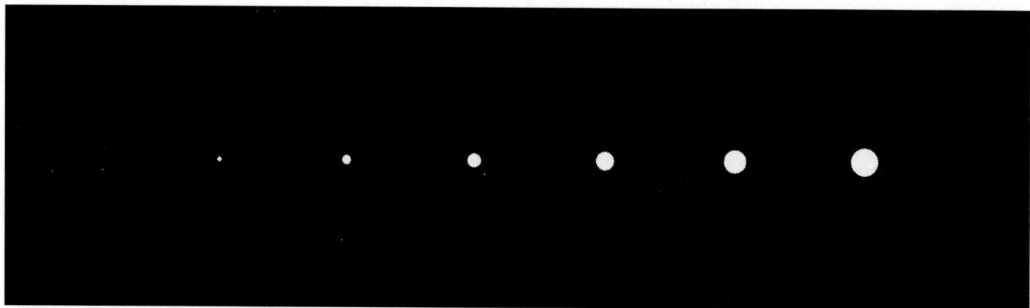

Note that in the preceding diagram, the points are now rendered as circles instead of squares with the anti-aliasing feature enabled. Readers are encouraged to disable and enable the features of the preceding diagram to see the effects of the operation.

See also

In this tutorial, we have focused on the C programming style due to its simplicity. In the upcoming chapters, we will migrate to an object-oriented programming style using C++. In addition, in this chapter, we focus on three basic primitives (and discuss the derivatives of these primitives where appropriate): `GL_POINTS`, `GL_LINES`, and `GL_TRIANGLES`. Here is a more extensive list of primitives supported by OpenGL (refer to `https://www.opengl.org/wiki/Primitive` for more information):

```
GL_POINTS, GL_LINES, GL_LINE_STRIP, GL_LINE_LOOP, GL_TRIANGLES,
GL_TRIANGLE_STRIP, GL_TRIANGLE_FAN, GL_QUADS, GL_QUAD_STRIP, and GL_
POLYGON
```

Drawing line segments

One natural extension now is to connect a line between data points and then to connect the lines together to form a grid for plotting. In fact, OpenGL natively supports drawing line segments, and the process is very similar to that of drawing a point.

Getting ready

In OpenGL, we can simply define a line segment with a set of 2 vertices, and a line will be automatically formed between them by choosing `GL_LINES` as the symbolic constant in the `glBegin` statement.

How to do it...

Here, we define a new line drawing function called `drawLineSegment` which users can test by simply replacing the `drawPointsDemo` function in the previous section:

1. Define the `drawLineSegment` function which takes in two vertices and the width of the line as inputs:

   ```
   void drawLineSegment(Vertex v1, Vertex v2, GLfloat width) {
   ```

2. Set the width of the line:

   ```
     glLineWidth(width);
   ```

3. Set the primitive type for line drawing:

   ```
     glBegin(GL_LINES);
   ```

4. Set the vertices and the color of the line:

```
      glColor4f(v1.r, v1.g, v1.b, v1.a);
      glVertex3f(v1.x, v1.y, v1.z);
      glColor4f(v2.r, v2.g, v2.b, v2.a);
      glVertex3f(v2.x, v2.y, v2.z);
      glEnd();
    }
```

In addition, we define a new grid drawing function called `drawGrid`, built on top of the `drawLineSegment` function as follows:

```
void drawGrid(GLfloat width, GLfloat height, GLfloat grid_width){
  //horizontal lines
  for(float i=-height; i<height; i+=grid_width){
    Vertex v1 = {-width, i, 0.0f, 1.0f, 1.0f, 1.0f, 1.0f};
    Vertex v2 = {width, i, 0.0f, 1.0f, 1.0f, 1.0f, 1.0f};
    drawLineSegment(v1, v2);
  }
  //vertical lines
  for(float i=-width; i<width; i+=grid_width){
    Vertex v1 = {i, -height, 0.0f, 1.0f, 1.0f, 1.0f, 1.0f};
    Vertex v2 = {i, height, 0.0f, 1.0f, 1.0f, 1.0f, 1.0f};
    drawLineSegment(v1, v2);
  }
}
```

Finally, we can execute the full demo by replacing the call for the `drawPointsDemo` function in the previous section with the following `drawLineDemo` function:

```
void drawLineDemo(){
  //draw a simple grid
  drawGrid(5.0f, 1.0f, 0.1f);
  //define the vertices and colors of the line segments
  Vertex v1 = {-5.0f, 0.0f, 0.0f, 1.0f, 0.0f, 0.0f, 0.7f};
  Vertex v2 = {5.0f, 0.0f, 0.0f, 0.0f, 1.0f, 0.0f, 0.7f};
  Vertex v3 = {0.0f, 1.0f, 0.0f, 0.0f, 0.0f, 1.0f, 0.7f};
  Vertex v4 = {0.0f, -1.0f, 0.0f, 0.0f, 0.0f, 1.0f, 0.7f};
  //draw the line segments
  drawLineSegment(v1, v2, 10.0f);
  drawLineSegment(v3, v4, 10.0f);
}
```

Here is a screenshot of the demo showing a grid with equal spacing and the *x* and *y* axes drawn with the line primitives:

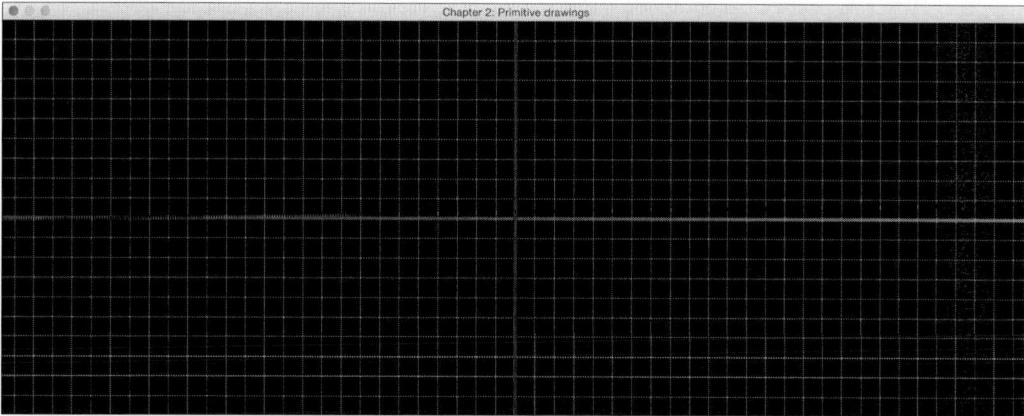

How it works...

There are multiple ways of drawing line segments in OpenGL. We have demonstrated the use of `GL_LINES` which takes every consecutive pair of vertices in the list to form an independent line segment for each pair. On the other hand, if you would like to draw a line without gaps, you can use the `GL_LINE_STRIP` option, which connects all the vertices in a consecutive fashion. Finally, to form a closed loop sequence in which the endpoints of the lines are connected, you would use the `GL_LINE_LOOP` option.

In addition, we can modify the width and the color of a line with the `glLineWidth` and `glColor4f` functions for each vertex, respectively.

Drawing triangles

We will now move on to another very commonly used primitive, namely a triangle, which forms the basis for drawing all possible polygons.

Getting ready

Similar to drawing a line segment, we can simply define a triangle with a set of 3 vertices, and line segments will be automatically formed by choosing `GL_TRIANGLES` as the symbolic constant in the `glBegin` statement.

How to do it...

Finally, we define a new function called `drawTriangle`, which users can test by simply replacing the `drawPointsDemo` function. We will also reuse the `drawGrid` function from the previous section:

1. Define the `drawTriangle` function, which takes in three vertices as the input:

   ```
   void drawTriangle(Vertex v1, Vertex v2, Vertex v3){
   ```

2. Set the primitive type to draw triangles:

   ```
     glBegin(GL_TRIANGLES);
   ```

3. Set the vertices and the color of the triangle:

   ```
     glColor4f(v1.r, v1.g, v1.b, v1.a);
     glVertex3f(v1.x, v1.y, v1.z);
     glColor4f(v2.r, v2.g, v2.b, v2.a);
     glVertex3f(v2.x, v2.y, v2.z);
     glColor4f(v3.r, v3.g, v3.b, v3.a);
     glVertex3f(v3.x, v3.y, v3.z);
     glEnd(),
   }
   ```

4. Execute the demo by replacing the call for the `drawPointsDemo` function in the full demo code with the following `drawTriangleDemo` function:

   ```
   void drawTriangleDemo(){
     //Triangle Demo
     Vertex v1 = {0.0f, 0.8f, 0.0f, 1.0f, 0.0f, 0.0f, 0.6f};
     Vertex v2 = {-1.0f, -0.8f, 0.0f, 0.0f, 1.0f, 0.0f, 0.6f};
     Vertex v3 = {1.0f, -0.8f, 0.0f, 0.0f, 0.0f, 1.0f, 0.6f};
     drawTriangle(v1, v2, v3);
   }
   ```

Here is the final result with a triangle rendered with 60 percent transparency overlaid on top of the grid lines:

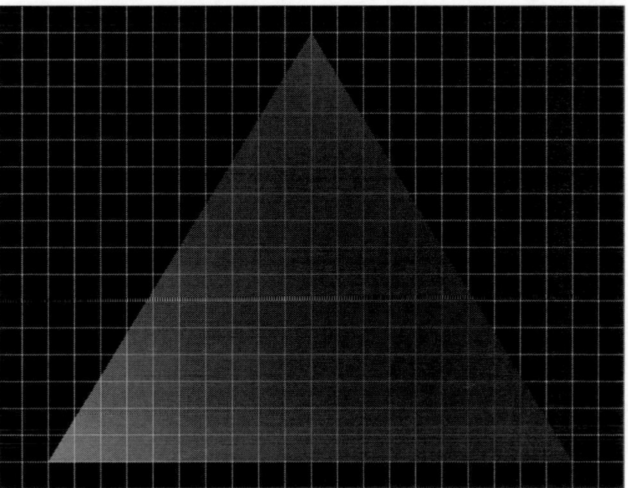

How it works...

While the process of drawing a triangle in OpenGL appears similar to previous examples, there are some subtle differences and further complexities that can be incorporated. There are three different modes in this primitive (`GL_TRIANGLES`, `GL_TRIANGLE_STRIP`, and `GL_TRIANGLE_FAN`), and each handles the vertices in a different manner. First, `GL_TRIANGLES` takes three vertices from a given list to create a triangle. The triangles are independently formed from each triplet of the vertices (that is, every three vertices are turned into a different triangle). On the other hand, `GL_TRIANGLE_STRIP` forms a triangle with the first three vertices, and each subsequent vertex forms a new triangle using the previous two vertices. Lastly, `GL_TRIANGLE_FAN` creates an arbitrarily complex convex polygon by creating triangles that have a common vertex in the center specified by the first vertex v_1, which forms a fan-shaped structure consisting of triangles. In other words, triangles will be generated in the grouping order specified as follows:

$$(v_1, v_2, v_3), (v_1, v_3, v_4), ..., (v_1, v_{n-1}, v_n)$$

```
for n vertices
```

Although a different color is set for each vertex, OpenGL handles color transition (linear interpolation) automatically, as shown in the triangle drawing in the previous example. The vertices are set to red, green, and blue, but the spectrum of colors can be clearly seen. Additionally, transparency can be set using the alpha channel, which enables us to clearly see the grid behind the triangle. With OpenGL, we can also add other elements, such as the advanced handling of color and shading, which will be discussed in the upcoming chapters.

Creating a 2D plot using primitives

Creating a 2D plot is a common way of visualizing trends in datasets in many applications. With OpenGL, we can render such plots in a much more dynamic way compared to conventional approaches (such as basic MATLAB plots) as we can gain full control over the graphics shader for color manipulation and we can also provide real-time feedback to the system. These unique features allow users to create highly interactive systems, so that, for example, time series such as an electrocardiogram can be visualized with minimal effort.

Here, we first demonstrate the visualization of a simple 2D dataset, namely a sinusoidal function in discrete time.

Getting ready

This demo requires a number of functions (including the `drawPoint`, `drawLineSegment`, and `drawGrid` functions) implemented earlier. In addition, we will reuse the code structure introduced in the *Chapter 1, Getting Started with OpenGL* to execute the demo.

How to do it...

We begin by generating a simulated data stream for a sinusoidal function over a time interval. In fact, the data stream can be any arbitrary signal or relationship:

1. Let's define an additional structure called `Data` to simplify the interface:

   ```
   typedef struct
   {
     GLfloat x, y, z;
   } Data;
   ```

2. Define a generic 2D data plotting function called `draw2DscatterPlot` with the input data stream and number of points as the input:

   ```
   void draw2DscatterPlot (const Data *data, int num_points){
   ```

3. Draw the *x* and *y* axes using the `drawLineSegment` function described earlier:

   ```
     Vertex v1 = {-10.0f, 0.0f, 0.0f, 1.0f, 1.0f, 1.0f, 1.0f};
     Vertex v2 = {10.0f, 0.0f, 0.0f, 1.0f, 1.0f, 1.0f, 1.0f};
     drawLineSegment(v1, v2, 2.0f);
     v1.x = 0.0f;
     v2.x = 0.0f;
     v1.y = -1.0f;
     v2.y = 1.0f;
     drawLineSegment(v1, v2, 2.0f);
   ```

4. Draw the data points one by one with the `drawPoint` function:

```
    for(int i=0; i<num_points; i++){
      GLfloat x=data[i].x;
      GLfloat y=data[i].y;
      Vertex v={x, y, 0.0f, 1.0f, 1.0f, 1.0f, 0.5f};
      drawPoint(v, 8.0f);
    }
  }
```

5. Create a similar function called `draw2DlineSegments` to connect the dots together with the line segments so that both the curve and the data points can be shown simultaneously:

```
  void draw2DlineSegments(const Data *data, int num_points){
    for(int i=0; i<num_points-1; i++){
      GLfloat x1=data[i].x;
      GLfloat y1=data[i].y;
      GLfloat x2=data[i+1].x;
      GLfloat y2=data[i+1].y;
      Vertex v1={x1, y1, 0.0f, 0.0f, 1.0f, 1.0f, 0.5f};
      Vertex v2={x2, y2, 0.0f, 0.0f, 1.0f, 0.0f, 0.5f};
      drawLineSegment(v1, v2, 4.0f);
    }
  }
```

6. Integrate everything into a full demo by creating the grid, generating the simulated data points using a cosine function and plotting the data points:

```
  void linePlotDemo(float phase_shift){
    drawGrid(5.0f, 1.0f, 0.1f);
    GLfloat range = 10.0f;
    const int num_points = 200;
    Data *data=(Data*)malloc(sizeof(Data)*num_points);
    for(int i=0; i<num_points; i++){
      data[i].x=((GLfloat)i/num_points)*range-range/2.0f;
      data[i].y= 0.8f*cosf(data[i].x*3.14f+phase_shift);
    }
    draw2DScatterPlot(data, num_points);
    draw2DLineSegments(data, num_points);
    free(data);
  }
```

7. Finally, in the main program, include the `math.h` header file for the cosine function and add a new variable called `phase_shift` outside the loop to execute this demo. You can download the code package from Packt Publishing website for the complete demo code:

```
#include <math.h>
...
int main(void){
  ...
  float phase_shift=0.0f;
  while (!glfwWindowShouldClose(window)){
    ...
    phase_shift+=0.02f;
    linePlotDemo(phase_shift);
    ...

    //finished all demo calls
    glfwSwapBuffers(window);
    glfwPollEvents();
  }
  ...
}
```

The final result simulating a real-time input data stream with a sinusoidal shape is plotted on top of grid lines using a combination of basic primitives discussed in previous sections.

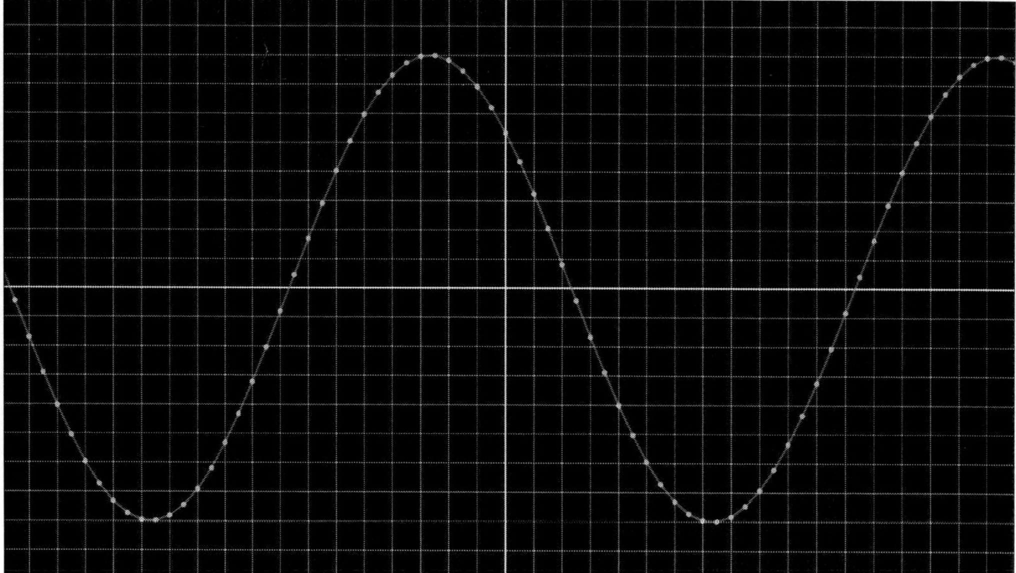

How it works...

Using the simple toolkit we created earlier using basic OpenGL primitives, we plotted a sinusoidal function with the data points (sampled at a constant time interval) overlaid on top of the curve. The smooth curve consists of many individual line segments drawn using the `draw2DlineSegments` function, while the samples were plotted using the `drawPoint` function. This intuitive interface serves as the basis for the visualization of more interesting time series for real-world applications in the next section.

Real-time visualization of time series

In this section, we further demonstrate the versatility of our framework to plot general time series data for biomedical applications. In particular, we will display an ECG in real time. As a brief introduction, an ECG is a very commonly used diagnostic and monitoring tool to detect abnormalities in the heart. ECG surface recording essentially probes the electrical activities of the heart. For example, the biggest spike (called a QRS complex) typically corresponds to the depolarization of the ventricles of the heart (the highly muscular chambers of the heart that pump blood). A careful analysis of the ECG can be a very powerful, noninvasive method for distinguishing many heart diseases clinically, including many forms of arrhythmia and heart attacks.

Getting ready

We begin by importing a computer-generated ECG data stream. The ECG data stream is stored in `data_ecg.h` (only a small portion of the data stream is provided here):

```
float data_ecg[]={0.396568808f, 0.372911844f, 0.311059085f, 0.220346775f,
0.113525529f, 0.002200333f, -0.103284775f, -0.194218528f, -0.266285973f,
-0.318075979f, -0.349670132f, -0.362640042f, -0.360047348f,
-0.346207663f, -0.325440887f, -0.302062532f, -0.279400804f, -0.259695686f
... };
```

How to do it...

1. Use the following code to plot the ECG data by drawing line segments:

```
void plotECGData(int offset, int size, float offset_y,
  float scale){
  //space between samples
  const float space = 2.0f/size*ratio;
  //initial position of the first vertex to render
  float pos = -size*space/2.0f;
  //set the width of the line
  glLineWidth(5.0f);
```

```
    glBegin(GL_LINE_STRIP);
    //set the color of the line to green
    glColor4f(0.1f, 1.0f, 0.1f, 0.8f);
    for (int i=offset; i<size+offset; i++){
      const float data = scale*data_ecg[i]+offset_y;
      glVertex3f(pos, data, 0.0f);
      pos += space;
    }
    glEnd();
  }
```

2. Display multiple ECG data streams (simulating recording from different leads):

```
void ecg_demo(int counter){
  const int data_size=ECG_DATA_BUFFER_SIZE;
  //Emulate the presence of multiple ECG leads (just for demo/
    display purposes)
  plotECGData(counter, data_size*0.5, -0.5f, 0.1f);
  plotECGData(counter+data_size, data_size*0.5, 0.0f, 0.5f);
  plotECGData(counter+data_size*2, data_size*0.5, 0.5f, -0.25f);
}
```

3. Finally, in the main program, include the `data_ecg.h` header file and add the following lines of code to the loop. You can download the code package from the Packt Publishing website for the complete demo code:

```
#include "data_ecg.h"
...
int main(void){
  ...
  while (!glfwWindowShouldClose(window)){
    ...
    drawGrid(5.0f, 1.0f, 0.1f);
    //reset counter to 0 after reaching the end of the
      sample data
    if(counter>5000){
      counter=0;
    }
    counter+=5;
    //run the demo visualizer
    ecg_demo(counter);
    ...
  }
}
```

Here are two snapshots of the real-time display across multiple ECG leads simulated at two different time points. If you execute the demo, you will see the ECG recording from multiple leads move across the screen as the data stream is processed for display.

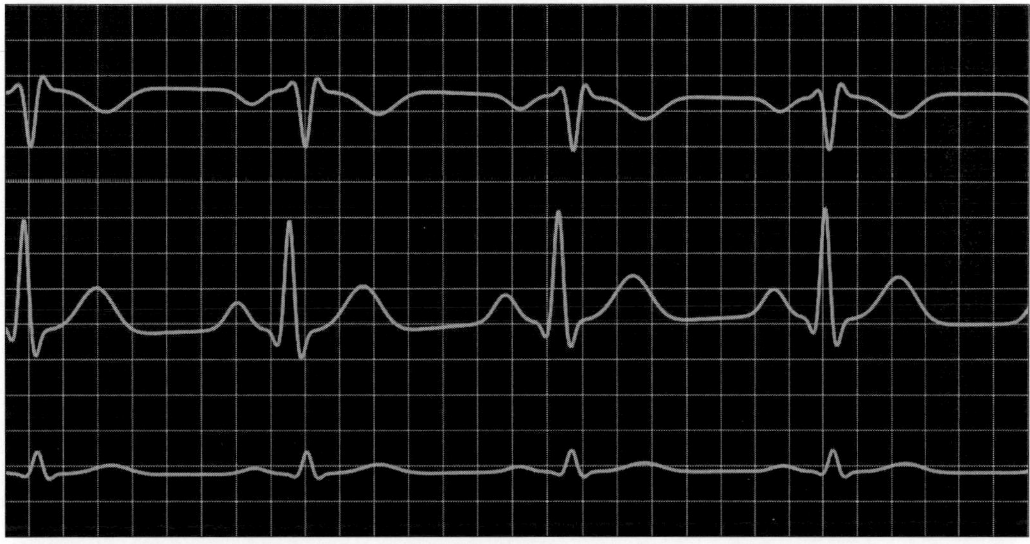

Here is the second snapshot at a later time point:

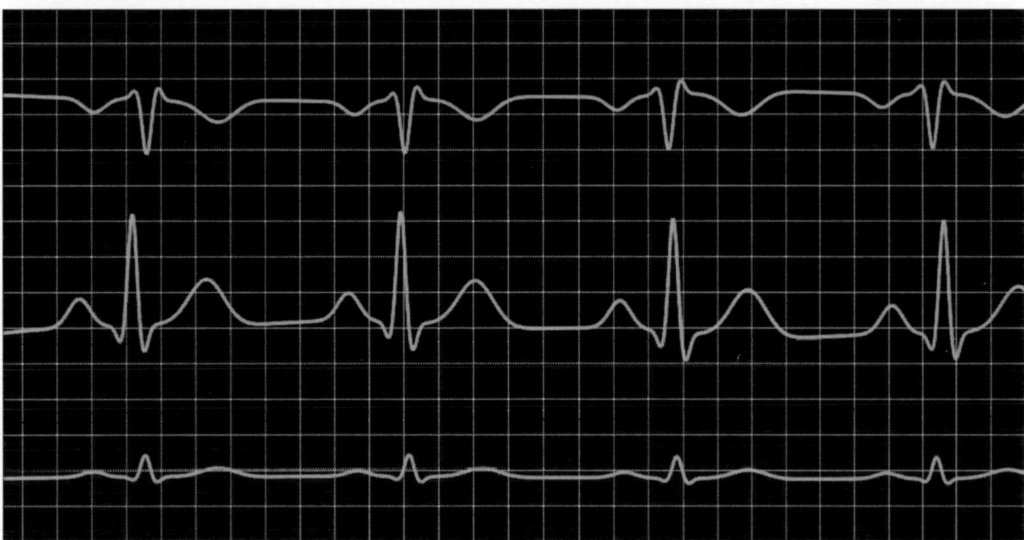

How it works...

This demo shows the use of the GL_LINE_STRIP option, described previously, to plot an ECG time series. Instead of drawing individual and independent line segments (using the GL_LINE option), we draw a continuous stream of data by calling the glVertex3f function for each data point. Additionally, the time series animates through the screen and provides dynamic updates on an interactive frame with minimal impact on the CPU computation cycles.

2D visualization of 3D/4D datasets

We have now learned multiple methods to generate plots on screen using points and lines. In the last section, we will demonstrate how to visualize a million data points in a 3D dataset using OpenGL in real time. A common strategy to visualize a complex 3D dataset is to encode the third dimension (for example, the *z* dimension) in the form of a heat map with a desirable color scheme. As an example, we show a heat map of a 2D Gaussian function with its height *z*, encoded using a simple color scheme. In general, a 2-D Gaussian function, $f(x,y)$, is defined as follows:

$$z = f(x,y) = Ae^{-\left(\frac{(x-x_0)^2}{2\sigma_x^2}+\frac{(y-y_0)^2}{2\sigma_y^2}\right)}$$

Here, *A* is the amplitude ($1/(2\pi\sigma_x\sigma_y)$) of the distribution centered at (x_0, y_0) and σ_x, σ_y are the standard deviations (spread) of the distribution in the *x* and *y* directions. To make this demo more interesting and more visually appealing, we vary the standard deviation or sigma term (equally in the *x* and *y* directions) over time. Indeed, we can apply the same method to visualize very complex 3D datasets.

Getting ready

By now, you should be very familiar with the basic primitives described in previous sections. Here, we employ the GL_POINTS option to generate a dense grid of data points with different colors encoding the *z* dimension.

How to do it...

1. Generate a million data points (1,000 x 1,000 grid) with a 2-D Gaussian function:

```
void gaussianDemo(float sigma){
  //construct a 1000x1000 grid
  const int grid_x = 1000;
  const int grid_y = 1000;
```

```
    const int num_points = grid_x*grid_y;
    Data *data=(Data*)malloc(sizeof(Data)*num_points);
    int data_counter=0;
    for(int x = -grid_x/2; x<grid_x/2; x+=1){
      for(int y = -grid_y/2; y<grid_y/2; y+=1){
        float x_data = 2.0f*x/grid_x;
        float y_data = 2.0f*y/grid_y;
        //compute the height z based on a
        //2D Gaussian function.
        float z_data = exp(-0.5f*(x_data*x_data)/(sigma*sigma)
          -0.5f*(y_data*y_data)/(sigma*sigma))/
            (sigma*sigma*2.0f*M_PI);
        data[data_counter].x = x_data;
        data[data_counter].y = y_data;
        data[data_counter].z = z_data;
        data_counter++;
      }
    }
    //visualize the result using a 2D heat map
    draw2DHeatMap(data, num_points);
    free(data);
  }
```

2. Draw the data points using a heat map function for color visualization:

```
void draw2DHeatMap(const Data *data, int num_points){
  //locate the maximum and minimum values in the dataset
  float max_value=-999.9f;
  float min_value=999.9f;
  for(int i=0; i<num_points; i++){
    const Data d = data[i];
    if(d.z > max_value){
      max_value = d.z;
    }
    if(d.z < min_value){
      min_value = d.z;
    }
  }
  const float halfmax = (max_value + min_value) / 2;

  //display the result
  glPointSize(2.0f);
  glBegin(GL_POINTS);
  for(int i = 0; i<num_points; i++){
```

```
      const Data d = data[i];
      float value = d.z;
      float b = 1.0f - value/halfmax;
      float r = value/halfmax - 1.0f;
      if(b < 0){
        b=0;
      }
      if(r < 0){
        r=0;
      }
      float g = 1.0f - b - r;
      glColor4f(r, g, b, 0.5f);
      glVertex3f(d.x, d.y, 0.0f);
    }
    glEnd();
  }
```

3. Finally, in the main program, include the `math.h` header file and add the following lines of code to the loop to vary the sigma term over time. You can download the example code from the Packt Publishing website for the complete demo code:

```
#define _USE_MATH_DEFINES // M_PI constant
#include <math.h>
...
int main(void){
  ...
  float sigma = 0.01f;
  while (!glfwWindowShouldClose(window)){
    ...
    drawGrid(5.0f, 1.0f, 0.1f);
    sigma+=0.01f;
    if(sigma>1.0f)
      sigma=0.01;
    gaussianDemo(sigma);
    ...
  }
}
```

Here are four figures illustrating the effect of varying the sigma term of the 2-D Gaussian function over time (from 0.01 to 1):

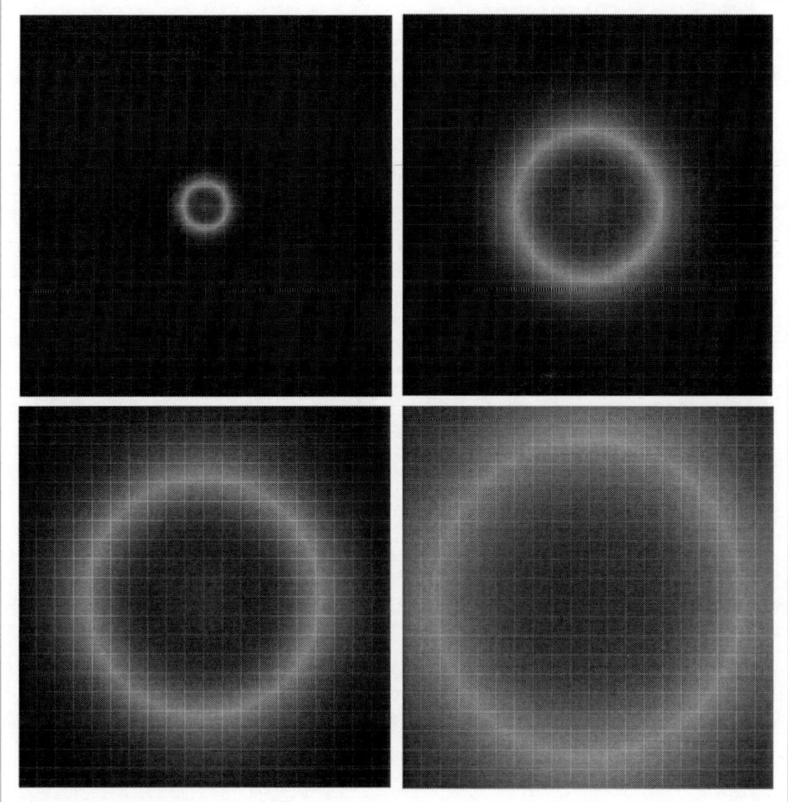

How it works...

We have demonstrated how to visualize a Gaussian function using a simple heat map in which the maximum value is represented by red, while the minimum value is represented by blue. In total, a million data points (1,000 x 1,000) were plotted using vertices for each Gaussian function with a specific sigma term. This sigma term was varied from 0.01 to 1 to show a time-varying Gaussian distribution. To reduce the overhead, vertex buffers can be implemented in the future (we can perform the memory copy operation all at once and remove the `glVertex3f` calls). Similar techniques can be applied to the color channel as well.

There's more...

The heat map we have described here provides a powerful visualization tool for complex 3D datasets seen in many scientific and biomedical applications. Indeed, we have actually extended our demo to the visualization of a 4D dataset, to be precise, since a time-varying 3D function; with the height encoded using a color map was displayed. This demo shows the many possibilities for displaying data in an interesting, dynamic way using just 2D techniques based on OpenGL primitives. In the next chapter, we will demonstrate the potential of OpenGL further by incorporating 3D rendering and adding user inputs to enable the 3D, interactive visualization of more complex datasets.

3
Interactive 3D Data Visualization

In this chapter, we will cover the following topics:

- Setting up a virtual camera for 3D rendering
- Creating a 3D plot with perspective rendering
- Creating an interactive environment with GLFW
- Rendering a volumetric dataset – MCML simulation

Introduction

OpenGL is a very attractive platform for creating dynamic, highly interactive tools for visualizing data in 3D. In this chapter, we will build upon the fundamental concepts discussed in the previous chapter and extend our demos to incorporate more sophisticated OpenGL features for 3D rendering. To enable 3D visualization, we will first introduce the basic steps of setting up a virtual camera in OpenGL. In addition, to create more interactive demos, we will introduce the use of GLFW callback functions for handling user inputs. Using these concepts, we will illustrate how to create an interactive 3D plot with perspective rendering using OpenGL. Finally, we will demonstrate how to render a 3D volumetric dataset generated from a Monte Carlo simulation of light transport in biological tissue. By the end of this chapter, readers will be able to visualize data in 3D with perspective rendering and interact with the environment dynamically through user inputs for a wide range of applications.

Setting up a virtual camera for 3D rendering

Rendering a 3D scene is similar to taking a photograph with a digital camera in the real world. The steps that are taken to create a photograph can also be applied in OpenGL.

For example, you can move the camera from one position to another and adjust the viewpoint freely in space, which is known as **viewing transformation**. You can also adjust the position and orientation of the the object of interest in the scene. However, unlike in the real world, in the virtual world you can position the object at any orientation freely without any physical constraints, termed as **modeling transformation**. Finally, we can exchange camera lenses to adjust the zoom and create different perspectives the process is called **projection transformation**.

When you take a photo applying the viewing and modeling transformation, the digital camera takes the information and creates an image on your screen. This process is called **rasterization**.

These sets of matrices—encompassing the viewing transformation, modeling transformation, and projection transformation—are the fundamental elements we can adjust at run-time, which allows us to create an interactive and dynamic rendering of the scene. To get started, we will first look into the setup of the camera matrix, and how we can create a scene with different perspectives.

Getting ready

The source code in this chapter is based on the final demo from the previous chapter. Basically, we will be modifying the previous implementation by setting up a camera model using a perspective matrix. In the upcoming chapters, we will explore the use of the **OpenGL Shading Language** (**GLSL**) to enable even more complex rendering techniques and higher performance.

How to do it...

Let's get started on the first new requirement for handling perspective transformation in OpenGL. Since the camera parameters depend on the window size, we need to first implement a callback function that handles a window resize event and updates the matrices accordingly:

1. Define the function prototype for the callback function:

   ```
   void framebuffer_size_callback(GLFWwindow* window, int width,
     int height)
   {
   ```

2. Preset the camera parameters: the vertical **field of view angle** (**fovY**), the distance to the **Near clipping plane** (front), the distance to **Far clipping plane** (back), and the screen aspect ratio (**width/height**):

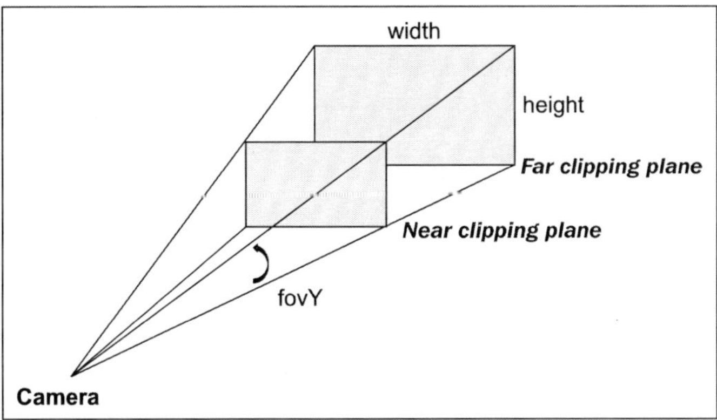


```
const float fovY = 45.0f;
const float front = 0.1f;
const float back = 128.0f;
float ratio = 1.0f;
if (height > 0)
  ratio = (float) width / (float) height;
```

3. Set up the viewport of the virtual camera (using the window size):

```
glViewport(0, 0, width, height);
```

4. Specify the matrix mode as `GL_PROJECTION` and allow subsequent matrix operations to be applied to the projection matrix stack:

```
glMatrixMode(GL_PROJECTION);
```

5. Load the identity matrix to the current matrix (that is, reset the matrix to its default state):

```
glLoadIdentity();
```

6. Set up the perspective projection matrix for the virtual camera:

```
  gluPerspective(fovY, ratio, front, back);
}
```

How it works...

The purpose of the framebuffer_size_callback function is to handle callback events from the GLFW library. Upon resizing the window, an event will be captured and the callback function provides a mechanism to update the virtual camera parameters accordingly. One important problem is that changing the aspect ratio of the screen can introduce distortion if we do not adjust our virtual camera rendering parameters appropriately. Therefore, the update function also calls the glViewport function to ensure that the graphic is rendered onto the new viewable area.

Furthermore, imagine we are taking a photo of a scene with a camera physically in the real world. The gluPerspective function basically controls the camera lens' zoom (that is, the field of view angle) as well as the camera sensor (that is, the image plane) aspect ratio. One major difference between the virtual and real camera is the concept of a near clipping and far clipping plane (front and back variables) that limits the viewable area of the rendered image. These constraints are related to more advanced topics (the depth buffer and depth testing) and how the graphical engine works with a virtual 3D scene. One rule of thumb is, we should never set an unnecessarily large value as it will affect the precision of the depth testing result, which can lead to z-fighting issue. **Z-fighting** is a phenomenon that occurs when objects share very similar depth values and the precision of the depth value is not sufficient to resolve the ambiguity (due to precision loss in the floating-point representation during the 3D rendering process). Setting a higher resolution depth buffer, or reducing the distance between the clipping planes, is often the simplest way to mitigate such problems.

The sample code provides perspective rendering of a scene that resembles how the human eye sees the world. For example, an object will appear larger if it is closer to the camera and smaller if it is farther away. This allows for a more realistic view of a scene. On the other hand, by controlling the field of view angle, we can exaggerate perspective distortion, similar to capturing a scene with an ultra-wide angle lens.

There's more...

Alternatively, we can set up the camera with the glFrustum() function by replacing the gluPerspective() function with the following code:

```
const double DEG2RAD = 3.14159265 / 180;
// tangent of half fovY
double tangent = tan(fovY/2 * DEG2RAD);
// half height of near plane
double height_f = front * tangent;
// half width of near plane
double width_f = height_f * ratio;
```

```
    //Create the projection matrix based on the near clipping
    //plane and the location of the corners
    glFrustum(-width_f, width_f, -height_f, height_f, front, back);
}
```

The `glFrustum` function takes the corners of the near clipping and far clipping planes to construct the projective matrix. Fundamentally, there is no difference between the `gluPerspective` and `glFrustum` functions, so they are interchangeable.

As we can see, the virtual camera in OpenGL can be updated upon changes to the screen frame buffer (window size) and these event updates are captured with the callback mechanism of the GLFW library. Of course, we can also handle other events such as keyboard and mouse inputs. Further details on how to handle additional events will be discussed later. In the next section, let's implement the rest of the demo to create our first 3D plot with perspective rendering.

Creating a 3D plot with perspective rendering

In the previous chapter, we showed a heat map of a 2D Gaussian distribution with varying standard deviation over time. Now, we will continue with more advanced rendering of the same dataset in 3D and demonstrate the effectiveness of visualizing multi-dimensional data with OpenGL. The code base from the previous chapter will be modified to enable 3D rendering.

Instead of rendering the 2D Gaussian distribution function on a plane, we take the output of the Gaussian function $f(x,y)$ as the z (height) value as follows:

$$z = f(x,y) = Ae^{-\left(\frac{(x-x_0)^2}{2\sigma_x^2}+\frac{(y-y_0)^2}{2\sigma_y^2}\right)}$$

Here **A** is the amplitude of the distribution centered at (x_0, y_0), and σ_x, σ_y are the standard deviations (spread) of the distribution in the *x* and *y* directions. In our example, we will vary the spread of the distribution over time to change its shape in 3D. Additionally, we will apply a heat map to each vertex based on the height for better visualization effect.

Getting ready

With the camera set up using the projection model, we can render our graph in 3D with the desired effects by changing some of the virtual camera parameters such as the field of view angle for perspective distortion as well as the rotation angles for different viewing angles. To reduce coding complexity, we will re-use the `draw2DHeatMap` and `gaussianDemo` functions implemented in *Chapter 2, OpenGL Primitives and 2D Data Visualization* with minor modifications. The rendering techniques will be based on the OpenGL primitives described in the previous chapter.

How to do it...

Let's modify the final demo in *Chapter 2, OpenGL Primitives and 2D Data Visualization* (`main_gaussian_demo.cpp` in the code package) to enable perspective rendering in 3D. The overall code structure is provided here to orient readers first and major changes will be discussed in smaller blocks sequentially:

```
#include <GLFW/glfw3.h>
...

// Window size
const int WINDOWS_WIDTH = 1280;
const int WINDOWS_HEIGHT = 720;

// NEW: Callback functions and helper functions for 3D plot
void framebuffer_size_callback(GLFWwindow* window, int width,
  int height);
void draw2DHeatMap(const Data *data, int num_points);
void gaussianDemo(float sigma);
...

int main(void)
{
  GLFWwindow* window;
  int width, height;
  if (!glfwInit()){
    exit(EXIT_FAILURE);
  }
  window = glfwCreateWindow(WINDOWS_WIDTH, WINDOWS_HEIGHT,
    "Chapter 3: 3D Data Plotting", NULL, NULL);
  if (!window){
    glfwTerminate();
    exit(EXIT_FAILURE);
  }
```

```
    glfwMakeContextCurrent(window);
    glfwSwapInterval(1);
    // NEW: Callback functions
    ...

    //enable anti-aliasing
    glEnable(GL_BLEND);
    //smooth the points
    glEnable(GL_LINE_SMOOTH);
    //smooth the lines
    glEnable(GL_POINT_SMOOTH);
    glHint(GL_LINE_SMOOTH_HINT, GL_NICEST);
    glHint(GL_POINT_SMOOTH_HINT, GL_NICEST);
    //needed for alpha blending
    glBlendFunc(GL_SRC_ALPHA, GL_ONE_MINUS_SRC_ALPHA);
    glEnable(GL_ALPHA_TEST) ;
    // NEW: Initialize parameters for perspective rendering
    ...
    while (!glfwWindowShouldClose(window))
    {
      glClear(GL_COLOR_BUFFER_BIT | GL_DEPTH_BUFFER_BIT);
      glClearColor(1.0f, 1.0f, 1.0f, 1.0f);
      // NEW: Perspective rendering
      ...
    }
    glfwDestroyWindow(window);
    glfwTerminate();
    exit(EXIT_SUCCESS);
  }
```

With the preceding framework in mind, inside the `main` function let's add the new `callback` function for handling window resizing implemented in the previous section:

```
glfwGetFramebufferSize(window, &width, &height);
framebuffer_size_callback(window, width, height);
```

Let's define several global variables and initialize them for perspective rendering, including the zoom level (`zoom`) and rotation angles around the *x* (`beta`) and *z* (`alpha`) axes, respectively:

```
GLfloat alpha=210.0f, beta=-70.0f, zoom=2.0f;
```

In addition, outside the `main` loop, let's initialize some parameters for rendering the Gaussian distribution, including the standard deviation (sigma), sign, and step size for dynamically changing the function over time:

```
float sigma = 0.1f;
float sign = 1.0f;
float step_size = 0.01f;
```

In the `while` loop, we perform the following transformations to render the Gaussian function in 3D:

1. Specify the matrix mode as `GL_MODELVIEW` to allow subsequent matrix operations to be applied to the `MODELVIEW` matrix stack:

   ```
   glMatrixMode(GL_MODELVIEW);
   ```

2. Perform the translation and rotation of the object:

   ```
   glLoadIdentity();
   glTranslatef(0.0, 0.0, -2.0);
   // rotate by beta degrees around the x-axis
   glRotatef(beta, 1.0, 0.0, 0.0);
   // rotate by alpha degrees around the z-axis
   glRotatef(alpha, 0.0, 0.0, 1.0);
   ```

3. Draw the origin (with the *x*, *y*, and *z* axes) and the Gaussian function in 3D. Dynamically plot a series of Gaussian functions with varying sigma values over time and reverse the sign once a certain threshold is reached:

   ```
   drawOrigin();
   sigma=sigma+sign*step_size;
   if(sigma>1.0f){
     sign = -1.0f;
   }
   if(sigma<0.1){
     sign = 1.0f;
   }
   gaussianDemo(sigma);
   ```

   For handling each of the preceding drawing tasks, we implement the origin visualizer, Guassian function generator, and 3D point visualizer in separate functions.

To visualize the origin, implement the following drawing function:

1. Define the function prototype:

   ```
   void drawOrigin(){
   ```

2. Draw the *x*, *y*, and *z* axes in red, green, and blue, respectively:

```
    glLineWidth(4.0f);
    glBegin(GL_LINES);
    float transparency = 0.5f;

    //draw a red line for the x-axis
    glColor4f(1.0f, 0.0f, 0.0f, transparency);
    glVertex3f(0.0f, 0.0f, 0.0f);
    glColor4f(1.0f, 0.0f, 0.0f, transparency);
    glVertex3f(0.3f, 0.0f, 0.0f);

    //draw a green line for the y-axis
    glColor4f(0.0f, 1.0f, 0.0f, transparency);
    glVertex3f(0.0f, 0.0f, 0.0f);
    glColor4f(0.0f, 1.0f, 0.0f, transparency);
    glVertex3f(0.0f, 0.0f, 0.3f);

    //draw a blue line for the z-axis
    glColor4f(0.0f, 0.0f, 1.0f, transparency);
    glVertex3f(0.0f, 0.0f, 0.0f);
    glColor4f(0.0f, 0.0f, 1.0f, transparency);
    glVertex3f(0.0f, 0.3f, 0.0f);
    glEnd();
  }
```

For the implementation of the Gaussian function demo, we have broken down the problem into two parts: a Gaussian data generator and a heat map visualizer function with point drawing. Together with 3D rendering and the heat map, we can now clearly see the shape of the Gaussian distribution and how the samples animate and move in space over time:

1. Generate the Gaussian distribution:

```
  void gaussianDemo(float sigma){
    const int grid_x = 400;
    const int grid_y = 400;
    const int num_points = grid_x*grid_y;
    Data *data=(Data*)malloc(sizeof(Data)*num_points);
    int data_counter=0;

    //standard deviation
    const float sigma2=sigma*sigma;
    //amplitude
    const float sigma_const = 10.0f*(sigma2*2.0f*(float)M_PI);

    for(float x = -grid_x/2.0f; x<grid_x/2.0f; x+=1.0f){
     for(float y = -grid_y/2.0f; y<grid_y/2.0f; y+=1.0f){
        float x_data = 2.0f*x/grid_x;
        float y_data = 2.0f*y/grid_y;
        //Set the mean to 0
```

```
        float z_data = exp(-0.5f*(x_data*x_data)/(sigma2)
          -0.5f*(y_data*y_data)/(sigma2)) /sigma_const;
        data[data_counter].x = x_data;
        data[data_counter].y = y_data;
        data[data_counter].z = z_data;
        data_counter++;
      }
    }
    draw2DHeatMap(data, num_points);
    free(data);
  }
```

2. Next, implement the `draw2DHeatMap` function to visualize the result. Note that, unlike in *Chapter 2, OpenGL Primitives and 2D Data Visualization*, we use the z value inside the `glVertex3f` function:

```
void draw2DHeatMap(const Data *data, int num_points){
  glPointSize(3.0f);
  glBegin(GL_POINTS);
  float transparency = 0.25f;
  //locate the maximum and minimum values in the dataset
  float max_value=-999.9f;
  float min_value=999.9f;
  for(int i=0; i<num_points; i++){
    Data d = data[i];
    if(d.z > max_value)
      max_value = d.z;
    if(d.z < min_value)
      min_value = d.z;
  }
  float halfmax = (max_value + min_value) / 2;
  //display the result
  for(int i = 0; i<num_points; i++){
    Data d = data[i];
    float value = d.z;
    float b = 1.0f - value/halfmax;
    float r = value/halfmax - 1.0f;
    if(b < 0)
      b=0;
    if(r < 0)
      r=0;
    float g = 1.0f - b - r;
    glColor4f(r, g, b, transparency);
    glVertex3f(d.x, d.y, d.z);
  }
  glEnd();
}
```

The rendered result is shown in the following screenshot. We can see that the transparency (alpha blending) allows us to see through the data points and provides a visually appealing result:

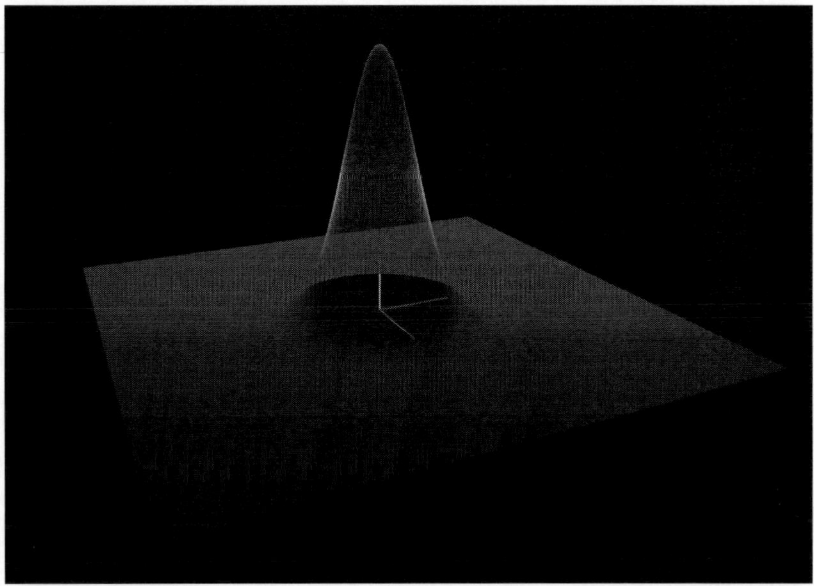

How it works...

This simple example demonstrates the use of perspective rendering as well as OpenGL transformation functions to rotate and translate the rendered objects in virtual space. As you can see, the overall code structure remains the same as in *Chapter 2, OpenGL Primitives and 2D Data Visualization* and the major changes primarily include setting up the camera parameters for perspective rendering (inside the `framebuffer_size_callback` function) and performing the required transformations to render the Gaussian function in 3D (after setting the matrix mode to `GL_MODELVIEW`). Two very commonly used transformation functions to manipulate virtual objects include `glRotatef` and `glTranslatef`, which allow us to position objects at any orientation and position. These functions can significantly improve the dynamics of your own application, with very minimal cost in development and computation time since they are heavily optimized.

The `glRotatef` function takes four parameters: the rotation angle and three components of the direction vector *(x, y, z)*, which define the axis of rotation. The function also replaces the current matrix with the product of the rotation matrix and the current matrix:

$$\begin{bmatrix} x^2(1-c)+c & xy(1-c)-zs & xz(1-c)+ys & 0 \\ yx(1-c)+zs & y^2(1-c)+c & yz(1-c)-xs & 0 \\ xz(1-c)-ys & yz(1-c)+xs & z^2(1-c)+c & 0 \\ 0 & 0 & 0 & 1 \end{bmatrix}$$

Here $c=\cos(angle), s=\sin(angle)$ and $|(x,y,z)|=1$.

There's more...

One may ask, what if we would like to position two objects at different orientations and positions? What if we would like to position many parts in space relative to one another? The answer to these is to use the `glPushMatrix` and `glPopMatrix` functions to control the stack of transformation matrices. The concept behind this can get relatively complex for a model with a large number of parts and keeping a history of the state machine with many components can be tedious. To address this issue, we will look into newer versions of GLSL support (OpenGL 3.x and higher).

Creating an interactive environment with GLFW

In the previous two sections, we focused on the creation of 3D objects and on utilizing basic OpenGL rendering techniques with a virtual camera. Now, we are ready to incorporate user inputs, such as mouse and keyboard inputs, to enable more dynamic interactions using camera control features such as zoom and rotate. These features will be the fundamental building blocks for the upcoming applications and the code will be reused in later chapters.

Getting ready

The GLFW library provides a mechanism to handle user inputs from different environments. The event handlers are implemented as callback functions in C/C++, and, in the previous tutorials, we bypassed these options for the sake of simplicity. To get started, we first need to enable these callback functions and implement basic features to control the rendering parameters.

How to do it...

To handle keyboard inputs, we attach our own implementation of the `callback` functions back to the event handler of GLFW. We will perform the following operations in the `callback` function:

1. Define the following global variables (including a new variable called `locked` to track whether the mouse button is pressed down, as well as the angles of rotation and zoom level) that will be updated by the `callback` functions:

   ```
   GLboolean locked = GL_FALSE;
   GLfloat alpha=210.0f, beta=-70.0f, zoom=2.0f;
   ```

2. Define the keyboard `callback` function prototype:

   ```
   void key_callback(GLFWwindow* window, int key, int scancode,
     int action, int mods)
   {
   ```

3. If we receive any event other than the key press event, ignore it:

   ```
     if (action != GLFW_PRESS)
       return;
   ```

4. Create a `switch` statement to handle each key press case:

   ```
     switch (key)
     {
   ```

5. If the *Esc* key is pressed, exit the program:

   ```
       case GLFW_KEY_ESCAPE:
         glfwSetWindowShouldClose(window, GL_TRUE);
         break;
   ```

6. If the space bar is pressed, start or stop the animation by toggling the variable:

   ```
       case GLFW_KEY_SPACE:
         freeze=!freeze;
         break;
   ```

7. If the direction keys (up, down, left, and right) are pressed, update the variables that control the angles of rotation for the rendered object:

   ```
       case GLFW_KEY_LEFT:
         alpha += 5.0f;
         break;
       case GLFW_KEY_RIGHT:
         alpha -= 5.0f;
         break;
       case GLFW_KEY_UP:
   ```

```
        beta -= 5.0f;
        break;
      case GLFW_KEY_DOWN:
        beta += 5.0f;
        break;
```

8. Lastly, if the *Page Up* or *Page Down* keys are pressed, zoom in and out from the object by updating the `zoom` variable:

```
      case GLFW_KEY_PAGE_UP:
        zoom -= 0.25f;
        if (zoom < 0.0f)
          zoom = 0.0f;
          break;
      case GLFW_KEY_PAGE_DOWN:
        zoom += 0.25f;
        break;
        default:
        break;
    }
  }
```

To handle mouse click events, we implement another `callback` function similar to the one for the keyboard. The mouse click event is rather simple as there is only a limited set of buttons available:

1. Define the mouse press `callback` function prototype:

```
void mouse_button_callback(GLFWwindow* window, int button,
  int action, int mods)
{
```

2. Ignore all inputs except for the left click event for simplicity:

```
  if (button != GLFW_MOUSE_BUTTON_LEFT)
    return;
```

3. Toggle the `lock` variable to store the mouse hold event. The `lock` variable will be used to determine whether the mouse movement is used for rotating the object:

```
  if (action == GLFW_PRESS)
  {
    glfwSetInputMode(window, GLFW_CURSOR,    GLFW_CURSOR_DISABLED);
    locked = GL_TRUE;
  }
  else
  {
```

```
      locked = GL_FALSE;
      glfwSetInputMode(window, GLFW_CURSOR,GLFW_CURSOR_NORMAL);
    }
  }
```

For handling mouse movement events, we need to create another `callback` function. The `callback` function for mouse movement takes the *x* and *y* coordinates from the window instead of unique key inputs:

1. Define the `callback` function prototype that takes in the mouse coordinates:

```
void cursor_position_callback(GLFWwindow* window, double x,
  double y)
{
```

2. Upon mouse press and mouse movement, we update the rotation angles of the object with the *x* and *y* coordinates of the mouse:

```
  //if the mouse button is pressed
  if (locked)
  {
    alpha += (GLfloat) (x - cursorX) / 10.0f;
    beta += (GLfloat) (y - cursorY) / 10.0f;
  }
  //update the cursor position
  cursorX = (int) x;
  cursorY = (int) y;
}
```

Finally, we will implement the mouse scroll callback function, which allows users to scroll up and down to zoom in and zoom out of the object.

1. Define the `callback` function prototype that captures the `x` and `y` scroll variables:

```
void scroll_callback(GLFWwindow* window, double x, double y)
{
```

2. Take the y parameter (up and down scroll) and update the zoom variable:

```
  zoom += (float) y / 4.0f;
  if (zoom < 0.0f)
    zoom = 0.0f;
}
```

With all of the `callback` functions implemented, we are now ready to link these functions to the GLFW library event handlers. The GLFW library provides a platform independent API for handling each of these events, so the same code will run in Windows, Linux, and Mac OS X seamlessly.

To integrate the callbacks with the GLFW library, call the following functions in the `main` function:

```
//keyboard input callback
glfwSetKeyCallback(window, key_callback);

//framebuffer size callback
glfwSetFramebufferSizeCallback(window, framebuffer_size_callback);

//mouse button callback
glfwSetMouseButtonCallback(window, mouse_button_callback);

//mouse movement callback
glfwSetCursorPosCallback(window, cursor_position_callback);

//mouse scroll callback
glfwSetScrollCallback(window, scroll_callback);
```

The end result is an interactive interface that allows the user to control the rendering object freely in space. First, when the user scrolls the mouse (see the following screenshots), we translate the object forward or backward. This creates the visual perception that the object is zoomed in or zoomed out of the camera:

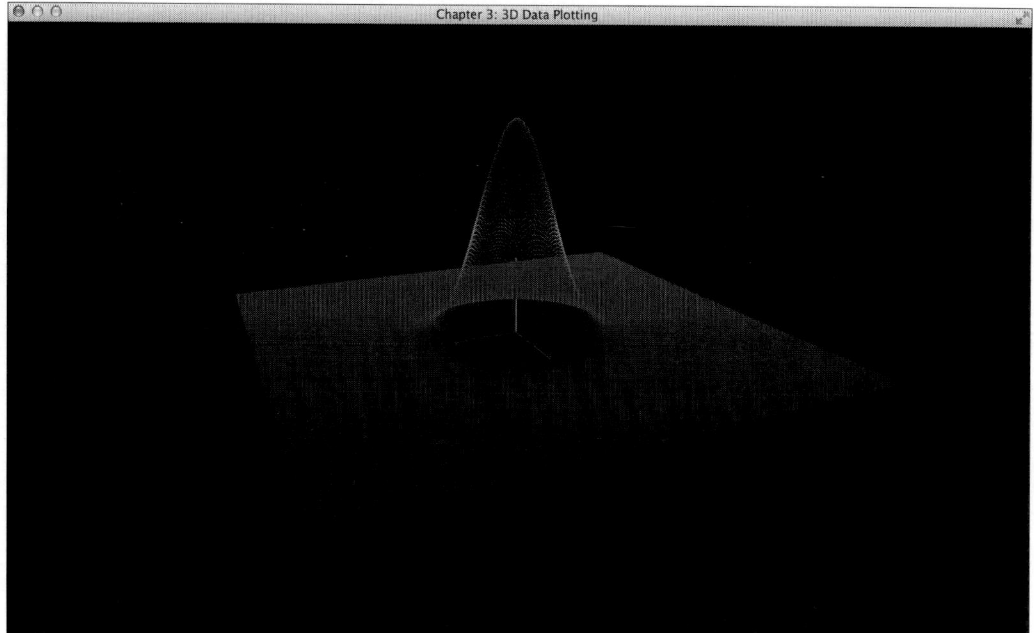

Here is another screenshot at a different zoom level:

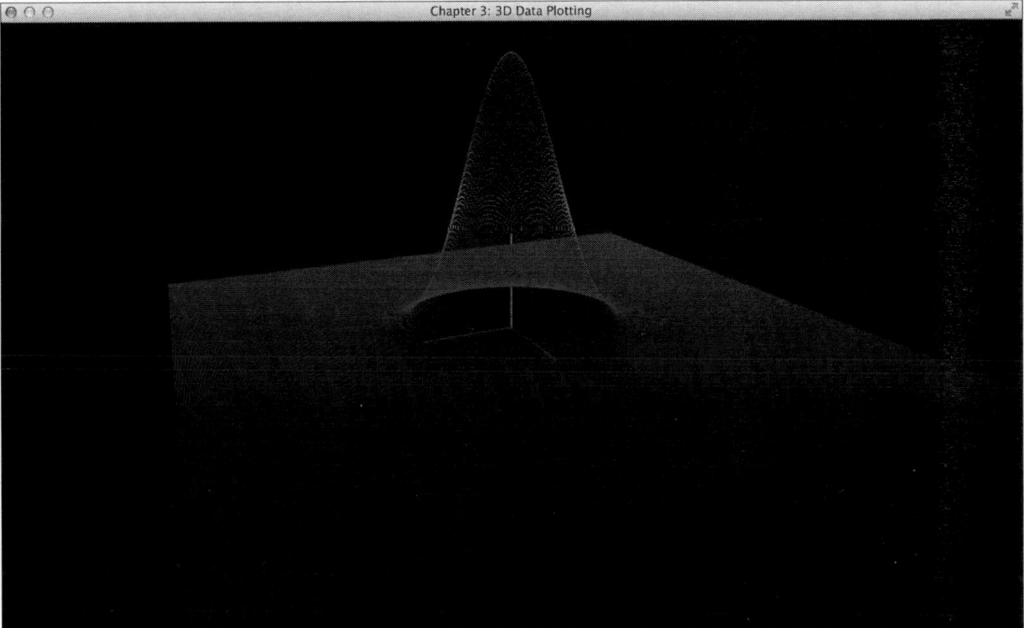

These simple yet powerful techniques allow users to manipulate virtual objects in real-time and can be extremely useful when visualizing complex datasets. Additionally, we can rotate the object at different angles by holding the mouse button and dragging the object in various directions. The screenshots below show how we can render the graph at any arbitrary angle to better understand the data distribution.

Here is a screenshot showing the side view of the Gaussian function:

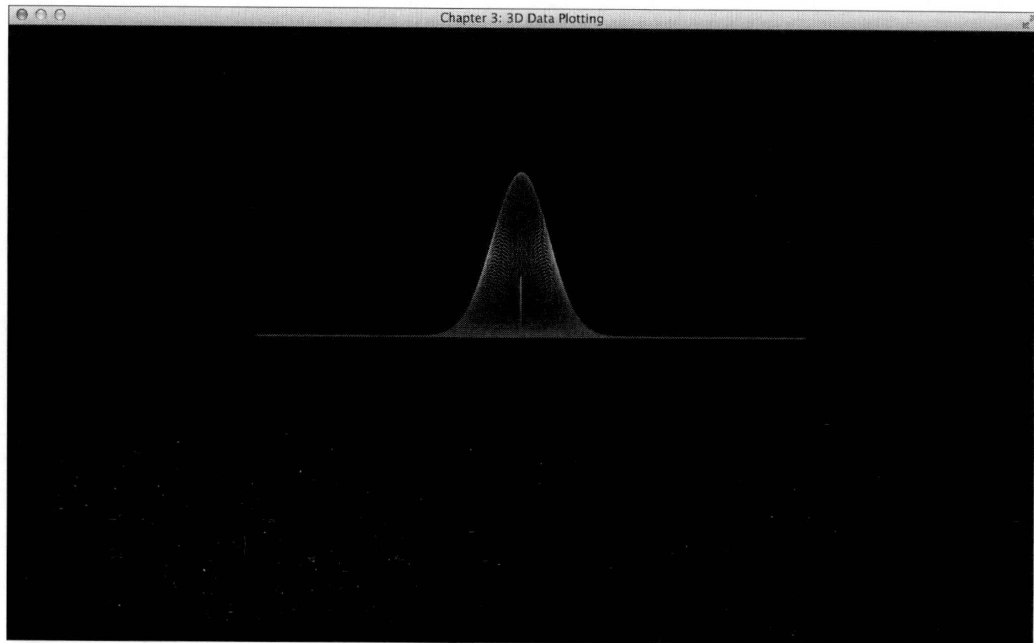

Here is a screenshot showing the Gaussian function from the top:

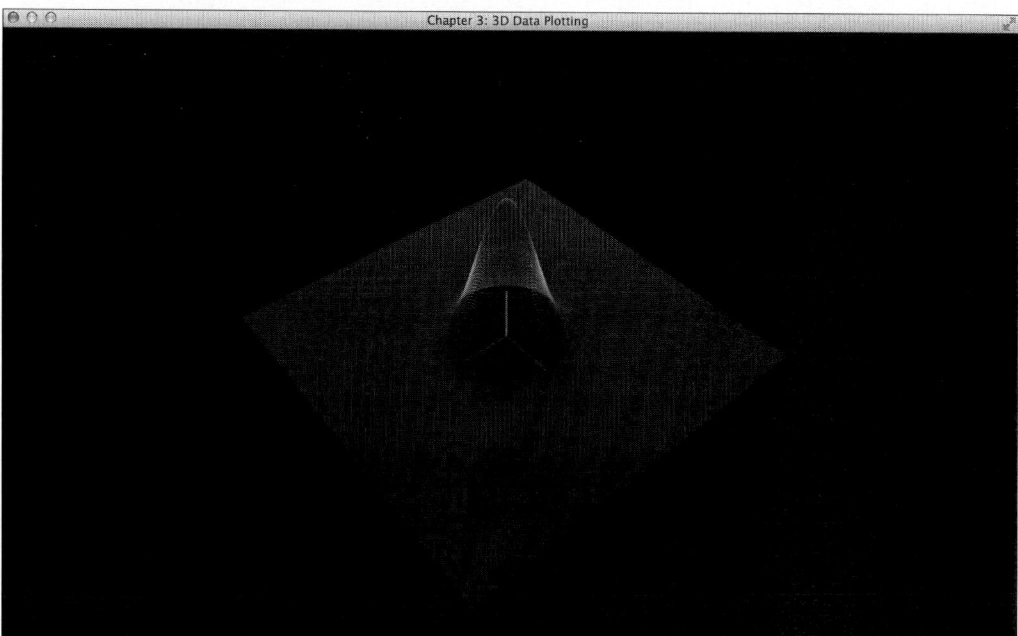

Finally, here is a screenshot showing the Gaussian function from the bottom:

How it works...

This sample code illustrates the basic interface needed to build interactive applications that are highly portable across multiple platforms using OpenGL and the GLFW library. The use of `callback` functions in the GLFW library allows non-blocking calls that run in parallel with the rendering engine. This concept is particularly useful since input devices such as the mouse, keyboard, and joysticks all have different input rates and latency. These `callback` functions allow for asynchronous execution without blocking the main rendering loop.

The `glfwSetKeyCallback`, `glfwSetFramebufferSizeCallback`, `glfwSetScrollCallback`, `glfwSetMouseBcuttonCallback`, and `glfwSetCursorPosCallback` functions provide controls over the mouse buttons and scrolling wheel, keyboard inputs, and window resizing events. These are only some of the many handlers we can implement with the GLFW library support. For example, we can further extend the error handling capabilities by adding additional `callback` functions. Also, we can handle window closing and opening events, thereby enabling even more sophisticated interfaces with multiple windows. With the examples provided thus far, we have introduced the basics of how to create interactive interfaces with relatively simple API calls.

See also

For complete coverage of GLFW library function calls, this website provides a comprehensive set of examples and documentation for all callback functions as well as the handling of inputs and other events: `http://www.glfw.org/docs/latest/`.

Rendering a volumetric dataset – MCML simulation

In this section, we will demonstrate the rendering of a 3D volumetric dataset generated from a Monte Carlo simulation of light transport in biological tissue, called **Monte Carlo for multi-layered media** (**MCML**). For simplicity, the simulation output file is included with the code bundle for this chapter so that readers can directly run the demo without setting up the simulation code. The source code for the Monte Carlo simulation is described in detail in a series of publications listed in the *See also* section and the GPU implementation is available online for interested readers (`https://code.google.com/p/gpumcml/`).

Light transport in biological tissue can be modeled with the **radiative transport equation** (**RTE**), which has proven difficult to solve analytically for complex geometry. The time-dependent RTE can be expressed as:

$$\frac{1}{\upsilon}\frac{\partial}{\partial t}L(\boldsymbol{r},\boldsymbol{\Omega},t)+\boldsymbol{\Omega}\cdot\nabla L(\boldsymbol{r},\boldsymbol{\Omega},t)+\left[\mu_a(\boldsymbol{r})+\mu_s(\boldsymbol{r})\right]L(\boldsymbol{r},\boldsymbol{\Omega},t)=$$
$$\int_{4\pi} L(\boldsymbol{r},\boldsymbol{\Omega}',t)\mu_s(\boldsymbol{r},\boldsymbol{\Omega}'\rightarrow\boldsymbol{\Omega})d\boldsymbol{\Omega}'+S(\boldsymbol{r},\boldsymbol{\Omega},t)$$

Here $L(r,\Omega,t)$ is the radiance [$W\,m^{-2}sr^{-1}$] defined as the radiant power [*W*] crossing an infinitesimal area at location *r* perpendicular to the direction Ω per unit solid angle, μ_s is the scattering coefficient, μ_a is the absorption coefficient, *v* is the speed of light, and $S(r,\Omega,t)$ is the source term. To solve the RTE numerically, Wilson and Adam introduced the **Monte Carlo** (**MC**) method, which is widely accepted as a gold-standard approach for photon migration modeling due to its accuracy and versatility (especially for complex tissue geometry).

The MC method is a statistical sampling technique that has been applied to a number of important problems in many different fields, ranging from radiation therapy planning in medicine to option pricing in finance. The name Monte Carlo is derived from the resort city in Monaco that is known for its casinos, among other attractions. As its name implies, the key feature of the MC method involves the exploitation of random chance (through the generation of random numbers with a particular probability distribution) to model the physical process in question.

In our case, we are interested in modeling photon propagation in biological tissue. The MCML algorithm provides an MC model of steady-state light transport in multi-layered media. In particular, we will simulate photon propagation in a homogeneous medium with a circular light source incident on the tissue surface in order to compute the light dose (absorbed energy) distribution. Such computations have a wide range of applications, including treatment planning for light therapies such as photodynamic therapy (this can be considered a light-activated chemotherapy for cancer).

Here, we demonstrate how to integrate our code base for displaying volumetric data with OpenGL rendering functions. We will take advantage of techniques such as alpha blending, perspective rendering, and heat map rendering. Together with the GLFW interface for capturing user inputs, we can create an interactive visualizer that can display a large volumetric dataset in real-time and control a slicer that magnifies a plane of data points within the volumetric dataset using a few simple key inputs.

Getting ready

The simulation result is stored in an ASCII text file that contains a 3D matrix. Each value in the matrix represents the absorbed photon energy density at some fixed position within the voxelized geometry. Here, we will provide a simple parser that extracts the simulation output matrix from the file and stores it in the local memory.

How to do it...

Let's get started by implementing the MCML data parser, the jet color scheme heat map generator, as well as the slicer in OpenGL:

1. Take the data from the simulation output text file and store it in floating-point arrays:

```
#define MCML_SIZE_X 50
#define MCML_SIZE_Y 50
#define MCML_SIZE_Z 200
float mcml_data[MCML_SIZE_X][MCML_SIZE_Y][MCML_SIZE_Z];
Vertex mcml_vertices[MCML_SIZE_X][MCML_SIZE_Y][MCML_SIZE_Z];
float max_data, min_data;
int slice_x = 0, slice_z = 0, slice_y = 0;
float point_size=5.0f;

//load the data from a text file
void loadMCML(){
  FILE *ifp;
  //open the file for reading
  ifp = fopen("MCML_output.txt", "r");
  if (ifp == NULL) {
```

```
    fprintf(stderr, "ERROR: Can't open MCML Data file!\n");
    exit(1);
  }
  float data;
  float max=0, min=9999999;
  for(int x=0; x<MCML_SIZE_X; x++){
    for(int z=0; z<MCML_SIZE_Z; z++){
      for(int y=0; y<MCML_SIZE_Y; y++){
        if (fscanf(ifp, "%f\n", &data) == EOF){
          fprintf(stderr, "ERROR: Missing MCML Data file!\n");
          exit(1);
        }
        //store the log compressed data point
        data = log(data+1);
        mcml_data[x][y][z]=data;
        //find the max and min from the data set for heatmap
        if(data>max){
          max=data;
        }
        if(data<min){
          min=data;
        }
        //normalize the coordinates
        mcml_vertices[x][y][z].x=(float)(x-MCML_SIZE_X/2.0f)/
          MCML_SIZE_X;
        mcml_vertices[x][y][z].y=(float)(y-MCML_SIZE_Y/2.0f)/
          MCML_SIZE_Y;
        mcml_vertices[x][y][z].z=(float)(z-MCML_SIZE_Z/2.0f)/
          MCML_SIZE_Z*2.0f;
      }
    }
  }
  fclose(ifp);
  max_data = max;
  min_data = min;
  halfmax= (max+min)/2.0f;
```

2. Encode the simulation output values using a custom color map for display:

```
  //store the heat map representation of the data
  for(int z=0; z<MCML_SIZE_Z; z++){
    for(int x=0; x<MCML_SIZE_X; x++){
      for(int y=0; y<MCML_SIZE_Y; y++){
        float value = mcml_data[x][y][z];
        COLOUR c = GetColour(value, min_data,max_data);
        mcml_vertices[x][y][z].r=c.r;
```

```
            mcml_vertices[x][y][z].g=c.g;
            mcml_vertices[x][y][z].b=c.b;
          }
        }
      }
    }
```

3. Implement the heat map generator with the jet color scheme:

```
Color getHeatMapColor(float value, float min, float max)
{
  //remapping the value to the JET color scheme
  Color c = {1.0f, 1.0f, 1.0f}; // default value
  float dv;
  //clamp the data
  if (value < min)
    value = min;
  if (value > max)
    value = max;
  range = max - min;
  //the first region (0%-25%)
  if (value < (min + 0.25f * range)) {
    c.r = 0.0f;
    c.g = 4.0f * (value - min) / range;
  }
  //the second region of value (25%-50%)
  else if (value < (min + 0.5f * range)) {
    c.r = 0.0f;
    c.b = 1.0f + 4.0f * (min + 0.25f * range - value) / range;
  }
  //the third region of value (50%-75%)
  else if (value < (min + 0.75f * range)) {
    c.r = 4.0f * (value - min - 0.5f * range) / range;
    c.b = 0.0f;
  }
  //the fourth region (75%-100%)
  else {
    c.g = 1.0f + 4.0f * (min + 0.75f * range - value) / range;
    c.b = 0.0f;
  }
  return(c);
}
```

4. Draw all data points on screen with transparency enabled:

```
void drawMCMLPoints(){
  glPointSize(point_size);
  glBegin(GL_POINTS);
  for(int z=0; z<MCML_SIZE_Z; z++){
    for(int x=0; x<MCML_SIZE_X; x++){
      for(int y=0; y<MCML_SIZE_Y; y++){
        glColor4f(mcml_vertices[x][y][z].r,mcml_vertices[x][y]
          [z].g,mcml_vertices[x][y][z].b, 0.15f);
        glVertex3f(mcml_vertices[x][y][z].x,mcml_vertices[x][y]
          [z].y,mcml_vertices[x][y][z].z);
      }
    }
  }
  glEnd();
}
```

5. Draw three slices of data points for cross-sectional visualization:

```
void drawMCMLSlices(){
  glPointSize(10.0f);
  glBegin(GL_POINTS);

  //display data on xy plane
  for(int x=0; x<MCML_SIZE_X; x++){
    for(int y=0; y<MCML_SIZE_Y; y++){
      int z = slice_z;
      glColor4f(mcml_vertices[x][y][z].r,mcml_vertices[x][y]
        [z].g,mcml_vertices[x][y][z].b, 0.9f);
      glVertex3f(mcml_vertices[x][y][z].x,mcml_vertices[x][y]
        [z].y,mcml_vertices[x][y][z].z);
    }
  }

  //display data on yz plane
  for(int z=0; z<MCML_SIZE_Z; z++){
    for(int y=0; y<MCML_SIZE_Y; y++){
      int x = slice_x;
      glColor4f(mcml_vertices[x][y][z].r,mcml_vertices[x][y]
        [z].g,mcml_vertices[x][y][z].b, 0.9f);
      glVertex3f(mcml_vertices[x][y][z].x,mcml_vertices[x][y]
        [z].y,mcml_vertices[x][y][z].z);
    }
  }

  //display data on xz plane
  for(int z=0; z<MCML_SIZE_Z; z++){
    for(int x=0; x<MCML_SIZE_X; x++){
      int y = slice_y;
```

```
        glColor4f(mcml_vertices[x][y][z].r,mcml_vertices[x][y]
          [z].g,mcml_vertices[x][y][z].b, 0.9f);
        glVertex3f(mcml_vertices[x][y][z].x,mcml_vertices[x][y]
          [z].y,mcml_vertices[x][y][z].z);
      }
    }
    glEnd();
  }
```

6. In addition, we need to update the `key_callback` function for moving the slices:

```
void key_callback(GLFWwindow* window, int key, int scancode,
  int action, int mods)
{
  if (action != GLFW_PRESS)
    return;
  switch (key)
  {
    case GLFW_KEY_ESCAPE:
      glfwSetWindowShouldClose(window, GL_TRUE);
      break;
    case GLFW_KEY_P:
      point_size+=0.5;
      break;
    case GLFW_KEY_O:
      point_size-=0.5;
      break;
    case GLFW_KEY_A:
      slice_y -=1;
      if(slice_y < 0)
        slice_y = 0;
      break;
    case GLFW_KEY_D:
      slice_y +=1;
      if(slice_y >= MCML_SIZE_Y-1)
        slice_y = MCML_SIZE_Y-1;
      break;
    case GLFW_KEY_W:
      slice_z +=1;
      if(slice_z >= MCML_SIZE_Z-1)
        slice_z = MCML_SIZE_Z-1;
      break;
    case GLFW_KEY_S:
      slice_z -= 1;
      if (slice_z < 0)
        slice_z = 0;
```

```
        break;
      case GLFW_KEY_E:
        slice_x -=1;
        if(slice_x < 0)
          slice_x = 0;
        break;
      case GLFW_KEY_Q:
        slice_x +=1;
        if(slice_x >= MCML_SIZE_X-1)
          slice_x = MCML_SIZE_X-1;
        break;
      case GLFW_KEY_PAGE_UP:
        zoom -= 0.25f;
        if (zoom < 0.f)
          zoom = 0.f;
        break;
      case GLFW_KEY_PAGE_DOWN:
        zoom += 0.25f;
        break;
      default:
        break;
    }
  }
```

7. Finally, to complete the demo, simply call the `drawMCMLPoints` and `drawMCMLSlices` functions inside the `main` loop using the same code structure for perspective rendering introduced in the previous demo for plotting a Gaussian function:

```
while (!glfwWindowShouldClose(window))
{
  glClear(GL_COLOR_BUFFER_BIT | GL_DEPTH_BUFFER_BIT);
  glClearColor(0.0f, 0.0f, 0.0f, 1.0f);

  glMatrixMode(GL_MODELVIEW);
  glLoadIdentity();
  glTranslatef(0.0, 0.0, -zoom);
  glRotatef(beta, 1.0, 0.0, 0.0);
  glRotatef(alpha, 0.0, 0.0, 1.0);
  //disable depth test so we can render the points with blending
  glDisable(GL_DEPTH_TEST);
  drawMCMLPoints();
  //must enable this to ensure the slides are rendered in the
    right order
```

```
    glEnable(GL_DEPTH_TEST);
    drawMCMLSlices();

    //draw the origin with the x,y,z axes for visualization
    drawOrigin();
    glfwSwapBuffers(window);
    glfwPollEvents();
  }
```

The simulation results, representing the photon absorption distribution in a voxelized geometry, are displayed in 3D in the following screenshot. The light source illuminates the tissue surface (*z=0* at the bottom) and propagates through the tissue (positive *z* direction) that is modeled as an infinitely wide homogeneous medium. The photon absorption distribution follows the expected shape for a finite-sized, flat, and circular beam:

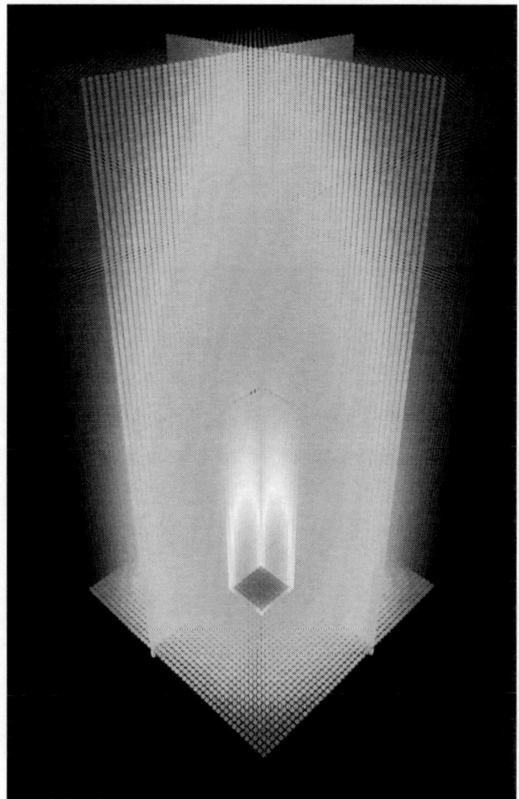

How it works...

This demo illustrates how we can take a volumetric dataset generated from a Monte Carlo simulation (and, more generally, a volumetric dataset from any application) and render it with a highly interactive interface using OpenGL. The data parser takes an ASCII text file as input. Then, we turn the floating-point data into individual vertices that can fit into our rendering pipeline. Upon initialization, the variables `mcml_vertices` and `mcml_data` store the pre-computed heat map data as well as the position of each data point. The `parser` function also computes the maximum and minimum value in the dataset for heat map visualization. The `getHeatMapColor` function takes the simulation output value and maps it to a color in the jet color scheme. The algorithm basically defines a color spectrum and we remap the value based on its range.

In the following screenshot, we show a top view of the simulation result, which allows us to visualize the symmetry of the light distribution:

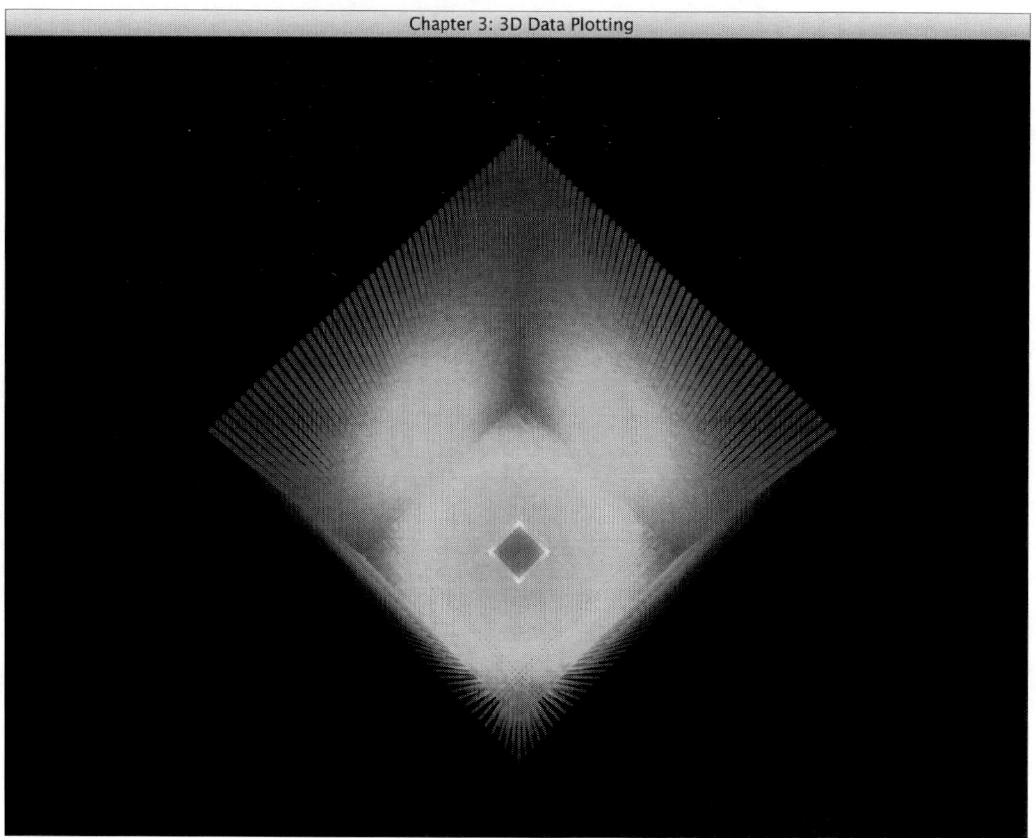

The `drawMCMLSlices` function takes a slice (that is, a plane) of data and renders the data points at the full opacity and a larger point size. This provides a useful and very common visualization method (especially in medical imaging) that allows users to examine the volumetric data in detail by moving the cross-sectional slices. As we can see in the following screenshot, we can shift the slicer in the *x*, *y*, and *z* directions to visualize the desired regions of interest:

There's more...

This demo provides an example of real-time volumetric data visualization for rendering simulation data in an interactive 3D environment. The current implementation can be easily modified for a wide range of applications that require volumetric dataset visualization. Our approach provides an intuitive way to render complex 3D datasets with a heat map generator and a slicer as well as 3D perspective rendering techniques using OpenGL.

One important observation is that this demo required a significant number of `glVertex3f` calls, which can become a major performance bottleneck. To address this, in the upcoming chapters, we will explore more sophisticated ways to handle memory transfer and draw even more complex models with **Vertex Buffer Objects** (**VBOs**), a memory buffer in your graphics card designed to store information about vertices. This will lead us towards fragment programs and custom vertex shader programs (that is, moving from OpenGL 2.0 to OpenGL 3.2 or higher). However, the simplicity of using classical OpenGL 2.0 calls is an important consideration if we are aiming for a short development cycle, minimal overhead, and backward compatibility with older hardware.

See also

For further information, please consult the following references:

- E. Alerstam & W. C. Y. Lo, T. Han, J. Rose, S. Andersson-Engels, and L. Lilge, "Next-generation acceleration and code optimization for light transport in turbid media using GPUs," *Biomed. Opt. Express 1*, 658-675 (2010).
- W. C. Y. Lo, K. Redmond, J. Luu, P. Chow, J. Rose, and L. Lilge, "Hardware acceleration of a Monte Carlo simulation for photodynamic therapy treatment planning," *J. Biomed. Opt. 14*, 014019 (2009).
- L. Wang, S. Jacques, and L. Zheng, "MCML - Monte Carlo modeling of light transport in multi-layered tissues," *Comput. Meth. Prog. Biol. 47*, 131–146 (1995).
- B. Wilson and G. Adam, "A Monte Carlo model for the absorption and flux distributions of light in tissue," *Med. Phys. 10*, 824 (1983).

4

Rendering 2D Images and Videos with Texture Mapping

In this chapter, we will cover the following topics:

- Getting started with modern OpenGL (3.2 or higher)
- Setting up the GLEW, GLM, SOIL, and OpenCV libraries in Windows
- Setting up the GLEW, GLM, SOIL, and OpenCV libraries in Mac OS X/Linux
- Creating your first vertex and fragment shader using GLSL
- Rendering 2D images with texture mapping
- Real-time video rendering with filters

Introduction

In this chapter, we will introduce OpenGL techniques to visualize another important class of datasets: those involving images or videos. Such datasets are commonly encountered in many fields, including medical imaging applications. To enable the rendering of images, we will discuss fundamental OpenGL concepts for texture mapping and transition to more advanced techniques that require newer versions of OpenGL (OpenGL 3.2 or higher). To simplify our tasks, we will also employ several additional libraries, including **OpenGL Extension Wrangler Library** (**GLEW**) for runtime OpenGL extension support, **Simple OpenGL Image Loader** (**SOIL**) to load different image formats, **OpenGL Mathematics** (**GLM**) for vector and matrix manipulation, as well as **OpenCV** for image/video processing. To get started, we will first introduce the features of modern OpenGL 3.2 and higher.

Getting started with modern OpenGL (3.2 or higher)

Continuous evolution of OpenGL APIs has led to the emergence of a modern standard. One of the biggest changes happened in 2008 with OpenGL version 3.0, in which a new context creation mechanism was introduced and most of the older functions, such as Begin/End primitive specifications, were marked as deprecated. The removal of these older standard features also implies a more flexible yet more powerful way of handling the graphics pipeline. In OpenGL 3.2 or higher, a core and a compatible profile were defined to differentiate the deprecated APIs from the current features. These profiles provide clear definitions for various features (core profile) while enabling backward compatibility (compatibility profile). In OpenGL 4.x, support for the latest graphics hardware that runs Direct3D 11 is provided, and a detailed comparison between OpenGL 3.x and OpenGL 4.x is available at `http://www.g-truc.net/post-0269.html`.

Getting ready

Starting from this chapter, we need compatible graphics cards with OpenGL 3.2 (or higher) support. Most graphics cards released before 2008 will most likely not be supported. For example, NVIDIA GeForce 100, 200, 300 series and higher support the OpenGL 3 standard. You are encouraged to consult the technical specifications of your graphics cards to confirm the compatibility (refer to `https://developer.nvidia.com/opengl-driver`).

How to do it...

To enable OpenGL 3.2 support, we need to incorporate the following lines of code at the beginning of every program for initialization:

```
glfwWindowHint(GLFW_CONTEXT_VERSION_MAJOR, 3);
glfwWindowHint(GLFW_CONTEXT_VERSION_MINOR, 2);
glfwWindowHint(GLFW_OPENGL_FORWARD_COMPAT, GL_TRUE);
glfwWindowHint(GLFW_OPENGL_PROFILE, GLFW_OPENGL_CORE_PROFILE);
```

How it works...

The `glfwWindowHint` function defines a set of constraints for the creation of the GLFW windows context (refer to *Chapter 1, Getting Started with OpenGL*). The first two lines of code here define the current version of OpenGL that will be used (3.2 in this case). The third line enables forward compatibility, while the last line specifies that the core profile will be used.

See also

Detailed explanation of the differences between various OpenGL versions can be found at `http://www.opengl.org/wiki/History_of_OpenGL`.

Setting up the GLEW, GLM, SOIL, and OpenCV libraries in Windows

In this section, we will provide step-by-step instructions to set up several popular libraries that will be used extensively in this chapter (and in subsequent chapters), including the GLEW, GLM, SOIL, and OpenCV libraries:

- The GLEW library is an open-source OpenGL extension library.
- The GLM library is a header-only C++ library that provides an easy-to-use set of common mathematical operations. It is built on the GLSL specifications and as it is a header-only library, it does not require tedious compilation steps.
- The SOIL library is a simple C library that is used to load images in a variety of common formats (such as BMP, PNG, JPG, TGA, TIFF, and HDR) in OpenGL textures.
- The OpenCV library is a very powerful open source computer vision library that we will use to simplify image and video processing in this chapter.

Getting ready

We will first need to download the prerequisite libraries from the following websites:

- **GLEW** (glew-1.10.0): `http://sourceforge.net/projects/glew/files/glew/1.10.0/glew-1.10.0-win32.zip`
- **GLM** (glm-0.9.5.4): `http://sourceforge.net/projects/ogl-math/files/glm-0.9.5.4/glm-0.9.5.4.zip`
- **SOIL**: `http://www.lonesock.net/files/soil.zip`
- **OpenCV** (opencv-2.4.9): `http://sourceforge.net/projects/opencvlibrary/files/opencv-win/2.4.9/opencv-2.4.9.exe`

How to do it...

To use the precompiled package from GLEW, follow these steps:

1. Unzip the package.
2. Copy the directory to `C:/Program Files (x86)`.

3. Ensure that the `glew32.dll` file (`C:\Program Files (x86)\glew-1.10.0\bin\Release\Win32`) can be found at runtime by placing it either in the same folder as the executable or including the directory in the Windows system `PATH` environment variable (Navigate to **Control Panel** | **System and Security** | **System** | **Advanced Systems Settings** | **Environment Variables**).

To use the header-only GLM library, follow these steps:

1. Unzip the package.
2. Copy the directory to `C:/Program Files (x86)`.
3. Include the desired header files in your source code. Here is an example:

```
#include <glm/glm.hpp>
```

To use the SOIL library, follow these steps:

1. Unzip the package.
2. Copy the directory to `C:/Program Files (x86)`.
3. Generate the `SOIL.lib` file by opening the Visual Studio solution file (`C:\Program Files (x86)\Simple OpenGL Image Library\projects\VC9\SOIL.sln`) and compiling the project files. Copy this file from `C:\Program Files (x86)\Simple OpenGL Image Library\projects\VC9\Debug` to `C:\Program Files (x86)\Simple OpenGL Image Library\lib`.
4. Include the header file in your source code:

```
#include <SOIL.h>
```

Finally, to install OpenCV, we recommend that you use prebuilt binaries to simplify the process:

1. Download the prebuilt binaries from `http://sourceforge.net/projects/opencvlibrary/files/opencv-win/2.4.9/opencv-2.4.9.exe` and extract the package.
2. Copy the directory (the `opencv` folder) to `C:\Program Files (x86)`.
3. Add this to the system `PATH` environment variable (Navigate to **Control Panel** | **System and Security** | **System** | **Advanced Systems Settings** | **Environment Variables**) - `C:\Program Files (x86)\opencv\build\x86\vc12\bin`.

4. Include the desired header files in your source code:

```
#include <opencv2/core/core.hpp>
#include <opencv2/highgui/highgui.hpp>
```

Now, we generate our Microsoft Visual Studio Solution files (the build environment) using `CMake`. We create the `CMakeList.txt` file within each project directory, which lists all the libraries and dependencies for the project. The following is a sample `CMakeList.txt` file for our first demo application:

```
cmake_minimum_required (VERSION 2.8)
set(CMAKE_CONFIGURATION_TYPES Debug Release)
set(PROGRAM_PATH "C:/Program Files \(x86\)")
set(OpenCV_DIR ${PROGRAM_PATH}/opencv/build)
project (code_simple)
#modify these path based on your configuration
#OpenCV
find_package(OpenCV REQUIRED )
INCLUDE_DIRECTORIES(${OpenCV_INCLUDE_DIRS})
INCLUDE_DIRECTORIES(${PROGRAM_PATH}/glm)
INCLUDE_DIRECTORIES(${PROGRAM_PATH}/glew-1.10.0/include)
LINK_DIRECTORIES(${PROGRAM_PATH}/glew-1.10.0/lib/Release)
INCLUDE_DIRECTORIES(${PROGRAM_PATH}/glfw-3.0.4/include)
LINK_DIRECTORIES(${PROGRAM_PATH}/glfw-3.0.4/lib)
INCLUDE_DIRECTORIES(${PROGRAM_PATH}/Simple\ OpenGL\ Image\ Library/
src)
LINK_DIRECTORIES(${PROGRAM_PATH}/Simple\ OpenGL\ Image\ Library/lib)
add_subdirectory (../common common)
add_executable (main main.cpp)
target_link_libraries (main LINK_PUBLIC shader controls texture
glew32s glfw3 opengl32 ${OpenCV_LIBS} SOIL)
```

As you can see in the `CMakeList.txt` file, the various dependencies, including the OpenCV, SOIL, GLFW, and GLEW libraries, are all included.

Finally, we run the `CMake` program to generate the Microsoft Visual Studio Solution for the project (refer to *Chapter 1, Getting Started with OpenGL* for details). Note that the output path for the binary must match the project folder due to dependencies of the shader programs. The following is a screenshot of the `CMake` window after generating the first sample project called `code_simple`:

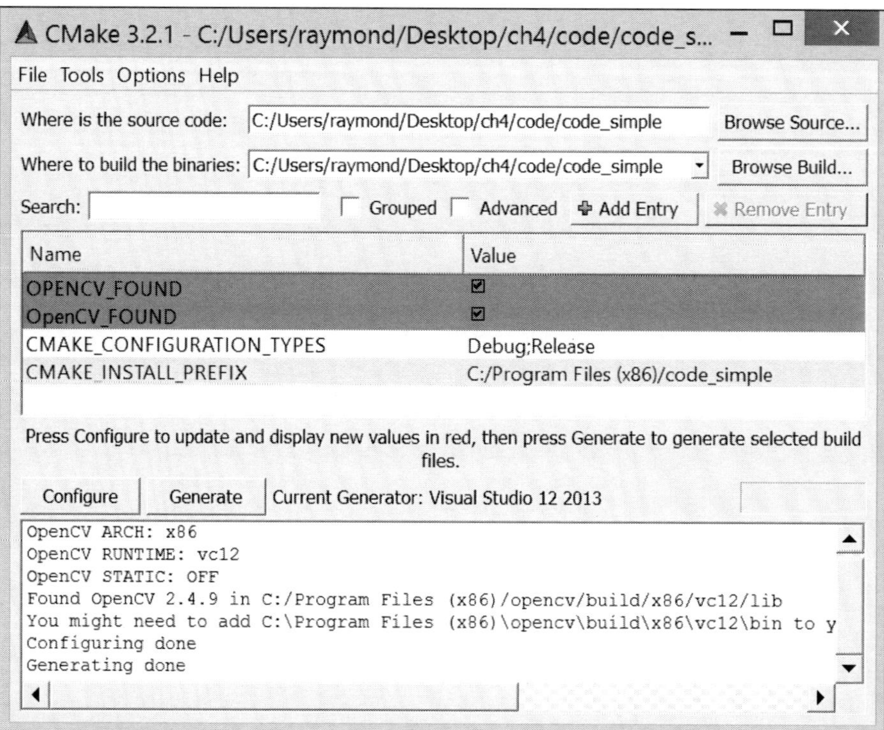

We will repeat this step for each project we create, and the corresponding Microsoft Visual Studio Solution file will be generated accordingly (for example, `code_simple.sln` in this case). To compile the code, open `code_simple.sln` with Microsoft Visual Studio 2013 and build the project using the Build (press *F7*) function as usual. Make sure that you set main as the start up project (by right-clicking on the *main* project in the **Solution Explorer** and left-clicking on the **Set as StartUp Project** option) before running the program, as shown follows:

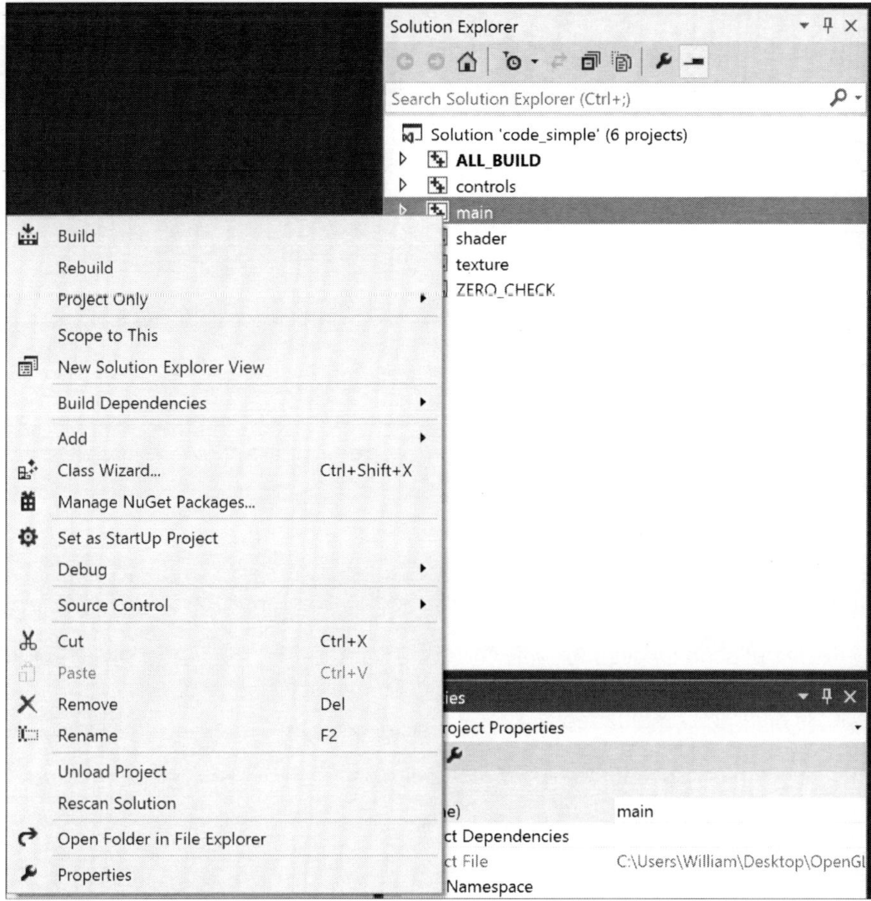

See also

Further documentation on each of the libraries installed can be found here:

- **GLEW**: `http://glew.sourceforge.net/`
- **GLM**: `http://glm.g-truc.net/0.9.5/index.html`
- **SOIL**: `http://www.lonesock.net/soil.html`
- **OpenCV**: `http://opencv.org/`

Setting up the GLEW, GLM, SOIL, and OpenCV libraries in Mac OS X/Linux

In this section, we will outline the steps required to set up the same libraries in Mac OS X and Linux.

Getting ready

We will first need to download the prerequisite libraries from the following websites:

1. **GLEW** (glew-1.10.0): `https://sourceforge.net/projects/glew/files/glew/1.10.0/glew-1.10.0.tgz`
2. **GLM** (glm-0.9.5.4): `http://sourceforge.net/projects/ogl-math/files/glm-0.9.5.4/glm-0.9.5.4.zip`
3. **SOIL**: `http://www.lonesock.net/files/soil.zip`
4. **OpenCV** (opencv-2.4.9): `http://sourceforge.net/projects/opencvlibrary/files/opencv-unix/2.4.9/opencv-2.4.9.zip`

To simplify the installation process for Mac OS X or Ubuntu users, the use of MacPorts in Mac OS X or the `apt-get` command in Linux (as described in *Chapter 1, Getting Started with OpenGL*) is highly recommended.

The following section assumes that the download directory is `~/opengl_dev` (refer to *Chapter 1, Getting Started with OpenGL*).

How to do it...

There are two methods to install the prerequisite libraries. The first method uses precompiled binaries. These binary files are fetched from remote repository servers and the version updates of the library are controlled externally. An important advantage of this method is that it simplifies the installation, especially in terms of resolving dependencies. However, in a release environment, it is recommended that you disable the automatic updates and thus protect the binary from version skewing. The second method requires users to download and compile the source code directly with various customizations. This method is recommended for users who would like to control the installation process (such as the paths), and it also provides more flexibility in terms of tracking and fixing bugs.

For beginners or developers who are looking for rapid prototyping, we recommend that you use the first method as it will simplify the workflow and have short-term maintenance. On an Ubuntu or Debian system, we can install the various libraries using the `apt-get` command. To install all the prerequisite libraries and dependencies on Ubuntu, simply run the following commands in the terminal:

```
sudo apt-get install libglm-dev libglew1.6-dev libsoil-dev libopencv
```

Similarly, on Mac OS X, we can install GLEW, OpenCV, and GLM with MacPorts through command lines in the terminal:

```
sudo port install opencv glm glew
```

However, the SOIL library is not currently supported by MacPorts, and thus, the installation has to be completed manually, as described in the following section.

For advanced users, we can install the latest packages by directly compiling from the source, and the upcoming steps are common among Mac OS as well as other Linux OS.

To compile the GLEW package, follow these steps:

1. Extract the `glew-1.10.0.tgz` package:

   ```
   tar xzvf glew-1.10.0.tgz
   ```

2. Install GLEW in `/usr/include/GL` and `/usr/lib`:

   ```
   cd glew-1.10.0
   make && sudo make install
   ```

To set up the header-only GLM library, follow these steps:

1. Extract the unzip `glm-0.9.5.4.zip` package:

   ```
   unzip glm-0.9.5.4.zip
   ```

2. Copy the header-only GLM library directory (`~/opengl_dev/glm/glm`) to `/usr/include/glm`:

   ```
   sudo cp -r glm/glm/ /usr/include/glm
   ```

To set up the SOIL library, follow these steps:

1. Extract the unzip `soil.zip` package:

   ```
   unzip soil.zip
   ```

2. Edit `makefile` (inside the `projects/makefile` directory) and add `-arch x86_64` and `-arch i386` to `CXXFLAGS` to ensure proper support:

   ```
   CXXFLAGS =-arch x86_64 -arch i386 -O2 -s -Wall
   ```

3. Compile the source code library:

```
cd Simple\ OpenGL\ Image\ Library/projects/makefile
mkdir obj
make && sudo make install
```

To set up the OpenCV library, follow these steps:

1. Extract the `opencv-2.4.9.zip` package:

```
unzip opencv-2.4.9.zip
```

2. Build the OpenCV library using `CMake`:

```
cd opencv-2.4.9/
mkdir build
cd build
cmake ../
make && sudo make install
```

3. Configure the library path:

```
sudo sh -c 'echo "/usr/local/lib" > /etc/ld.so.conf.d/opencv.conf'
sudo ldconfig -v
```

4. With the development environment fully configured, we can now create the compilation script (`Makefile`) within each project folder:

```
CFILES = ../common/shader.cpp ../common/texture.cpp ../common/
controls.cpp main.cpp
CFLAGS = -O3 -c -Wall
INCLUDES = -I/usr/include -I/usr/include/SOIL -I../common  `pkg-
config --cflags glfw3` `pkg-config --cflags opencv`
LIBS = -lm -L/usr/local/lib -lGLEW -lSOIL  `pkg-config --static
--libs glfw3` `pkg-config --libs opencv`
CC = g++
OBJECTS=$(CFILES:.cpp=.o)
EXECUTABLE=main
all: $(CFILES) $(EXECUTABLE)
$(EXECUTABLE): $(OBJECTS)
  $(CC) $(INCLUDES) $(OBJECTS) -o $@ $(LIBS)
.cpp.o:
  $(CC) $(CFLAGS) $(INCLUDES) $< -o $@

clean:
  rm -v -f *~ ../common/*.o *.o *.obj $(EXECUTABLE)
```

To compile the code, we simply run the `make` command in the project directory and it generates the executable (`main`) automatically.

See also

Further documentation on each of the libraries installed can be found here:

- **GLEW**: `http://glew.sourceforge.net/`
- **GLM**: `http://glm.g-truc.net/0.9.5/index.html`
- **SOIL**: `http://www.lonesock.net/soil.html`
- **OpenCV**: `http://opencv.org/`
- **MacPorts**: `http://www.macports.org/`

Creating your first vertex and fragment shader using GLSL

Before we can render images using OpenGL, we need to first understand the basics of the GLSL. In particular, the concept of shader programs is essential in GLSL. Shaders are simply programs that run on graphics processors (GPUs), and a set of shaders is compiled and linked to form a program. This concept emerges as a result of the increasing complexity of various common processing tasks in modern graphics hardware, such as vertex and fragment processing, which necessitates greater programmability of specialized processors. Accordingly, the vertex and fragment shader are two important types of shaders that we will cover here, and they run on the vertex processor and fragment processor, respectively. A simplified diagram illustrating the overall processing pipeline is shown as follows:

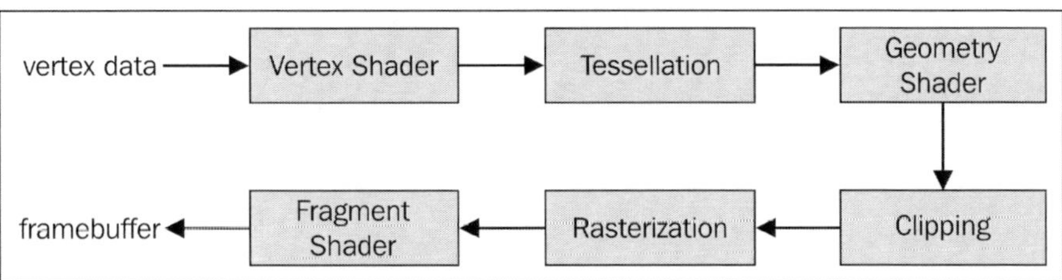

The main purpose of the vertex shader is to perform the processing of a stream of vertex data. An important processing task involves the transformation of the position of each vertex from the 3D virtual space to a 2D coordinate for display on the screen. Vertex shaders can also manipulate the color and texture coordinates. Therefore, vertex shaders serve as an important component of the OpenGL pipeline to control movement, lighting, and color.

A fragment shader is primarily designed to compute the final color of an individual pixel (fragment). Oftentimes, we implement various image post-processing techniques, such as blurring or sharpening, at this stage; the end results are stored in the framebuffer, which will be displayed on screen.

For readers interested in understanding the rest of the pipeline, a detailed summary of these stages, such as the clipping, rasterization, and tessellation, can be found at `https://www.opengl.org/wiki/Rendering_Pipeline_Overview`. Additionally, a detailed documentation of GLSL can be found at `https://www.opengl.org/registry/doc/GLSLangSpec.4.40.pdf`.

Getting ready

At this point, we should have all the prerequisite libraries, such as GLEW, GLM, and SOIL. With GLFW configured for the OpenGL core profile, we are now ready to implement the first simple example code, which takes advantage of the modern OpenGL pipeline.

How to do it...

To keep the code simple, we will divide the program into two components: the main program (`main.cpp`) and shader programs (`shader.cpp`, `shader.hpp`, `simple.vert`, and `simple.frag`). The main program performs the essential tasks to set up the simple demo, while the shader programs perform the specialized processing in the modern OpenGL pipeline. The complete sample code can be found in the `code_simple` folder.

First, let's take a look at the shader programs. We will create two extremely simple vertex and fragment shader programs (specified inside the `simple.vert` and `simple.frag` files) that are compiled and loaded by the program at runtime.

For the `simple.vert` file, enter the following lines of code:

```
#version 150
in vec3 position;
in vec3 color_in;
out vec3 color;
void main() {
  color = color_in;
  gl_Position = vec4(position, 1.0);
}
```

For the `simple.frag` file, enter the following lines of code:

```
#version 150
in vec3 color;
out vec4 color_out;
void main() {
  color_out = vec4(Color, 1.0);
}
```

First, let's define a function to compile and load the shader programs (`simple.frag` and `simple.vert`) called `LoadShaders` inside `shader.hpp`:

```
#ifndef SHADER_HPP
#define SHADER_HPP
GLuint LoadShaders(const char * vertex_file_path,const char *
  fragment_file_path);
#endif
```

Next, we will create the `shader.cpp` file to implement the `LoadShaders` function and two helper functions to handle file I/O (`readSourceFile`) and the compilation of the shaders (`CompileShader`):

1. Include prerequisite libraries and the `shader.hpp` header file:

   ```
   #include <iostream>
   #include <fstream>
   #include <algorithm>
   #include <vector>
   #include "shader.hpp"
   ```

2. Implement the `readSourceFile` function as follows:

   ```
   std::string readSourceFile(const char *path){
     std::string code;
     std::ifstream file_stream(path, std::ios::in);
     if(file_stream.is_open()){
       std::string line = "";
       while(getline(file_stream, line))
       code += "\n" + line;
       file_stream.close();
       return code;
     }else{
       printf("Failed to open \"%s\".\n", path);
       return "";
     }
   }
   ```

3. Implement the `CompileShader` function as follows:

```
void CompileShader(std::string program_code, GLuint
  shader_id){
  GLint result = GL_FALSE;
  int infolog_length;
  char const * program_code_pointer = program_code.c_str();
  glShaderSource(shader_id, 1, &program_code_pointer ,
    NULL);
  glCompileShader(shader_id);
  //check the shader for successful compile
  glGetShaderiv(shader_id, GL_COMPILE_STATUS, &result);
  glGetShaderiv(shader_id, GL_INFO_LOG_LENGTH,
    &infolog_length);
  if ( infolog_length > 0 ){
    std::vector<char> error_msg(infolog_length+1);
    glGetShaderInfoLog(shader_id, infolog_length, NULL,
      &error_msg[0]);
    printf("%s\n", &error_msg[0]);
  }
}
```

4. Now, let's implement the `LoadShaders` function. First, create the shader ID and read the shader code from two files specified by `vertex_file_path` and `fragment_file_path`:

```
GLuint LoadShaders(const char * vertex_file_path,const char
  * fragment_file_path){
  GLuint vertex_shader_id =
    glCreateShader(GL_VERTEX_SHADER);
  GLuint fragment_shader_id =
    glCreateShader(GL_FRAGMENT_SHADER);
  std::string vertex_shader_code =
    readSourceFile(vertex_file_path);
  if(vertex_shader_code == ""){
    return 0;
  }
  std::string fragment_shader_code =
    readSourceFile(fragment_file_path);
  if(fragment_shader_code == ""){
    return 0;
  }
```

5. Compile the vertex shader and fragment shader programs:

```
printf("Compiling Vertex shader : %s\n",
  vertex_file_path);
CompileShader(vertex_shader_code, vertex_shader_id);
printf("Compiling Fragment shader :
  %s\n",fragment_file_path);
CompileShader(fragment_shader_code, fragment_shader_id);
```

6. Link the programs together, check for errors, and clean up:

```
GLint result = GL_FALSE;
int infolog_length;
printf("Linking program\n");
GLuint program_id = glCreateProgram();
glAttachShader(program_id, vertex_shader_id);
glAttachShader(program_id, fragment_shader_id);
glLinkProgram(program_id);
//check the program and ensure that the program is linked properly
glGetProgramiv(program_id, GL_LINK_STATUS, &result);
glGetProgramiv(program_id, GL_INFO_LOG_LENGTH,
  &infolog_length);
if ( infolog_length > 0 ){
  std::vector<char> program_error_msg(infolog_length+1);
  glGetProgramInfoLog(program_id, infolog_length, NULL,
    &program_error_msg[0]);
  printf("%s\n", &program_error_msg[0]);
}else{
  printf("Linked Successfully\n");
}

//flag for delete, and will free all memories
//when the attached program is deleted
glDeleteShader(vertex_shader_id);
glDeleteShader(fragment_shader_id);
return program_id;
}
```

Finally, let's put everything together with the `main.cpp` file:

1. Include prerequisite libraries and the shader program header file inside the common folder:

```
#include <stdio.h>
#include <stdlib.h>
//GLFW and GLEW libraries
#include <GL/glew.h>
#include <GLFW/glfw3.h>
#include "common/shader.hpp"
```

2. Create a global variable for the GLFW window:

```
//Global variables
GLFWwindow* window;
```

3. Start the main program with the initialization of the GLFW library:

```
int main(int argc, char **argv)
{
  //Initialize GLFW
  if(!glfwInit()){
    fprintf( stderr, "Failed to initialize GLFW\n" );
    exit(EXIT_FAILURE);
  }
```

4. Set up the GLFW window:

```
  //enable anti-aliasing 4x with GLFW
  glfwWindowHint(GLFW_SAMPLES, 4);
  /* specify the client API version that the created context
    must be compatible with. */
  glfwWindowHint(GLFW_CONTEXT_VERSION_MAJOR, 3);
  glfwWindowHint(GLFW_CONTEXT_VERSION_MINOR, 2);
  //make the GLFW forward compatible
  glfwWindowHint(GLFW_OPENGL_FORWARD_COMPAT, GL_TRUE);
  //use the OpenGL Core
  glfwWindowHint(GLFW_OPENGL_PROFILE,
    GLFW_OPENGL_CORE_PROFILE);
```

5. Create the GLFW window object and make the context of the specified window current on the calling thread:

```
  window = glfwCreateWindow(640, 480, "Chapter 4 - GLSL",
    NULL, NULL);
  if(!window){
    fprintf( stderr, "Failed to open GLFW window. If you
      have an Intel GPU, they are not 3.3 compatible. Try
        the 2.1 version of the tutorials.\n" );
```

```
    glfwTerminate();
    exit(EXIT_FAILURE);
  }
  glfwMakeContextCurrent(window);
  glfwSwapInterval(1);
```

6. Initialize the GLEW library and include support for experimental drivers:

```
glewExperimental = true;
if (glewInit() != GLEW_OK) {
  fprintf(stderr, "Final to Initialize GLEW\n");
  glfwTerminate();
  exit(EXIT_FAILURE);
}
```

7. Set up the shader programs:

```
GLuint program = LoadShaders("simple.vert",
  "simple.frag");
glBindFragDataLocation(program, 0, "color_out");
glUseProgram(program);
```

8. Set up Vertex Buffer Object (and color buffer) and copy the vertex data to it:

```
GLuint vertex_buffer;
GLuint color_buffer;
glGenBuffers(1, &vertex_buffer);
glGenBuffers(1, &color_buffer);
const GLfloat vertices[] = {
  -1.0f, -1.0f, 0.0f,
  1.0f, -1.0f, 0.0f,
  1.0f, 1.0f, 0.0f,
  -1.0f, -1.0f, 0.0f,
  1.0f, 1.0f, 0.0f,
  -1.0f, 1.0f, 0.0f
};
const GLfloat colors[]={
  0.0f, 0.0f, 1.0f,
  0.0f, 1.0f, 0.0f,
  1.0f, 0.0f, 0.0f,
  0.0f, 0.0f, 1.0f,
  1.0f, 0.0f, 0.0f,
  0.0f, 1.0f, 0.0f
};

glBindBuffer(GL_ARRAY_BUFFER, vertex_buffer);
glBufferData(GL_ARRAY_BUFFER, sizeof(vertices), vertices,
  GL_STATIC_DRAW);
```

```
glBindBuffer(GL_ARRAY_BUFFER, color_buffer);
glBufferData(GL_ARRAY_BUFFER, sizeof(colors), colors,
  GL_STATIC_DRAW);
```

9. Specify the layout of the vertex data:

```
GLint position_attrib = glGetAttribLocation(program,
  "position");
glEnableVertexAttribArray(position_attrib);
glBindBuffer(GL_ARRAY_BUFFER, vertex_buffer);
glVertexAttribPointer(position_attrib, 3, GL_FLOAT,
  GL_FALSE, 0, (void*)0);

GLint color_attrib = glGetAttribLocation(program,
  "color_in");
glEnableVertexAttribArray(color_attrib);
glBindBuffer(GL_ARRAY_BUFFER, color_buffer);
glVertexAttribPointer(color_attrib, 3, GL_FLOAT,
  GL_FALSE, 0, (void*)0);
```

10. Run the drawing program:

```
while(!glfwWindowShouldClose(window)){
  // Clear the screen to black
  glClearColor(0.0f, 0.0f, 0.0f, 1.0f);
  glClear(GL_COLOR_BUFFER_BIT);
  // Draw a rectangle from the 2 triangles using 6
  vertices
  glDrawArrays(GL_TRIANGLES, 0, 6);
  glfwSwapBuffers(window);
  glfwPollEvents();
}
```

11. Clean up and exit the program:

```
  //clean up the memories
  glDisableVertexAttribArray(position_attrib);
  glDisableVertexAttribArray(color_attrib);
  glDeleteBuffers(1, &vertex_buffer);
  glDeleteBuffers(1, &color_buffer);
  glDeleteVertexArrays(1, &vertex_array);
  glDeleteProgram(program);
  // Close OpenGL window and terminate GLFW
  glfwDestroyWindow(window);
  glfwTerminate();
  exit(EXIT_SUCCESS);
}
```

Now we have created the first GLSL program by defining custom shaders:

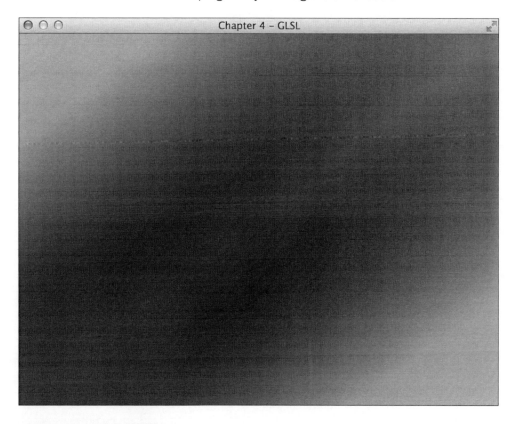

How it works...

As there are multiple components in this implementation, we will highlight the key features inside each component separately, organized in the same order as the previous section using the same file name for simplicity.

Inside `simple.vert`, we defined a simple vertex shader. In the first simple implementation, the vertex shader simply passes information forward to the rest of the rendering pipeline. First, we need to define the GLSL version that corresponds to the OpenGL 3.2 support, which is 1.50 (`#version 150`). The vertex shader takes two parameters: the position of the vertex (`in vec3 position`) and the color (`in vec3 color_in`). Note that only the color is defined explicitly in an output variable (`out vec3 color`) as `gl_Position` is a built-in variable. In general, variable names with the prefix `gl` should not be used inside shader programs in OpenGL as these are reserved for built-in variables. Notice that the final position, `gl_Position`, is expressed in homogeneous coordinates.

Inside `simple.frag`, we defined the fragment shader, which again passes the color information forward to the output framebuffer. Notice that the final output (`color_out`) is expressed in the RGBA format, where A is the alpha value (transparency).

Next, in `shader.cpp`, we created a framework to compile and link shader programs. The workflow shares some similarity with conventional code compilation in C/C++. Briefly, there are six major steps:

1. Create a shader object (`glCreateShader`).
2. Read and set the shader source code (`glShaderSource`).
3. Compile (`glCompileShader`).
4. Create the final program ID (`glCreateProgram`).
5. Attach a shader to the program ID (`glAttachShader`).
6. Link everything together (`glLinkProgram`).

Finally, in `main.cpp`, we set up a demo to illustrate the use of the compiled shader program. As described in the *Getting Started with Modern OpenGL* section of this chapter, we need to use the `glfwWindowHint` function to properly create the GLFW window context in OpenGL 3.2. An interesting aspect to point out about this demo is that even though we defined only six vertices (three vertices for each of the two triangles drawn using the `glDrawArrays` function) and their corresponding colors, the final result is an interpolated color gradient.

Rendering 2D images with texture mapping

Now that we have introduced the basics of GLSL using a simple example, we will incorporate further complexity to provide a complete framework that enables users to modify any part of the rendering pipeline in the future.

The code in this framework is divided into smaller modules to handle the shader programs (`shader.cpp` and `shader.hpp`), texture mapping (`texture.cpp` and `texture.hpp`), and user inputs (`controls.hpp` and `controls.hpp`). First, we will reuse the mechanism to load shader programs in OpenGL introduced previously and incorporate new shader programs for our purpose. Next, we will introduce the steps required for texture mapping. Finally, we will describe the main program, which integrates all the logical pieces and prepares the final demo. In this section, we will show how we can load an image and convert it into a texture object to be rendered in OpenGL. With this framework in mind, we will further demonstrate how to render a video in the next section.

Getting ready

To avoid redundancy here, we will refer readers to the previous section for part of this demo (in particular, `shader.cpp` and `shader.hpp`).

How to do it...

First, we aggregate all the common libraries used in our program into the common.h header file. The common.h file is then included in shader.hpp, controls.hpp, texture.hpp, and main.cpp:

```
#ifndef _COMMON_h
#define _COMMON_h
#include <stdlib.h>
#include <string.h>
#include <stdio.h>
#include <string>
#include <GL/glew.h>
#include <GLFW/glfw3.h>
using namespace std;
#endif
```

We previously implemented a mechanism to load a fragment and vertex shader program from files, and we will reuse the code here (shader.cpp and shader.hpp). However, we will modify the actual vertex and shader programs as follows.

For the vertex shader (transform.vert), we will implement the following:

```
#version 150
in vec2 UV;
out vec4 color;
uniform sampler2D textureSampler;
void main(){
  color = texture(textureSampler, UV).rgba;
}
```

For the fragment shader (texture.frag), we will implement the following:

```
#version 150
in vec3 vertexPosition_modelspace;
in vec2 vertexUV;
out vec2 UV;
uniform mat4 MVP;
void main(){
  //position of the vertex in clip space
  gl_Position = MVP * vec4(vertexPosition_modelspace,1);
  UV = vertexUV;
}
```

For the texture objects, in `texture.cpp`, we provide a mechanism to load images or video stream into the texture memory. We also take advantage of the SOIL library for simple image loading and the OpenCV library for more advanced video stream handling and filtering (refer to the next section).

In `texture.cpp`, we will implement the following:

1. Include the `texture.hpp` header and SOIL library header for simple image loading:

   ```
   #include "texture.hpp"
   #include <SOIL.h>
   ```

2. Define the initialization of texture objects and set up all parameters:

   ```
   GLuint initializeTexture(const unsigned char *image_data,
     int width, int height, GLenum format){
     GLuint textureID=0;
     //create and bind one texture element
     glGenTextures(1, &textureID);
     glBindTexture(GL_TEXTURE_2D, textureID);
     glPixelStorei(GL_UNPACK_ALIGNMENT,1);
     /* Specify target texture. The parameters describe the
       format and type of the image data */
     glTexImage2D(GL_TEXTURE_2D, 0, GL_RGBA, width, height, 0,
       format, GL_UNSIGNED_BYTE, image_data);
     /* Set the wrap parameter for texture coordinate s & t to
       GL_CLAMP, which clamps the coordinates within [0, 1] */
     glTexParameteri(GL_TEXTURE_2D, GL_TEXTURE_WRAP_S,
       GL_CLAMP_TO_EDGE);
     glTexParameteri(GL_TEXTURE_2D, GL_TEXTURE_WRAP_T,
       GL_CLAMP_TO_EDGE);
     /* Set the magnification method to linear and return
       weighted average of four texture elements closest to
         the center of the pixel */
     glTexParameteri(GL_TEXTURE_2D, GL_TEXTURE_MAG_FILTER,
       GL_LINEAR);
     /* Choose the mipmap that most closely matches the size of
       the pixel being textured and use the GL_NEAREST
         criterion (the texture element nearest to the center
           of the pixel) to produce a texture value. */
     glTexParameteri(GL_TEXTURE_2D, GL_TEXTURE_MIN_FILTER,
       GL_LINEAR_MIPMAP_LINEAR);
     glGenerateMipmap(GL_TEXTURE_2D);
     return textureID;
   }
   ```

3. Define the routine to update the texture memory:

```
void updateTexture(const unsigned char *image_data, int width, int
height, GLenum format){
  // Update Texture
  glTexSubImage2D (GL_TEXTURE_2D, 0, 0, 0, width, height,
    format, GL_UNSIGNED_BYTE, image_data);
  /* Sets the wrap parameter for texture coordinate s & t to
    GL_CLAMP, which clamps the coordinates within [0, 1]. */
  glTexParameteri(GL_TEXTURE_2D, GL_TEXTURE_WRAP_S,
    GL_CLAMP_TO_EDGE);
  glTexParameteri(GL_TEXTURE_2D, GL_TEXTURE_WRAP_T,
    GL_CLAMP_TO_EDGE);
  /* Set the magnification method to linear and return
    weighted average of four texture elements closest to
      the center of the pixel */
  glTexParameteri(GL_TEXTURE_2D, GL_TEXTURE_MAG_FILTER,
    GL_LINEAR);
  /* Choose the mipmap that most closely matches the size of
    the pixel being textured and use the GL_NEAREST
      criterion (the texture element nearest to the center
        of the pixel) to produce a texture value. */
  glTexParameteri(GL_TEXTURE_2D, GL_TEXTURE_MIN_FILTER,
    GL_LINEAR_MIPMAP_LINEAR);
  glGenerateMipmap(GL_TEXTURE_2D);
}
```

4. Finally, implement the texture-loading mechanism for images. The function takes the image path and automatically converts the image into various compatible formats for the texture object:

```
GLuint loadImageToTexture(const char * imagepath){
  int width, height, channels;
  GLuint textureID=0;
  //Load the images and convert them to RGBA format
  unsigned char* image = SOIL_load_image(imagepath, &width,
    &height, &channels, SOIL_LOAD_RGBA);
  if(!image){
    printf("Failed to load image %s\n", imagepath);
    return textureID;
  }
  printf("Loaded Image: %d x %d - %d channels\n", width,
    height, channels);
  textureID=initializeTexture(image, width, height,
    GL_RGBA);
  SOIL_free_image_data(image);
  return textureID;
}
```

On the controller front, we capture the arrow keys and modify the camera model parameter in real time. This allows us to change the position and orientation of the camera as well as the angle of view. In `controls.cpp`, we implement the following:

1. Include the GLM library header and the `controls.hpp` header for the projection matrix and view matrix computations:

   ```
   #define GLM_FORCE_RADIANS
   #include <glm/glm.hpp>
   #include <glm/gtc/matrix_transform.hpp>
   #include "controls.hpp"
   ```

2. Define global variables (camera parameters as well as view and projection matrices) to be updated after each frame:

   ```
   //initial position of the camera
   glm::vec3 g_position = glm::vec3( 0, 0, 2 );
   const float speed = 3.0f; // 3 units / second
   float g_initial_fov = glm::pi<float>()*0.4f;
   //the view matrix and projection matrix
   glm::mat4 g_view_matrix;
   glm::mat4 g_projection_matrix;
   ```

3. Create helper functions to return the most updated view matrix and projection matrix:

   ```
   glm::mat4 getViewMatrix(){
     return g_view_matrix;
   }
   glm::mat4 getProjectionMatrix(){
     return g_projection_matrix;
   }
   ```

4. Compute the view matrix and projection matrix based on the user input:

   ```
   void computeViewProjectionMatrices(GLFWwindow* window){
     static double last_time = glfwGetTime();
     // Compute time difference between current and last frame
     double current_time = glfwGetTime();
     float delta_time = float(current_time - last_time);
     int width, height;
     glfwGetWindowSize(window, &width, &height);
     //direction vector for movement
     glm::vec3 direction(0, 0, -1);
     //up vector
     glm::vec3 up = glm::vec3(0,-1,0);
     if (glfwGetKey(window, GLFW_KEY_UP) == GLFW_PRESS){
       g_position += direction * delta_time * speed;
     }
   ```

```
    else if (glfwGetKey(window, GLFW_KEY_DOWN) ==
      GLFW_PRESS){
      g_position -= direction * delta_time * speed;
    }
    else if (glfwGetKey(window, GLFW_KEY_RIGHT) ==
      GLFW_PRESS){
      g_initial_fov -= 0.1 * delta_time * speed;
    }
    else if (glfwGetKey(window, GLFW_KEY_LEFT) ==
      GLFW_PRESS){
      g_initial_fov += 0.1 * delta_time * speed;
    }
    /* update projection matrix: Field of View, aspect ratio,
      display range : 0.1 unit <-> 100 units */
    g_projection_matrix = glm::perspective(g_initial_fov,
      (float)width/(float)height, 0.1f, 100.0f);

    // update the view matrix
    g_view_matrix = glm::lookAt(
      g_position,       // camera position
      g_position+direction, // viewing direction
      up         // up direction
    );
    last_time = current_time;
  }
```

In `main.cpp`, we will use the various previously defined functions to complete the implementation:

1. Include the GLFW and GLM libraries as well as our helper functions, which are stored in separate files inside a folder called the `common` folder:

```
#define GLM_FORCE_RADIANS
#include <stdio.h>
#include <stdlib.h>
#include <GL/glew.h>
#include <GLFW/glfw3.h>
#include <glm/glm.hpp>
#include <glm/gtc/matrix_transform.hpp>
using namespace glm;
#include <common/shader.hpp>
#include <common/texture.hpp>
#include <common/controls.hpp>
#include <common/common.h>
```

2. Define all global variables for the setup:

```
GLFWwindow* g_window;
const int WINDOWS_WIDTH = 1280;
const int WINDOWS_HEIGHT = 720;
float aspect_ratio = 3.0f/2.0f;
float z_offset = 2.0f;
float rotateY = 0.0f;
float rotateX = 0.0f;
//Our vertices
static const GLfloat g_vertex_buffer_data[] = {
  -aspect_ratio,-1.0f,z_offset,
  aspect_ratio,-1.0f,z_offset,
  aspect_ratio,1.0f,z_offset,
  -aspect_ratio,-1.0f,z_offset,
  aspect_ratio,1.0f,z_offset,
  -aspect_ratio,1.0f,z_offset
};
//UV map for the vertices
static const GLfloat g_uv_buffer_data[] = {
  1.0f, 0.0f,
  0.0f, 0.0f,
  0.0f, 1.0f,
  1.0f, 0.0f,
  0.0f, 1.0f,
  1.0f, 1.0f
};
```

3. Define the keyboard `callback` function:

```
static void key_callback(GLFWwindow* window, int key, int
  scancode, int action, int mods)
{
  if (action != GLFW_PRESS && action != GLFW_REPEAT)
  return;
  switch (key)
  {
    case GLFW_KEY_ESCAPE:
      glfwSetWindowShouldClose(window, GL_TRUE);
      break;
    case GLFW_KEY_SPACE:
      rotateX=0;
      rotateY=0;
      break;
    case GLFW_KEY_Z:
      rotateX+=0.01;
```

```
        break;
      case GLFW_KEY_X:
        rotateX-=0.01;
        break;
      case GLFW_KEY_A:
        rotateY+=0.01;
        break;
      case GLFW_KEY_S:
        rotateY-=0.01;
        break;
      default:
        break;
    }
  }
```

4. Initialize the GLFW library with the OpenGL core profile enabled:

```
int main(int argc, char **argv)
{
  //Initialize the GLFW
  if(!glfwInit()){
    fprintf( stderr, "Failed to initialize GLFW\n" );
    exit(EXIT_FAILURE);
  }

  //enable anti-alising 4x with GLFW
  glfwWindowHint(GLFW_SAMPLES, 4);
  //specify the client API version
  glfwWindowHint(GLFW_CONTEXT_VERSION_MAJOR, 3);
  glfwWindowHint(GLFW_CONTEXT_VERSION_MINOR, 2);
  //make the GLFW forward compatible
  glfwWindowHint(GLFW_OPENGL_FORWARD_COMPAT, GL_TRUE);
  //enable the OpenGL core profile for GLFW
  glfwWindowHint(GLFW_OPENGL_PROFILE,
    GLFW_OPENGL_CORE_PROFILE);
```

5. Set up the GLFW windows and keyboard input handlers:

```
  //create a GLFW windows object
  window = glfwCreateWindow(WINDOWS_WIDTH, WINDOWS_HEIGHT,
    "Chapter 4 - Texture Mapping", NULL, NULL);
  if(!window){
    fprintf( stderr, "Failed to open GLFW window. If you
      have an Intel GPU, they are not 3.3 compatible. Try
      the 2.1 version of the tutorials.\n" );
    glfwTerminate();
    exit(EXIT_FAILURE);
```

```
}
/* make the context of the specified window current for
  the calling thread */
glfwMakeContextCurrent(window);
glfwSwapInterval(1);
glewExperimental = true; // Needed for core profile
if (glewInit() != GLEW_OK) {
  fprintf(stderr, "Final to Initialize GLEW\n");
  glfwTerminate();
  exit(EXIT_FAILURE);
}
//keyboard input callback
glfwSetInputMode(window,GLFW_STICKY_KEYS,GL_TRUE);
glfwSetKeyCallback(window, key_callback);
```

6. Set a black background and enable alpha blending for various visual effects:

```
glClearColor(0.0f, 0.0f, 0.0f, 1.0f);
glEnable(GL_BLEND);
glBlendFunc(GL_SRC_ALPHA,GL_ONE_MINUS_SRC_ALPHA);
```

7. Load the vertex shader and fragment shader:

```
GLuint program_id = LoadShaders( "transform.vert",
  "texture.frag" );
```

8. Load an image file into the texture object using the SOIL library:

```
char *filepath;
//load the texture from image with SOIL
if(argc<2){
  filepath = (char*)malloc(sizeof(char)*512);
  sprintf(filepath, "texture.png");
}
else{
  filepath = argv[1];
}

int width;
int height;
GLuint texture_id = loadImageToTexture(filepath, &width,
  &height);

aspect_ratio = (float)width/(float)height;
if(!texture_id){
  //if we get 0 with no texture
  glfwTerminate();
  exit(EXIT_FAILURE);
}
```

9. Get the locations of the specific variables in the shader programs:

```
//get the location for our "MVP" uniform variable
GLuint matrix_id = glGetUniformLocation(program_id,
  "MVP");
//get a handler for our "myTextureSampler" uniform
GLuint texture_sampler_id =
  glGetUniformLocation(program_id, "textureSampler");
//attribute ID for the variables
GLint attribute_vertex, attribute_uv;
attribute_vertex = glGetAttribLocation(program_id,
  "vertexPosition_modelspace");
attribute_uv = glGetAttribLocation(program_id,
  "vertexUV");
```

10. Define our **Vertex Array Objects** (**VAO**):

```
GLuint vertex_array_id;
glGenVertexArrays(1, &vertex_array_id);
glBindVertexArray(vertex_array_id);
```

11. Define our VAO for vertices and UV mapping:

```
//initialize the vertex buffer memory.
GLuint vertex_buffer;
glGenBuffers(1, &vertex_buffer);
glBindBuffer(GL_ARRAY_BUFFER, vertex_buffer);
glBufferData(GL_ARRAY_BUFFER,
  sizeof(g_vertex_buffer_data), g_vertex_buffer_data,
    GL_STATIC_DRAW);
//initialize the UV buffer memory
GLuint uv_buffer;
glGenBuffers(1, &uv_buffer);
glBindBuffer(GL_ARRAY_BUFFER, uv_buffer);
glBufferData(GL_ARRAY_BUFFER, sizeof(g_uv_buffer_data),
  g_uv_buffer_data, GL_STATIC_DRAW);
```

12. Use the shader program and bind all texture units and attribute buffers:

```
glUseProgram(program_id);
//binds our texture in Texture Unit 0
glActiveTexture(GL_TEXTURE0);
glBindTexture(GL_TEXTURE_2D, texture_id);
glUniform1i(texture_sampler_id, 0);
//1st attribute buffer: vertices for position
glEnableVertexAttribArray(attribute_vertex);
glBindBuffer(GL_ARRAY_BUFFER, vertex_buffer);
glVertexAttribPointer(attribute_vertex, 3, GL_FLOAT,
  GL_FALSE, 0, (void*)0);
```

```
//2nd attribute buffer: UVs mapping
glEnableVertexAttribArray(attribute_uv);
glBindBuffer(GL_ARRAY_BUFFER, uv_buffer);
glVertexAttribPointer(attribute_uv, 2, GL_FLOAT,
  GL_FALSE, 0, (void*)0);
```

13. In the main loop, clear the screen and depth buffers:

```
//time-stamping for performance measurement
double previous_time = glfwGetTime();
do{
  //clear the screen
  glClear(GL_COLOR_BUFFER_BIT | GL_DEPTH_BUFFER_BIT);
  glClearColor(1.0f, 1.0f, 1.0f, 0.0f);
```

14. Compute the transforms and store the information in the shader variables:

```
//compute the MVP matrix from keyboard and mouse input
computeMatricesFromInputs(g_window);
//obtain the View and Model Matrix for rendering
glm::mat4 projection_matrix = getProjectionMatrix();
glm::mat4 view_matrix = getViewMatrix();
glm::mat4 model_matrix = glm::mat4(1.0);
model_matrix = glm::rotate(model_matrix,
  glm::pi<float>() * rotateY, glm::vec3(0.0f, 1.0f,
    0.0f));
model_matrix = glm::rotate(model_matrix,
  glm::pi<float>() * rotateX, glm::vec3(1.0f, 0.0f,
    0.0f));
glm::mat4 mvp = projection_matrix * view_matrix *
  model_matrix;
//send our transformation to the currently bound shader
//in the "MVP" uniform variable
glUniformMatrix4fv(matrix_id, 1, GL_FALSE, &mvp[0][0]);
```

15. Draw the elements and flush the screen:

```
glDrawArrays(GL_TRIANGLES, 0, 6); //draw a square
//swap buffers
glfwSwapBuffers(window);
glfwPollEvents();
```

16. Finally, define the conditions to exit the `main` loop and clear all the memory to exit the program gracefully:

```
  } // Check if the ESC key was pressed or the window was closed
  while(!glfwWindowShouldClose(window) &&
    glfwGetKey(window, GLFW_KEY_ESCAPE )!=GLFW_PRESS);
  glDisableVertexAttribArray(attribute_vertex);
  glDisableVertexAttribArray(attribute_uv);
  // Clean up VBO and shader
  glDeleteBuffers(1, &vertex_buffer);
  glDeleteBuffers(1, &uv_buffer);
  glDeleteProgram(program_id);
  glDeleteTextures(1, &texture_id);
  glDeleteVertexArrays(1, &vertex_array_id);
  // Close OpenGL window and terminate GLFW
  glfwDestroyWindow(g_window);
  glfwTerminate();
  exit(EXIT_SUCCESS);
}
```

How it works...

To demonstrate the use of the framework for data visualization, we will apply it to the visualization of a histology slide (an H&E cross-section of a skin sample), as shown in the following screenshot:

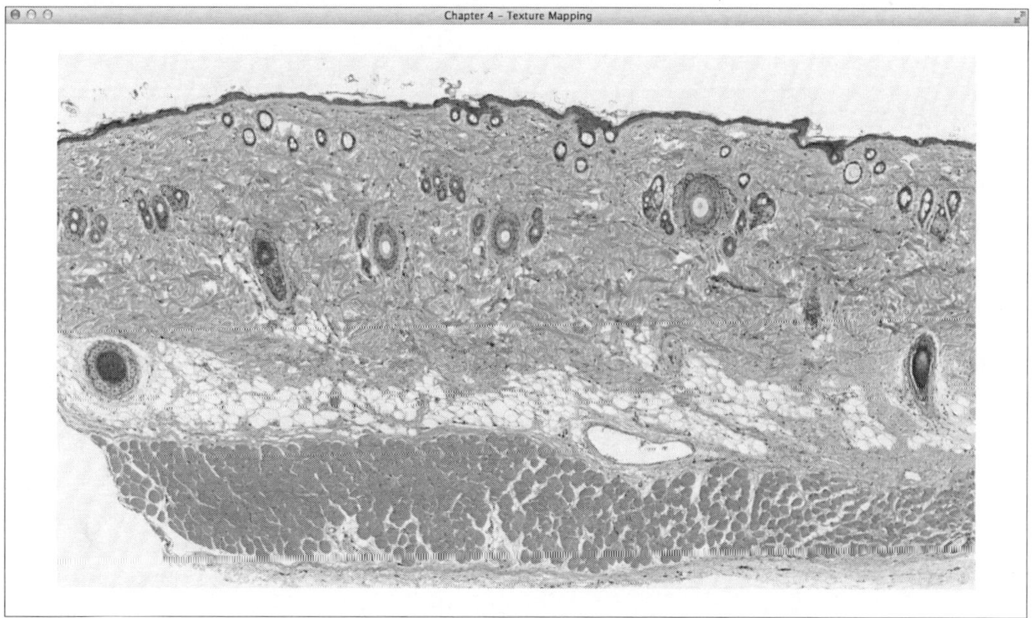

An important difference between this demo and the previous one is that here, we actually load an image into the texture memory (`texture.cpp`). To facilitate this task, we use the SOIL library call (`SOIL_load_image`) to load the histology image in the RGBA format (`GL_RGBA`) and the `glTexImage2D` function call to generate a texture image that can be read by shaders.

Another important difference is that we can now dynamically recompute the view (`g_view_matrix`) and projection (`g_projection_matrix`) matrices to enable an interactive and interesting visualization of an image in the 3D space. Note that the GLM library header is included to facilitate the matrix computations. Using the keyboard inputs (up, down, left, and right) defined in `controls.cpp` with the GLFW library calls, we can zoom in and out of the slide as well as adjust the view angle, which gives an interesting perspective of the histology image in the 3D virtual space. Here is a screenshot of the image viewed with a different perspective:

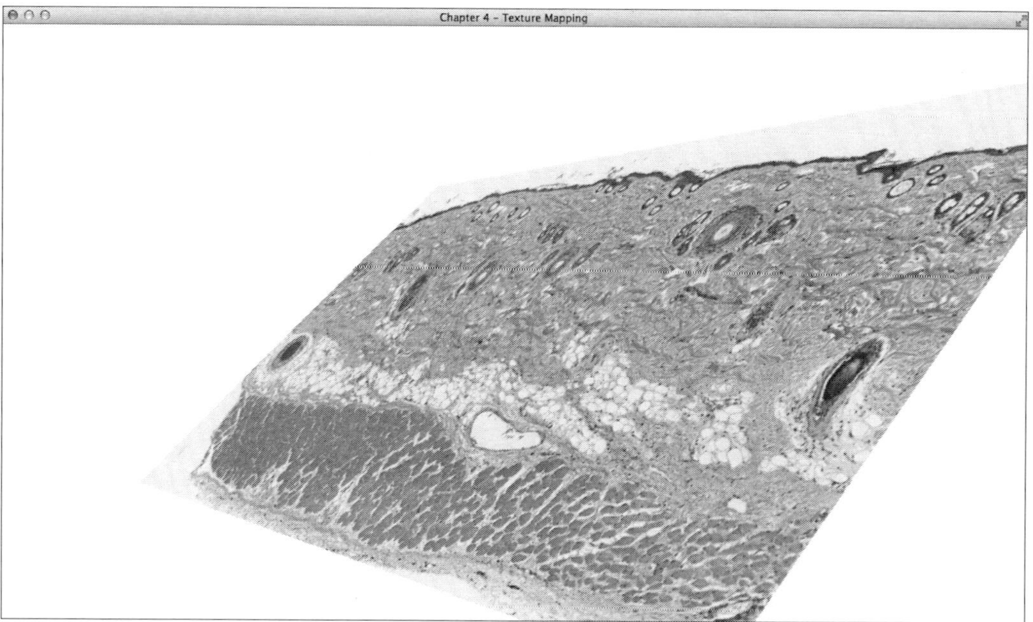

Yet another unique feature of the current OpenGL-based framework is illustrated by the following screenshot, which is generated with a new image filter implemented into the fragment shader that highlights the edges in the image. This shows the endless possibilities for the real-time interactive visualization and processing of 2D images using OpenGL rendering pipeline without compromising on CPU performance. The filter implemented here will be discussed in the next section.

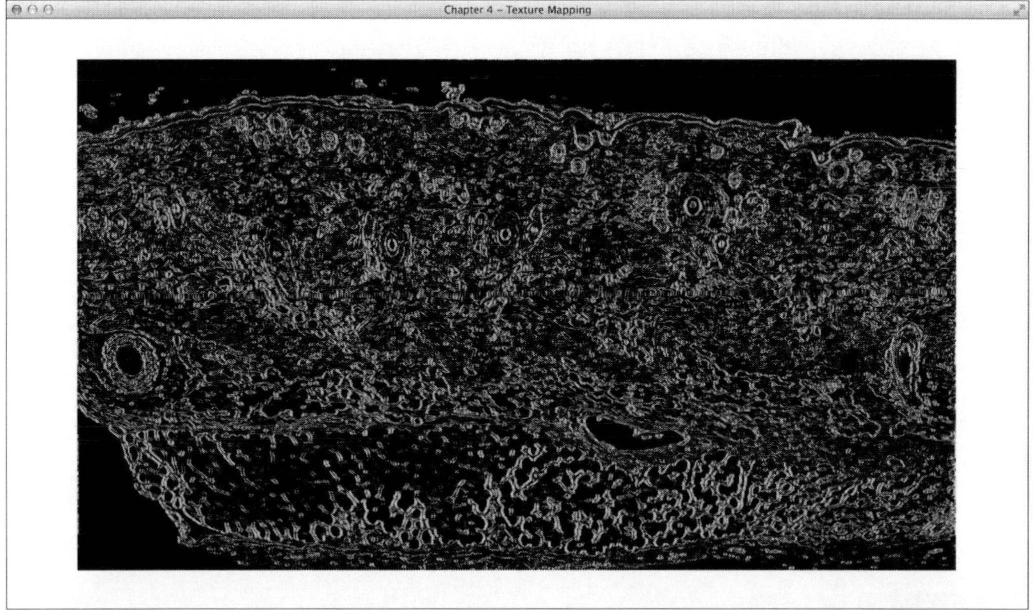

Real-time video rendering with filters

The GLSL shader provides a simple way to perform highly parallelized processing. On top of the texture mapping shown previously, we will demonstrate how to implement a simple video filter that postprocesses the end results of the buffer frame using the fragment shader. To illustrate this technique, we implement the Sobel Filter along with a heat map rendered using the OpenGL pipeline. The heat map function that was previously implemented in *Chapter 3, Interactive 3D Data Visualization*, will now be directly ported to GLSL with very minor changes.

The Sobel operator is a simple image processing technique frequently used in computer vision algorithms such as edge detection. This operator can be defined as a convolution operation with a 3 x 3 kernel, shown as follows:

$$G_x = \begin{bmatrix} -1 & 0 & 1 \\ -2 & 0 & 2 \\ -1 & 0 & 1 \end{bmatrix} * I(x,y), \quad G_y = \begin{bmatrix} 1 & 2 & 1 \\ 0 & 0 & 0 \\ -1 & -2 & -1 \end{bmatrix} * I(x,y)$$

G_x and G_y are results of the horizontal and vertical derivatives of an image, respectively, from the convolution operation of image *I* at the pixel location *(x, y)*.

We can also perform a sum of squares operation to approximate the gradient magnitude of the image:

$$G^2 = {G_x}^2 + {G_y}^2$$

Getting ready

This demo builds on top of the previous section, where an image was rendered. In this section, we will demonstrate the rendering of an image sequence or a video with the use of OpenCV library calls to handle videos. Inside `common.h`, we will add the following lines to include the OpenCV libraries:

```
#include <opencv2/opencv.hpp>
using namespace cv;
```

How to do it...

Now, let's complete the implementation as follows:

1. First, modify `main.cpp` to enable video processing using OpenCV. Essentially, instead of loading an image, feed the individual frames of a video into the same pipeline:

```
char *filepath;
if(argc<2){
  filepath = (char*)malloc(sizeof(char)*512);
  sprintf(filepath, "video.mov");
}
else{
  filepath = argv[1];
}
//Handling Video input with OpenCV
VideoCapture cap(filepath); // open the default camera
Mat frame;
if (!cap.isOpened()){ // check if we succeeded
  printf("Cannot open files\n");
  glfwTerminate();
  exit(EXIT_FAILURE);
  }else{
    cap >> frame; // get a new frame from camera
```

```
    printf("Got Video, %d x %d\n",frame.size().width,
      frame.size().height);
  }
  cap >> frame; // get a new frame from camera
  GLuint texture_id = initializeTexture(frame.data,
    frame.size().width, frame.size().height, GL_BGR);
  aspect_ratio = (float)frame.size().width/
    (float)frame.size().height;
```

2. Then, add the `update` function in the `main` loop to update the texture in every frame:

```
/* get the video feed, reset to beginning if it reaches
  the end of the video */
if(!cap.grab()){
  printf("End of Video, Resetting\n");
  cap.release();
  cap.open(filepath); // open the default camera
}
cap >> frame; // get a new frame from camera
//update the texture with the new frame
updateTexture(frame.data, frame.size().width,
  frame.size().height, GL_BGR);
```

3. Next, modify the fragment shader and rename it `texture_sobel.frag` (from `texture.frag`). In the `main` function, we will outline the overall processing (process the texture buffers with the Sobel filter and heat map renderer):

```
void main(){
  //compute the results of Sobel filter
  float graylevel = sobel_filter();
  color = heatMap(graylevel, 0.1, 3.0);
}
```

4. Now, implement the Sobel filter algorithm that takes the neighboring pixels to compute the result:

```
float sobel_filter()
{
  float dx = 1.0 / float(1280);
  float dy = 1.0 / float(720);

  float s00 = pixel_operator(-dx, dy);
  float s10 = pixel_operator(-dx, 0);
  float s20 = pixel_operator(-dx,-dy);
  float s01 = pixel_operator(0.0,dy);
  float s21 = pixel_operator(0.0, -dy);
  float s02 = pixel_operator(dx, dy);
```

```
    float s12 = pixel_operator(dx, 0.0);
    float s22 = pixel_operator(dx, -dy);
    float sx = s00 + 2 * s10 + s20 - (s02 + 2 * s12 + s22);
    float sy = s00 + 2 * s01 + s02 - (s20 + 2 * s21 + s22);
    float dist = sx * sx + sy * sy;
    return dist;
  }
```

5. Define the helper function that computes the brightness value:

```
float rgb2gray(vec3 color ) {
  return 0.2126 * color.r + 0.7152 * color.g + 0.0722 *
    color.b;
}
```

6. Create a helper function for the per-pixel operator operations:

```
float pixel_operator(float dx, float dy){
  return rgb2gray(texture( textureSampler, UV +
    vec2(dx,dy)).rgb);
}
```

7. Lastly, define the heat map renderer prototype and implement the algorithm for better visualization of the range of values:

```
vec4 heatMap(float v, float vmin, float vmax){
  float dv;
  float r, g, b;
  if (v < vmin)
    v = vmin;
  if (v > vmax)
    v = vmax;
  dv = vmax - vmin;
  if(v == 0){
    return vec4(0.0, 0.0, 0.0, 1.0);
}
if (v < (vmin + 0.25f * dv)) {
  r = 0.0f;
  g = 4.0f * (v - vmin) / dv;
} else if (v < (vmin + 0.5f * dv)) {
  r = 0.0f;
  b = 1.0f + 4.0f * (vmin + 0.25f * dv - v) / dv;
} else if (v < (vmin + 0.75f * dv)) {
```

```
        r = 4.0f * (v - vmin - 0.5f * dv) / dv;
        b = 0.0f;
      } else {
        g = 1.0f + 4.0f * (vmin + 0.75f * dv - v) / dv;
        b = 0.0f;
      }
      return vec4(r, g, b, 1.0);
    }
```

How it works...

This demo effectively opens up the possibility of rendering any image sequence with real-time processing using the OpenGL pipeline at the fragment shading stage. The following screenshot is an example that illustrates the use of this powerful OpenGL framework to display one frame of a video (showing the authors of the book) without the Sobel filter enabled:

Now, with the Sobel filter and heat map rendering enabled, we see an interesting way to visualize the world using real-time OpenGL texture mapping and processing using custom shaders:

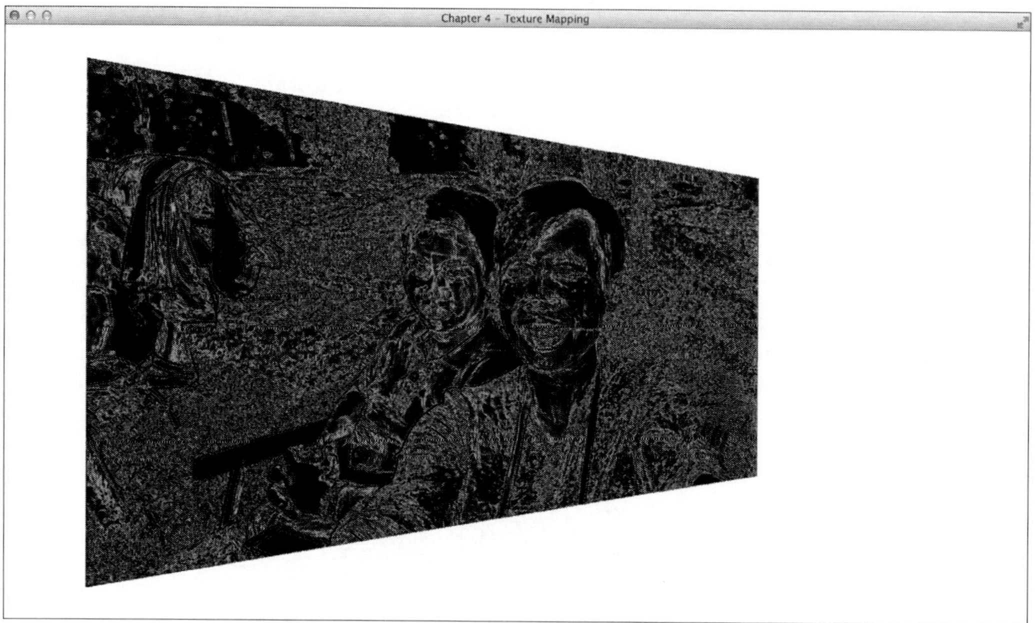

Further fine-tuning of the threshold parameters and converting the result into grayscale (in the `texture_sobel.frag` file) leads to an aesthetically interesting output:

```
void main(){
  //compute the results of Sobel filter
  float graylevel = sobel_filter();
  color = vec4(graylevel, graylevel, graylevel, 1.0);
}
```

In addition, we can blend these results with the original video feed to create filtered effects in real time by modifying the main function in the shader program (`texture_sobel.frag`):

```
void main(){
  //compute the results of Sobel filter
  float graylevel = sobel_filter();
  //process the right side of the image
    if(UV.x > 0.5)
      color = heatMap(graylevel, 0.0, 3.0) + texture
        (textureSampler, UV);
```

```
        else
        color = vec4(graylevel, graylevel, graylevel, 1.0) + texture
          (textureSampler, UV);
    }
```

To illustrate the use of the exact same program to visualize imaging datasets, here is an example that shows a volumetric dataset of a human finger imaged with **Optical Coherence Tomography** (**OCT**), simply by changing the input video's filename:

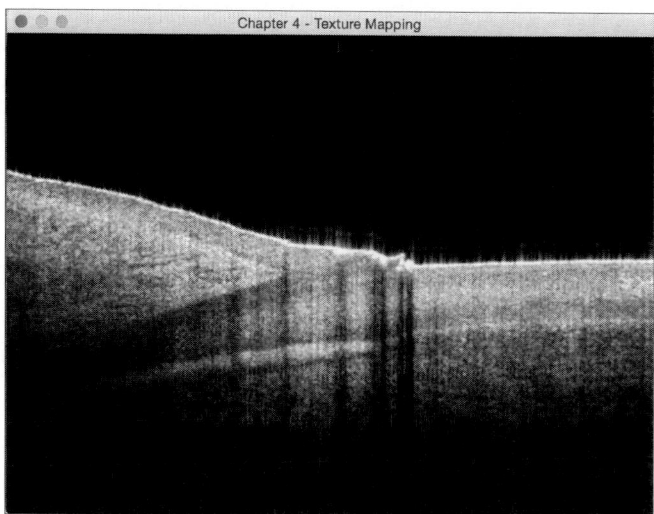

This screenshot represents one of 256 cross-sectional images of the nail bed in this volumetric OCT dataset (which is exported in a movie file format).

Here is another example that shows a volumetric dataset of a scar specimen imaged with **Polarization-Sensitive Optical Coherence Tomography** (**PS-OCT**), which provides label-free, intrinsic contrast to the scar region:

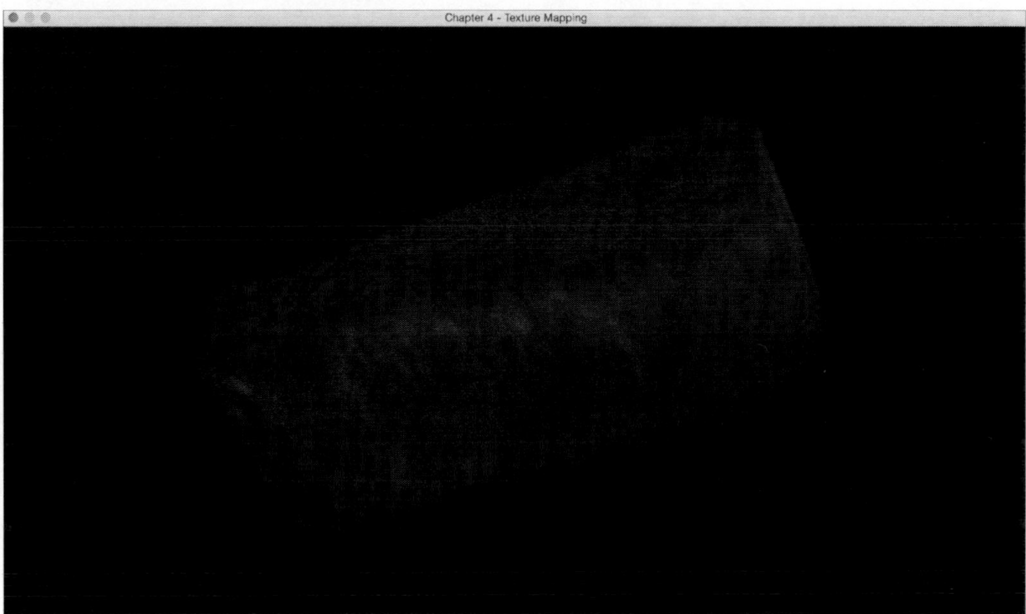

In this case, the volumetric PS-OCT dataset was rendered with the ImageJ 3D Viewer and converted into a movie file. The colors denote the **Degree of Polarization** (**DOP**), which is a measure of the randomness of the polarization states of light (a low DOP in yellow/green and a high DOP in blue), in the skin. The scar region is characterized by a high DOP compared to the normal skin.

As we have demonstrated here, this program can be easily adopted (by changing the input video source) to display many types of datasets, such as endoscopy videos or other volumetric imaging datasets. The utility of OpenGL becomes apparent in demanding applications that require real-time processing of very large datasets.

5

Rendering of Point Cloud Data for 3D Range-sensing Cameras

In this chapter, we will cover the following topics:

- Getting started with the Microsoft Kinect (PrimeSense) 3D range-sensing camera
- Capturing raw data from depth-sensing cameras
- OpenGL point cloud rendering with texture mapping and overlays

Introduction

The purpose of this chapter is to introduce the techniques to visualize another interesting and emerging class of data: depth information from 3D range-sensing cameras. Devices with 3D depth sensors are hitting the market everyday, and companies such as Intel, Microsoft, SoftKinetic, PMD, Structure Sensor, and Meta (wearable Augmented Reality eyeglasses) are all using these novel 3D sensing devices to track user inputs, such as hand gestures for interaction and/or tracking a user's environment. An interesting integration of 3D sensors with OpenGL is the ability to look at a scene in 3D from different perspectives, thereby enabling a virtual 3D fly-through of a scene captured with the depth sensors. In our case, for data visualization, being able to walk through a massive 3D dataset could be particularly powerful in scientific computing, urban planning, and many other applications that involve the visualization of 3D structures of a scene.

In this chapter, we propose a simplified pipeline that takes any 3D point data (*X*, *Y*, *Z*) with color (*r*, *g*, *b*) and renders these point clouds on the screen in real time. The point clouds will be obtained directly from real-world data using a 3D range-sensing camera. We will also provide ways to fly around the point cloud and have dynamic ways to adjust the camera's parameters. This chapter will build on the OpenGL graphics rendering pipeline discussed in the previous chapter, and we will show you a few additional tricks to filter the data with GLSL. We will display our depth information using our heat map generator to see the depth in 2D and remap this data to a 3D point cloud using texture mapping and perspective projection. This will allow us to see the real-life depth-based rendering of a scene and navigate around the scene from any perspective.

Getting started with the Microsoft Kinect (PrimeSense) 3D range-sensing camera

The Microsoft Kinect 3D range-sensing camera based on the PrimeSense technology is an interesting piece of equipment that enables the estimation of the 3D geometry of a scene through depth-sensing using light patterns. The 3D sensor has an active infrared laser projector, which emits encoded speckle light patterns. The sensors allow users to capture color images and provide a 3D depth map at a resolution of 640 x 480. Since the Kinect sensor is an active sensor, it is invariant to indoor lighting condition (that is, it even works in the dark) and enables many applications, such as gesture and pose tracking as well as 3D scanning and reconstruction.

In this section, we will demonstrate how to set up this type of range-sensing camera, as an example. While we do not require readers to purchase a 3D range-sensing camera for this chapter (since we will provide the raw data captured on this device for the purpose of running our demos), we will demonstrate how one can set up the device to capture data directly, primarily for those who are interested in further experimenting with real-time 3D data.

How to do it...

Windows users can download the OpenNI 2 SDK and driver from `http://structure.io/openni` (or using the direct download link: `http://com.occipital.openni.s3.amazonaws.com/OpenNI-Windows-x64-2.2.0.33.zip`) and follow the on-screen instructions. Linux users can download the OpenNI 2 SDK from the same website at `http://structure.io/openni`.

Mac users can install the OpenNI2 driver as follows:

1. Install libraries with Macport:

   ```
   sudo port install libtool
   sudo port install libusb +universal
   ```

2. Download OpenNI2 from `https://github.com/occipital/openni2`.
3. Compile the source code with the following commands:

```
cd OpenNI2-master
make
cd Bin/x64-Release/
```

4. Run the `SimpleViewer` executable:

```
./SimpleViewer
```

If you are using a computer with a USB 3.0 interface, it is important that you first upgrade the firmware for the PrimeSense sensor to version 1.0.9 (`http://dasl.mem.drexel.edu/wiki/images/5/51/FWUpdate_RD109-112_5.9.2.zip`). This upgrade requires a Windows platform. Note that the Windows driver for the PrimeSense sensor must be installed (`http://structure.io/openni`) for you to proceed. Execute the `FWUpdate_RD109-112_5.9.2.exe` file, and the firmware will be automatically upgraded. Further details on the firmware can be found at `http://dasl.mem.drexel.edu/wiki/index.php/4._Updating_Firmware_for_Primesense`.

See also

Detailed technical specifications of the Microsoft Kinect 3D system can be obtained from `http://msdn.microsoft.com/en-us/library/jj131033.aspx`, and further installation instructions and prerequisites to build OpenNI2 drivers can be found at `https://github.com/occipital/openni2`.

In addition, Microsoft Kinect V2 is also available and is compatible with Windows. The new sensor provides higher resolution images and better depth fidelity. More information about the sensor, as well as the Microsoft Kinect SDK, can be found at `https://www.microsoft.com/en-us/kinectforwindows`.

Capturing raw data from depth-sensing cameras

Now that you have installed the prerequisite libraries and drivers, we will demonstrate how to capture raw data from your depth-sensing camera.

How to do it...

To capture sensor data directly in a binary format, implement the following function:

```
void writeDepthBuffer(openni::VideoFrameRef depthFrame){
  static int depth_buffer_counter=0;
  char file_name [512];
  sprintf(file_name, "%s%d.bin", "depth_frame",
    depth_buffer_counter);
  openni::DepthPixel *depthPixels = new
    openni::DepthPixel[depthFrame.getHeight()*depthFrame.getWidth()];
  memcpy(depthPixels, depthFrame.getData(),
    depthFrame.getHeight()*depthFrame.getWidth()*sizeof(uint16_t));
  std::fstream myFile (file_name, std::ios::out
    |std::ios::binary);
  myFile.write ((char*)depthPixels,
    depthFrame.getHeight()*depthFrame.getWidth()*sizeof(uint16_t));
  depth_buffer_counter++;
  printf("Dumped Depth Buffer %d\n",depth_buffer_counter);
  myFile.close();
  delete depthPixels;
}
```

Similarly, we also capture the raw RGB color data with the following implementation:

```
void writeColorBuffer(openni::VideoFrameRef colorFrame){
  static int color_buffer_counter=0;
  char file_name [512];
  sprintf(file_name, "%s%d.bin", "color_frame",
    color_buffer_counter);
  //basically unsigned char*
  const openni::RGB888Pixel* imageBuffer = (const
    openni::RGB888Pixel*)colorFrame.getData();
  std::fstream myFile (file_name, std::ios::out |
    std::ios::binary);
  myFile.write ((char*)imageBuffer,
    colorFrame.getHeight()*colorFrame.getWidth()*sizeof(uint8_t)*3);
  color_buffer_counter++;
  printf("Dumped Color Buffer %d, %d, %d\n",
    colorFrame.getHeight(), colorFrame.getWidth(),
      color_buffer_counter);
  myFile.close();
}
```

The preceding code snippet can be added to any sample code within the OpenNI2 SDK that provides depth and color data visualization (to enable raw data capture). We recommend that you modify the `Viewer.cpp` file in the `OpenNI2-master/Samples/SimpleViewer` folder. The modified sample code is included in our code package. To capture raw data, press *R* and the data will be stored in the `depth_frame0.bin` and `color_frame0.bin` files.

How it works...

The depth sensor returns two streams of data in real time. One data stream is a 3D depth map, which is stored in 16-bits unsigned short data type (see the following figure on the left-hand side). Another data stream is a color image (see the following figure on the right-hand side), which is stored in a 24 bits per pixel, RGB888 format (that is, the memory is aligned in the R, G, and B order, and *8 bits * 3 channels = 24 bits* are used per pixel).

The binary data is written directly to the hard disk without compression or modification to the data format. On the client side, we read the binary files as if there is a continuous stream of data and color data pairs arriving synchronously from the hardware device. The OpenNI2 driver provides the mechanism to interface with the PrimeSense-based sensors (Microsoft Kinect or PS1080).

The `openni::VideoFrameRef depthFrame` variable, for example, stores the reference to the depth data buffer. By calling the `depthFrame.getData()` function, we obtain a pointer to the buffer in the `DepthPixel` format, which is equivalent to the unsigned short data type. Then, we write the binary data to a file using the `write()` function in the `fstream` library. Similarly, we perform the same task with the color image, but the data is stored in the RGB888 format.

Additionally, we can enable the `setImageRegistrationMode(openni::IMAGE_REGISTRATION_DEPTH_TO_COLOR)` depth map registration function in OpenNI2 to automatically compute and map a depth value onto the color image. The depth map is overlaid onto the color image and is shown in the following figure:

In the next section, we will assume that the raw depth map is precalibrated with image registration by OpenNI2 and can be used to compute the real-world coordinates and UV mapping indices directly.

OpenGL point cloud rendering with texture mapping and overlays

We will build on the OpenGL framework discussed in the previous chapter for point cloud rendering in this section. The texture mapping technique introduced in the previous chapter can also be applied in the point cloud format. Basically, the depth sensor provides a set of vertices in real-world space (the depth map), and the color camera provides us with the color information of the vertices. UV mapping is a simple lookup table once the depth map and color camera are calibrated.

Getting ready

Readers should use the raw data provided for the subsequent demo or obtain their own raw data from a 3D range-sensing camera. In either case, we assume these filenames will be used to denote the raw data files: `depth_frame0.bin` and `color_frame0.bin`.

How to do it...

Similar to the previous chapter, we will divide the program into three major components: the main program (`main.cpp`), shader programs (`shader.cpp`, `shader.hpp`, `pointcloud.vert`, `pointcloud.frag`), and texture-mapping functions (`texture.cpp`, `texture.hpp`). The main program performs the essential tasks to set up the demo, while the shader programs perform the specialized processing. The texture-mapping functions provide a mechanism to load and map the color information onto the vertices. Finally, we modify the `control.cpp` file to provide more refined controls over the **fly-through** experience through various additional keyboard inputs (using the up, down, left, and right arrow keys to zoom in and out in addition to adjusting the rotation angles using the *a*, *s*, *x*, and *z* keys).

First, let's take a look at the shader programs. We will create two vertex and fragment shader programs inside the `pointcloud.vert` and `pointcloud.frag` files that are compiled and loaded by the program at runtime by using the `LoadShaders` function in the `shader.cpp` file.

For the `pointcloud.vert` file, we implement the following:

```
#version 150 core
// Input vertex data
in vec3 vertexPosition_modelspace;
in vec2 vertexUV;
// Output data: interpolated for each fragment.
out vec2 UV;
out vec4 color_based_on_position;
// Values that stay constant for the whole mesh
uniform mat4 MVP;
//heat map generator
vec4 heatMap(float v, float vmin, float vmax){
  float dv;
  float r=1.0f, g=1.0f, b=1.0f;
  if (v < vmin)
    v = vmin;
  if (v > vmax)
    v = vmax;
  dv = vmax - vmin;
  if (v < (vmin + 0.25f * dv)) {
    r = 0.0f;
    g = 4.0f * (v - vmin) / dv;
  } else if (v < (vmin + 0.5f * dv)) {
    r = 0.0f;
    b = 1.0f+4.0f*(vmin+0.25f*dv-v)/dv;
  } else if (v < (vmin + 0.75f * dv)) {
    r = 4.0f*(v-vmin-0.5f*dv)/dv;
```

```
      b = 0.0f;
    } else {
      g = 1.0f+4.0f*(vmin+0.75f*dv-v)/dv;
      b = 0.0f;
    }
    return vec4(r, g, b, 1.0);
  }
  void main(){
    // Output position of the vertex, in clip space: MVP * position
    gl_Position =  MVP * vec4(vertexPosition_modelspace,1);
    color_based_on_position = heatMap(vertexPosition_modelspace.z, -
      3.0, 0.0f);
    UV = vertexUV;
  }
```

For the `pointcloud.frag` file, we implement the following:

```
#version 150 core
in vec2 UV;
out vec4 color;
uniform sampler2D textureSampler;
in vec4 color_based_on_position;
void main(){
  //blend the depth map color with RGB
  color = 0.5f*texture(textureSampler,
    UV).rgba+0.5f*color_based_on_position;
}
```

Finally, let's put everything together with the `main.cpp` file:

1. Include prerequisite libraries and the shader program header files inside the common folder:

   ```
   #include <stdio.h>
   #include <stdlib.h>
   //GLFW and GLEW libraries
   #include <GL/glew.h>
   #include <GLFW/glfw3.h>
   //GLM library
   #include <glm/glm.hpp>
   #include <glm/gtc/matrix_transform.hpp>
   #include "../common/shader.hpp"
   #include "../common/texture.hpp"
   #include "../common/controls.hpp"
   #include "../common/common.h"
   #include <fstream>
   ```

2. Create a global variable for the GLFW window:

```
GLFWwindow* window;
```

3. Define the width and height of the input depth dataset as well as other window/camera properties for rendering:

```
const int WINDOWS_WIDTH = 640;
const int WINDOWS_HEIGHT = 480;
const int IMAGE_WIDTH = 320;
const int IMAGE_HEIGHT = 240;
float z_offset = 0.0f;
float rotateY = 0.0f;
float rotateX = 0.0f;
```

4. Define helper functions to parse the raw depth and color data:

```
unsigned short *readDepthFrame(const char *file_path){
  int depth_buffer_size =
    DEPTH_WIDTH*DEPTH_HEIGHT*sizeof(unsigned short);
  unsigned short *depth_frame = (unsigned
    short*)malloc(depth_buffer_size);
  char *depth_frame_pointer = (char*)depth_frame;
  //read the binary file
  ifstream myfile;
  myfile.open (file_path, ios::binary | ios::in);
  myfile.read(depth_frame_pointer, depth_buffer_size);
  return depth_frame;
}
unsigned char *readColorFrame(const char *file_path){
  int color_buffer_size =
    DEPTH_WIDTH*DEPTH_HEIGHT*sizeof(unsigned char)*3;
  unsigned char *color_frame = (unsigned
    char*)malloc(color_buffer_size);
  //read the binary file
  ifstream myfile;
  myfile.open (file_path, ios::binary | ios::in);
  myfile.read((char *)color_frame, color_buffer_size);
  return color_frame;
}
```

5. Create callback functions to handle key strokes:

```
static void key_callback(GLFWwindow* window, int key, int
  scancode, int action, int mods)
{
  if (action != GLFW_PRESS && action != GLFW_REPEAT)
    return;
```

```
    switch (key)
    {
      case GLFW_KEY_ESCAPE:
        glfwSetWindowShouldClose(window, GL_TRUE);
        break;
      case GLFW_KEY_SPACE:
        rotateX=0;
        rotateY=0;
        break;
      case GLFW_KEY_Z:
        rotateX+=0.01;
        break;
      case GLFW_KEY_X:
        rotateX-=0.01;
        break;
      case GLFW_KEY_A:
        rotateY+=0.01;
        break;
      case GLFW_KEY_S:
        rotateY-=0.01;
        break;
      default:
        break;
    }
  }
```

6. Start the main program with the initialization of the GLFW library:

```
int main(int argc, char **argv)
{
  if(!glfwInit()){
    fprintf( stderr, "Failed to initialize GLFW\n" );
    exit(EXIT_FAILURE);
  }
```

7. Set up the GLFW window:

```
  glfwWindowHint(GLFW_SAMPLES, 4);
  glfwWindowHint(GLFW_CONTEXT_VERSION_MAJOR, 3);
  glfwWindowHint(GLFW_CONTEXT_VERSION_MINOR, 2);
  glfwWindowHint(GLFW_OPENGL_FORWARD_COMPAT, GL_TRUE);
  glfwWindowHint(GLFW_OPENGL_PROFILE,
    GLFW_OPENGL_CORE_PROFILE);
```

8. Create the GLFW window object and make it current for the calling thread:

```
g_window = glfwCreateWindow(WINDOWS_WIDTH,
  WINDOWS_HEIGHT, "Chapter 5 - 3D Point Cloud
    Rendering", NULL, NULL);
if(!g_window){
  fprintf( stderr, "Failed to open GLFW window. If you
    have an Intel GPU, they are not 3.3 compatible. Try
      the 2.1 version of the tutorials.\n" );
  glfwTerminate();
  exit(EXIT_FAILURE);
}
glfwMakeContextCurrent(g_window);
glfwSwapInterval(1);
```

9. Initialize the GLEW library and include support for experimental drivers:

```
glewExperimental = true;
if (glewInit() != GLEW_OK) {
  fprintf(stderr, "Final to Initialize GLEW\n");
  glfwTerminate();
  exit(EXIT_FAILURE);
}
```

10. Set up keyboard callback:

```
glfwSetInputMode(g_window,GLFW_STICKY_KEYS,GL_TRUE);
glfwSetKeyCallback(g_window, key_callback);
```

11. Set up the shader programs:

```
GLuint program_id = LoadShaders("pointcloud.vert",
  "pointcloud.frag");
```

12. Create the vertex (*x*, *y*, *z*) for all depth pixels:

```
GLfloat *g_vertex_buffer_data =
  (GLfloat*)malloc(IMAGE_WIDTH*IMAGE_HEIGHT *
    3*sizeof(GLfloat));
GLfloat *g_uv_buffer_data =
  (GLfloat*)malloc(IMAGE_WIDTH*IMAGE_HEIGHT *
    2*sizeof(GLfloat));
```

13. Read the raw data using the helper functions defined previously:

```
unsigned short *depth_frame =
  readDepthFrame("depth_frame0.bin");
unsigned char *color_frame =
  readColorFrame("color_frame0.bin");
```

14. Load the color information into a texture object:

```
GLuint texture_id = loadRGBImageToTexture(color_frame,
  IMAGE_WIDTH, IMAGE_HEIGHT);
```

15. Create a set of vertices in a real-world space based on the depth map and also define the UV mapping for the color mapping:

```
//divided by two due to 320x240 instead of 640x480 resolution
float cx = 320.0f/2.0f;
float cy = 240.0f/2.0f;
float fx = 574.0f/2.0f;
float fy = 574.0f/2.0f;
for(int y=0; y<IMAGE_HEIGHT; y++){
  for(int x=0; x<IMAGE_WIDTH; x++){
    int index = y*IMAGE_WIDTH+x;
    float depth_value =
      (float)depth_frame[index]/1000.0f; //in meter
    int ver_index = index*3;
    int uv_index = index*2;
    if(depth_value != 0){
      g_vertex_buffer_data[ver_index+0] = ((float)x-
        cx)*depth_value/fx;
      g_vertex_buffer_data[ver_index+1] = ((float)y-
        cy)*depth_value/fy;
      g_vertex_buffer_data[ver_index+2] = -depth_value;
      g_uv_buffer_data[uv_index+0] =
        (float)x/IMAGE_WIDTH;
      g_uv_buffer_data[uv_index+1] =
        (float)y/IMAGE_HEIGHT;
    }
  }
}
//Enable depth test to ensure occlusion:
//uncommented glEnable(GL_DEPTH_TEST);
```

16. Get the location for various uniform and attribute variables:

```
GLuint matrix_id = glGetUniformLocation(program_id,
  "MVP");
GLuint texture_sampler_id =
  glGetUniformLocation(program_id, "textureSampler");
GLint attribute_vertex, attribute_uv;
attribute_vertex = glGetAttribLocation(program_id,
  "vertexPosition_modelspace");
attribute_uv = glGetAttribLocation(program_id,
  "vertexUV");
```

17. Generate the vertex array object:

```
GLuint vertex_array_id;
glGenVertexArrays(1, &vertex_array_id);
glBindVertexArray(vertex_array_id);
```

18. Initialize the vertex buffer memory:

```
  GLuint vertex_buffer;
  glGenBuffers(1, &vertex_buffer);
  glBindBuffer(GL_ARRAY_BUFFER, vertex_buffer);
  glBufferData(GL_ARRAY_BUFFER,
IMAGE_WIDTH*IMAGE_HEIGHT*2* sizeof(GLfloat),
g_uv_buffer_data, GL_STATIC_DRAW);
```

19. Create and bind the UV buffer memory:

```
  GLuint uv_buffer;
  glGenBuffers(1, &uv_buffer);
  glBindBuffer(GL_ARRAY_BUFFER, uv_buffer);
  glBufferData(GL_ARRAY_BUFFER,
IMAGE_WIDTH*IMAGE_HEIGHT*3* sizeof(GLfloat),
g_vertex_buffer_data, GL_STATIC_DRAW);
```

20. Use our shader program:

```
glUseProgram(program_id);
```

21. Bind the texture in Texture Unit 0:

```
glActiveTexture(GL_TEXTURE0);
glBindTexture(GL_TEXTURE_2D, texture_id);
glUniform1i(texture_sampler_id, 0);
```

22. Set up attribute buffers for vertices and UV mapping:

```
glEnableVertexAttribArray(attribute_vertex);
glBindBuffer(GL_ARRAY_BUFFER, vertex_buffer);
glVertexAttribPointer(attribute_vertex, 3, GL_FLOAT,
  GL_FALSE, 0, (void*)0);
glEnableVertexAttribArray(attribute_uv);
glBindBuffer(GL_ARRAY_BUFFER, uv_buffer);
glVertexAttribPointer(attribute_uv, 2, GL_FLOAT,
  GL_FALSE, 0, (void*)0);
```

23. Run the draw functions and loop:

```
do{
  //clear the screen
  glClear(GL_COLOR_BUFFER_BIT | GL_DEPTH_BUFFER_BIT);
  glClearColor(1.0f, 1.0f, 1.0f, 0.0f);
```

```
        //compute the MVP matrix from keyboard and mouse input
        computeViewProjectionMatrices(g_window);
        //get the View and Model Matrix and apply to the rendering
        glm::mat4 projection_matrix = getProjectionMatrix();
        glm::mat4 view_matrix = getViewMatrix();
        glm::mat4 model_matrix = glm::mat4(1.0);
        model_matrix = glm::rotate(model_matrix,
          glm::pi<float>() * rotateY, glm::vec3(0.0f, 1.0f, 0.0f));
          model_matrix = glm::rotate(model_matrix,
          glm::pi<float>() * rotateX, glm::vec3(1.0f, 0.0f, 0.0f));
        glm::mat4 mvp = projection_matrix * view_matrix *
          model_matrix;
        //send our transformation to the currently bound
        //shader in the "MVP" uniform variable
        glUniformMatrix4fv(matrix_id, 1, GL_FALSE,
          &mvp[0][0]);
        glPointSize(2.0f);
        //draw all points in space
        glDrawArrays(GL_POINTS, 0, IMAGE_WIDTH*IMAGE_HEIGHT);
        //swap buffers
        glfwSwapBuffers(g_window);
        glfwPollEvents();
      }
      // Check if the ESC key was pressed or the window was closed
      while(!glfwWindowShouldClose(g_window) &&
        glfwGetKey(g_window, GLFW_KEY_ESCAPE )!=GLFW_PRESS);
```

24. Clean up and exit the program:

```
      glDisableVertexAttribArray(attribute_vertex);
      glDisableVertexAttribArray(attribute_uv);
      glDeleteBuffers(1, &vertex_buffer);
      glDeleteBuffers(1, &uv_buffer);
      glDeleteProgram(program_id);
      glDeleteTextures(1, &texture_id);
      glDeleteVertexArrays(1, &vertex_array_id);
      glfwDestroyWindow(g_window);
      glfwTerminate();
      exit(EXIT_SUCCESS);
    }
```

25. In `texture.cpp`, we implement the additional image-loading functions based on the previous chapter:

```
/* Handle loading images to texture memory and setting
  up the parameters */
GLuint loadRGBImageToTexture(const unsigned char *
  image_buffer, int width, int height){
  int channels;
  GLuint textureID=0;
  textureID=initializeTexture(image_buffer, width,
    height, GL_RGB);
  return textureID;
}
GLuint initializeTexture(const unsigned char *image_data,
  int width, int height, GLenum input_format){
  GLuint textureID=0;
  //for the first time we create the image,
  //create one texture element
  glGenTextures(1, &textureID);
  //bind the one element
  glBindTexture(GL_TEXTURE_2D, textureID);
  glPixelStorei(GL_UNPACK_ALIGNMENT,1);
  /* Specify the target texture. Parameters describe the
    format and type of image data */
  glTexImage2D(GL_TEXTURE_2D, 0, GL_RGBA, width, height, 0,
    input_format, GL_UNSIGNED_BYTE, image_data);
  /* Set the magnification method to linear, which returns
    an weighted average of 4 texture elements */
  glTexParameteri(GL_TEXTURE_2D, GL_TEXTURE_WRAP_S,
    GL_CLAMP);
  glTexParameteri(GL_TEXTURE_2D, GL_TEXTURE_WRAP_T,
    GL_CLAMP);
  /* Set the magnification method to linear, which //returns
    an weighted average of 4 texture elements */
  //closest to the center of the pixel
  glTexParameteri(GL_TEXTURE_2D, GL_TEXTURE_MAG_FILTER,
    GL_LINEAR);
  /* Choose the mipmap that most closely matches the size
    of the pixel being textured and use the GL_NEAREST
      criterion (texture element nearest to the center of
        the pixel) to produce texture value. */
  glTexParameteri(GL_TEXTURE_2D, GL_TEXTURE_MIN_FILTER,
    GL_LINEAR_MIPMAP_LINEAR);
  glGenerateMipmap(GL_TEXTURE_2D);
  return textureID;
}
```

26. In `texture.hpp`, we simply define the function prototypes:

```
GLuint loadRGBImageToTexture(const unsigned char
  *image_data, int width, int height);
GLuint initializeTexture(const unsigned char *image_data,
  int width, int height, GLenum input_format = GL_RGBA);
```

27. In `control.cpp`, we modify the `computeViewProjectionMatrices` function with the following code to support additional translation controls:

```
//initial position of the camera
glm::vec3 g_position = glm::vec3( 0, 0, 3.0 );
const float speed = 3.0f; // 3 units / second
float g_initial_fov = glm::pi<float>()*0.25f;
//compute the view matrix and projection matrix based on
//user input
void computeViewProjectionMatrices(GLFWwindow* window){
  static double last_time = glfwGetTime();
  // Compute time difference between current and last frame
  double current_time = glfwGetTime();
  float delta_time = float(current_time - last_time);
  int width, height;
  glfwGetWindowSize(window, &width, &height);
  //direction vector for movement
  glm::vec3 direction_z(0, 0, -0.5);
  glm::vec3 direction_y(0, 0.5, 0);
  glm::vec3 direction_x(0.5, 0, 0);
  //up vector
  glm::vec3 up = glm::vec3(0,-1,0);
  if (glfwGetKey( window, GLFW_KEY_UP ) == GLFW_PRESS){
    g_position += direction_y * delta_time * speed;
  }
  else if (glfwGetKey( window, GLFW_KEY_DOWN ) ==
    GLFW_PRESS){
    g_position -= direction_y * delta_time * speed;
  }
  else if (glfwGetKey( window, GLFW_KEY_RIGHT ) ==
    GLFW_PRESS){
    g_position += direction_z * delta_time * speed;
  }
  else if (glfwGetKey( window, GLFW_KEY_LEFT ) ==
    GLFW_PRESS){
    g_position -= direction_z * delta_time * speed;
  }
  else if (glfwGetKey( window, GLFW_KEY_PERIOD ) ==
    GLFW_PRESS){
    g_position -= direction_x * delta_time * speed;
  }
```

```
    else if (glfwGetKey( window, GLFW_KEY_COMMA ) ==
      GLFW_PRESS){
      g_position += direction_x * delta_time * speed;
    }
    /* update projection matrix: Field of View, aspect ratio,
      display range : 0.1 unit <-> 100 units */
    g_projection_matrix = glm::perspective(g_initial_fov,
      (float)width/(float)height, 0.01f, 100.0f);

    // update the view matrix
    g_view_matrix = glm::lookAt(
      g_position,           // camera position
      g_position+direction_z, //viewing direction
      up                    // up direction
    );
    last_time = current_time;
  }
```

Now we have created a way to visualize the depth sensor information in a 3D fly-through style; the following figure shows the rendering of the point cloud with a virtual camera at the central position of the frame:

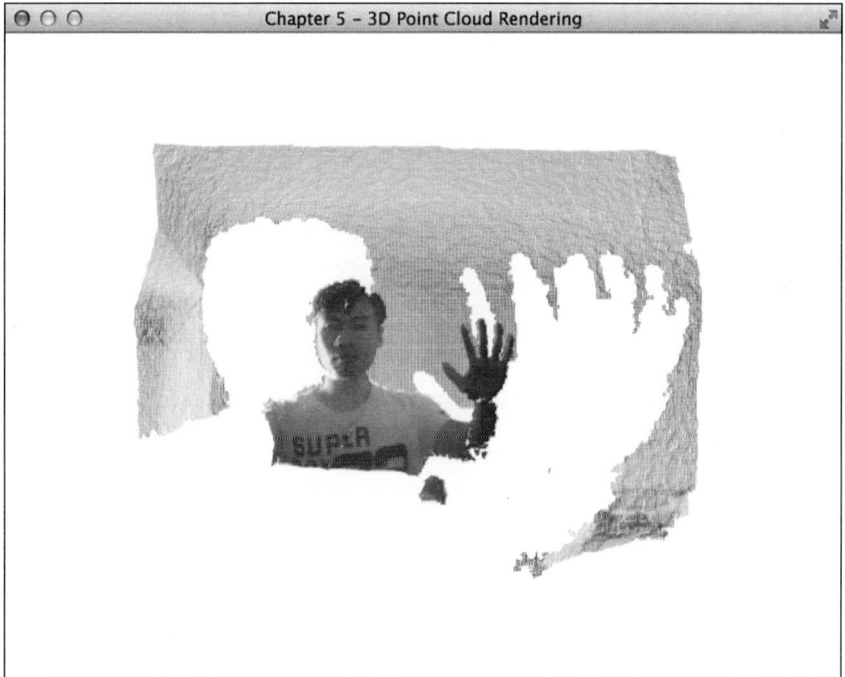

By rotating and translating the virtual camera, we can create various representations of the scene from different perspectives. With a bird's eye view or side view of the scene, we can see the contour of the face and hand more apparently from these two angles, respectively:

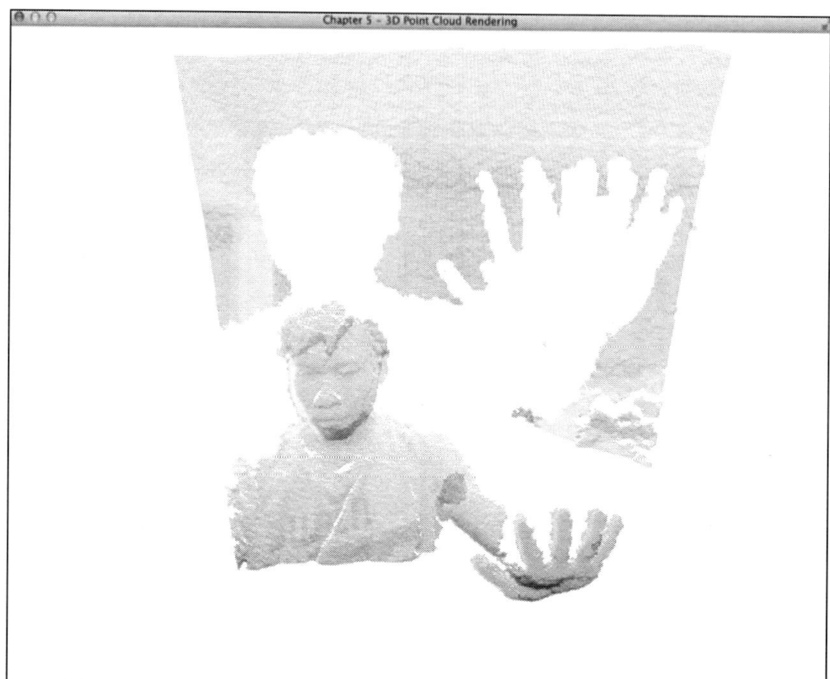

This is the side view of the same scene:

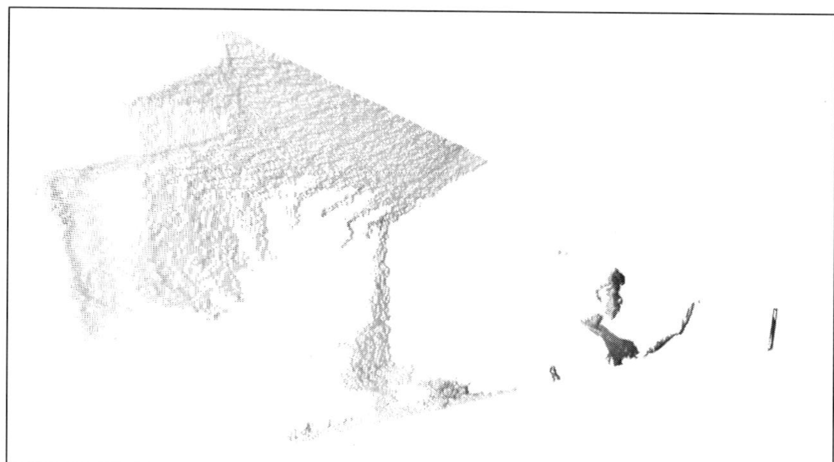

By adding an additional condition to the remapping loop, we can render the unknown regions (holes) from the scene where the depth camera fails to reconstruct due to occlusion, field of view limitation, range limitation, and/or surface properties such as reflectance:

```
if(depth_value != 0){
  g_vertex_buffer_data[ver_index+0] = ((float)x-cx)*depth_value/fx;
  g_vertex_buffer_data[ver_index+1] = ((float)y-cy)*depth_value/fy;
  g_vertex_buffer_data[ver_index+2] = -depth_value;
  g_uv_buffer_data[uv_index+0] = (float)x/IMAGE_WIDTH;
  g_uv_buffer_data[uv_index+1] = (float)y/IMAGE_HEIGHT;
}
else{
  g_vertex_buffer_data[ver_index+0] = ((float)x-cx)*0.2f/fx;
  g_vertex_buffer_data[ver_index+1] = ((float)y-cy)*0.2f/fy;
  g_vertex_buffer_data[ver_index+2] = 0;
}
```

This condition allows us to segment the region and project the regions with depth values of 0 onto a plane that is 0.2 meters away from the virtual camera, as shown in the following figure:

How it works...

In this chapter, we exploited the GLSL pipeline and texture-mapping technique to create an interactive point cloud visualization tool that enables the 3D navigation of a scene captured with a 3D range-sensing camera. The shader program also combines the result with the color image to produce our desired effect. The program reads two binary images: the calibrated depth map image and the RGB color image. The color is loaded into a texture object directly using the new `loadRGBImageToTexture()` function, which converts the data from `GL_RGB` to `GL_RGBA`. Then, the depth map data is converted into point cloud data in real-world coordinates based on the intrinsic value of the cameras as well as the depth value at each pixel, as follows:

$$(X,Y,Z)=d(x-c_x)/f_x, d(y-c_y)/f_y, d/1000)$$

Here, *d* is the depth value in millimeter, *x* and *y* are the positions of the depth value in pixel (projective) space, c_x and c_y are the principle axes of the depth camera, f_x and f_y are the focal lengths of the camera, and (X,Y,Z) is the position of the point cloud in the real-world coordinate.

In our example, we do not require fine alignment or registration as our visualizer uses a primitive estimation of the intrinsic parameters:

$$c_x = 320, c_y = 240,$$
$$f_x = 574, f_y = 574$$

These numbers could be estimated with the camera calibration tools in OpenCV. The details of these tools are beyond the scope of this chapter.

For our application, we are provided a set of 3D points (*x*, *y*, *z*) as well as the corresponding color information (*r*, *g*, *b*) to compute the point cloud representation. However, the point visualization does not support dynamic lighting and other more advanced rendering techniques. To address this, we can extend the point cloud further into a mesh (that is, a set of triangles to represent surfaces), which will be discussed in the next chapter.

6
Rendering Stereoscopic 3D Models using OpenGL

In this chapter, we will cover the following topics:

- Installing the Open Asset Import Library (Assimp)
- Loading the first 3D model in the Wavefront Object (.obj) format
- Rendering 3D models with points, lines, and triangles
- Stereoscopic 3D rendering

Introduction

In this chapter, we will demonstrate how to visualize data with stunning stereoscopic 3D technology using OpenGL. Stereoscopic 3D devices are becoming increasingly popular, and the latest generation's wearable computing devices (such as the 3D vision glasses from NVIDIA, Epson, and more recently, the augmented reality 3D glasses from Meta) can now support this feature natively.

The ability to visualize data in a stereoscopic 3D environment provides a powerful and highly intuitive platform for the interactive display of data in many applications. For example, we may acquire data from the 3D scan of a model (such as in architecture, engineering, and dentistry or medicine) and would like to visualize or manipulate 3D objects in real time.

Unfortunately, OpenGL does not provide any mechanism to load, save, or manipulate 3D models. Thus, to support this, we will integrate a new library named **Open Asset Import Library** (**Assimp**) into our code. The source code in this chapter is built on top of the *OpenGL point cloud rendering with texture mapping and overlays* recipe in *Chapter 5, Rendering of Point Cloud Data for 3D Range-sensing Cameras*. The main dependencies include the GLFW library that requires OpenGL version 3.2 and higher. We will assume that you have all the prerequisite packages installed from earlier chapters.

Installing the Open Asset Import Library (Assimp)

Assimp is an open source library that loads and processes 3D geometric scenes from various 3D model data formats. The library provides a unified interface to load many different data formats, such as **Wavefront Object** (**.obj**), **3ds Max 3DS** (**.3ds**), and **Stereolithography** (**.stl**). Moreover, this library is written in portable, ISO-compliant C++, and thus, it allows further customization and long-term support. Since the library is cross-platform, we can easily install it in Mac OS X, Linux, as well as Windows with the instructions given in the next section.

How to do it...

To obtain the library source files or binary library for Assimp 3.0, download them directly from Assimp's official website at `http://sourceforge.net/projects/assimp/files/assimp-3.0/`. Alternatively, for Linux and Mac OS X users, use the command-line interface to simplify the installation steps described next.

In Mac OS X, install Assimp using the MacPort's command-line interface. It automatically resolves all dependencies, so this is recommended:

```
sudo port install assimp
```

In Linux, install Assimp using the `apt-get` command interface:

```
sudo apt-get install install libassimp-dev
```

After the installation, modify the Makefile to ensure the libraries are linked to the source files by appending the following to the `LIBS` variable:

```
`pkg-config --static --libs assimp`
```

and the `INCLUDES` path variable, respectively:

```
`pkg-config --cflags assimp`
```

The final Makefile is shown here for your reference:

```
PKG_CONFIG_PATH=/usr/local/lib/pkgconfig/
CFILES = ../common/shader.cpp ../common/controls.cpp ../common/ObjLoader.
cpp main.cpp
CFLAGS = -c
OPT = -O3
INCLUDES = -I../common -I/usr/include -I/usr/include/SOIL -I.  `pkg-
config --cflags glfw3` `pkg-config --cflags assimp`
LIBS = -lm -L/usr/local/lib -lGLEW `pkg-config --static --libs glfw3`
`pkg-config --static --libs assimp`
CC = g++
OBJECTS=$(CFILES:.cpp=.o)
EXECUTABLE=main
all: $(CFILES) $(EXECUTABLE)
$(EXECUTABLE): $(OBJECTS)
$(CC) $(OPT) $(INCLUDES) $(OBJECTS) -o $@ $(LIBS)
.cpp.o:
$(CC) $(OPT) $(CFLAGS) $(INCLUDES) $< -o $@
clean:
rm -v -f *~ ../common/*.o *.o $(EXECUTABLE)
```

To install Assimp in Windows, first, download the binary library from this link: `http://sourceforge.net/projects/assimp/files/assimp-3.0/assimp--3.0.1270-full.zip/download`.

Then, we configure the environment with the following steps:

1. Unpack `assimp--3.0.1270-full.zip` and save it in `C:/Program Files (x86)/`.
2. Add the DLL path, `C:/Program Files (x86)/assimp--3.0.1270-sdk/bin/assimp_release-dll_win32`, to the PATH environment variable.
3. Include the `CMakeLists.txt` file to the project:

```
cmake_minimum_required (VERSION 2.8)
set(CMAKE_CONFIGURATION_TYPES Debug Release)
set(PROGRAM_PATH "C:/Program Files \(x86\)")
set(OpenCV_DIR ${PROGRAM_PATH}/opencv/build)
project (code)
#modify these path based on your configuration
#OpenCV
find_package(OpenCV REQUIRED )
INCLUDE_DIRECTORIES(${OpenCV_INCLUDE_DIRS})
INCLUDE_DIRECTORIES(${PROGRAM_PATH}/glm)
```

```
INCLUDE_DIRECTORIES(${PROGRAM_PATH}/glew-1.10.0/include)
LINK_DIRECTORIES(${PROGRAM_PATH}/glew-
  1.10.0/lib/Release/Win32)
INCLUDE_DIRECTORIES(${PROGRAM_PATH}/glfw-3.0.4/include)
LINK_DIRECTORIES(${PROGRAM_PATH}/glfw-3.0.4/lib)
INCLUDE_DIRECTORIES(${PROGRAM_PATH}/Simple\ OpenGL\ Image\
  Library/src)
INCLUDE_DIRECTORIES(${PROGRAM_PATH}/assimp--3.0.1270-
  sdk/include/assimp)
LINK_DIRECTORIES(${PROGRAM_PATH}/assimp--3.0.1270-
  sdk/lib/assimp_release-dll_win32)
add_subdirectory (../common common)
add_executable (main main.cpp)
target_link_libraries (main LINK_PUBLIC shader controls
  texture glew32s glfw3 opengl32 assimp ObjLoader)
```

Finally, generate the build files with the same steps as described in *Chapter 4, Rendering 2D Images and Videos with Texture Mapping* and *Chapter 5, Rendering of Point Cloud Data for 3D Range-sensing Cameras*.

See also

In addition to importing 3D model objects, Assimp also supports the exporting of 3D models in `.obj`, `.stl`, and `.ply` formats. By combining this library with the OpenGL graphics rendering engine, we have created a simple yet powerful mechanism to visualize and exchange 3D models collaboratively or remotely. The Assimp library can also handle some postprocessing tasks of 3D scenes after importing the model (for example, splitting large meshes to overcome certain GPU limitations on vertex count). These additional features are documented on the official website and may be of interest to advanced users (`http://assimp.sourceforge.net/lib_html/index.html`).

Loading the first 3D model in the Wavefront Object (.obj) format

Now, we are ready to integrate a 3D object loader into our code. The first step is to create an empty class called `ObjLoader` along with the source (`.cpp`) and header (`.h`) files. This class handles all the functions related to 3D object loading, parsing, and drawing using the OpenGL and Assimp libraries. The headers of the class will include the Assimp core functions for the handling of the data structures and all I/O mechanisms of the 3D data format:

```
#include <cimport.h>
#include <scene.h>
#include <postprocess.h>
```

In the ObjLoader.h file, we provide interfaces for the main program to create, destroy, load, and display the 3D data. In the ObjLoader.cpp file, we implement a set of functions to parse the scene (a hierarchical representation of the 3D objects in terms of meshes and faces) using the built-in functions from Assimp.

The Assimp library can support various 3D model data formats; however, in our example, we will focus on the Wavefront Object (.obj) format due to its simplicity. The .obj file is a simple geometric definition file that was first developed by Wavefront Technologies. The file contains the core elements of graphics, such as vertex, vertex position, normal face and so on, and is stored in a simple text format. Since the files are stored in ASCII text, we can easily open and examine the files without any parsers. For example, the following is the .obj file of a front-facing square:

```
# This is a comment.
# Front facing square.
# vertices [x, y, z]
v 0 0 0   # Bottom left.
v 1 0 0   # Bottom right.
v 1 1 0   # Top    right.
v 0 1 0   # Top    left.
# List of faces:
f 1 2 3 4       # Square.
```

As we can see from the preceding example, the representation is quite simple and intuitive for beginners. The vertices can be read and extracted one line at a time, and then they can be modified.

In the next section, we will show the full implementation, which allows users to load the .obj file, store the scene in a vertex buffer object, and display the scene.

How to do it...

First, we create the ObjLoader.h file in the common folder and append the class function definitions and variables that will be used in our implementation:

```
#ifndef OBJLOADER_H_
#define OBJLOADER_H_
/* Assimp include files. These three are usually needed. */
#include <cimport.h>
#include <scene.h>
#include <postprocess.h>
#include <common.h>
#define aisgl_min(x,y) (x<y?x:y)
#define aisgl_max(x,y) (y>x?y:x)
class ObjLoader {
```

```
  public:
  ObjLoader();
  virtual ~ObjLoader();
  int loadAsset(const char* path);
  void setScale(float scale);
  unsigned int getNumVertices();
  void draw(const GLenum draw_mode);
  void loadVertices(GLfloat *g_vertex_buffer_data);
private:
  //helper functions and variables
  const struct aiScene* scene;
  GLuint scene_list;
  aiVector3D scene_min, scene_max, scene_center;
  float g_scale;
  unsigned int num_vertices;
  unsigned int recursiveDrawing(const struct aiNode* nd,
    unsigned int v_count, const GLenum);
  unsigned int recursiveVertexLoading(const struct aiNode *nd,
    GLfloat *g_vertex_buffer_data, unsigned int v_counter);
  unsigned int recursiveGetNumVertices(const struct aiNode *nd);
  void get_bounding_box (aiVector3D* min, aiVector3D* max);
  void get_bounding_box_for_node (const struct aiNode* nd,
    aiVector3D* min, aiVector3D* max, aiMatrix4x4* trafo);
};
#endif
```

The names of classes from the Assimp library are preceded by the prefix `ai-` (for example, `aiScene` and `aiVector3D`). The `ObjLoader` file provides ways to dynamically load and draw the object loaded into the memory. It also handles simple dynamic scaling so that the object will fit on the screen.

In the source file, `ObjLoader.cpp`, we start by adding the constructor for the class:

```
#include <ObjLoader.h>
ObjLoader::ObjLoader() {
  g_scale=1.0f;
  scene = NULL; //empty scene
  scene_list = 0;
  num_vertices = 0;
}
```

Then, we implement the file-loading mechanism with the `aiImportFile` function. The scene is processed to extract the bounding box size for proper scaling to fit the screen. The number of vertices of the scene is then used to allow dynamic vertex buffer creation in later steps:

```
int ObjLoader::loadAsset(const char *path){
  scene = aiImportFile(path,
    aiProcessPreset_TargetRealtime_MaxQuality);
  if (scene) {
    get_bounding_box(&scene_min,&scene_max);
    scene_center.x = (scene_min.x + scene_max.x) / 2.0f;
    scene_center.y = (scene_min.y + scene_max.y) / 2.0f;
    scene_center.z = (scene_min.z + scene_max.z) / 2.0f;
    printf("Loaded file %s\n", path);
    g_scale =4.0/(scene_max.x-scene_min.x);

    printf("Scaling: %lf", g_scale);
    num_vertices = recursiveGetNumVertices(scene->mRootNode);
    printf("This Scene has %d vertices.\n", num_vertices);
    return 0;
  }
  return 1;
}
```

To extract the total number of vertices required to draw the scene, we recursively walk through every node in the tree hierarchy. The implementation requires a simple recursive function that returns the number of vertices in each node, and then the total is calculated based on the summation of all nodes upon the return of the function:

```
unsigned int ObjLoader::recursiveGetNumVertices(const struct
  aiNode *nd){
  unsigned int counter=0;
  unsigned int i;
  unsigned int n = 0, t;
  // draw all meshes assigned to this node
  for (; n < nd->mNumMeshes; ++n) {
    const struct aiMesh* mesh = scene-> mMeshes[nd->mMeshes[n]];
    for (t = 0; t < mesh->mNumFaces; ++t) {
      const struct aiFace* face = &mesh-> mFaces[t];
      counter+=3*face->mNumIndices;
    }
    printf("recursiveGetNumVertices: mNumFaces    %d\n",
      mesh->mNumFaces);
  }
```

```
    //traverse all children nodes
    for (n = 0; n < nd->mNumChildren; ++n) {
      counter+=recursiveGetNumVertices(nd-> mChildren[n]);
    }
    printf("recursiveGetNumVertices: counter %d\n", counter);
    return counter;
  }
```

Similarly, to calculate the size of the bounding box (that is, the minimum volume that is required to contain the scene), we recursively examine each node and extract the points that are farthest away from the center of the object:

```
  void ObjLoader::get_bounding_box (aiVector3D* min,
    aiVector3D* max)
  {
    aiMatrix4x4 trafo;
    aiIdentityMatrix4(&trafo);
    min->x = min->y = min->z =  1e10f;
    max->x = max->y = max->z = -1e10f;
    get_bounding_box_for_node(scene-> mRootNode,min,max,&trafo);
  }
  void ObjLoader::get_bounding_box_for_node (const struct aiNode*
    nd, aiVector3D* min, aiVector3D* max, aiMatrix4x4* trafo)
  {
    aiMatrix4x4 prev;
    unsigned int n = 0, t;
    prev = *trafo;
    aiMultiplyMatrix4(trafo,&nd->mTransformation);
    for (; n < nd->mNumMeshes; ++n) {
      const struct aiMesh* mesh = scene-> mMeshes[nd->mMeshes[n]];
      for (t = 0; t < mesh->mNumVertices; ++t) {
        aiVector3D tmp = mesh->mVertices[t];
        aiTransformVecByMatrix4(&tmp,trafo);
        min->x = aisgl_min(min->x,tmp.x);
        min->y = aisgl_min(min->y,tmp.y);
        min->z = aisgl_min(min->z,tmp.z);
        max->x = aisgl_max(max->x,tmp.x);
        max->y = aisgl_max(max->y,tmp.y);
        max->z = aisgl_max(max->z,tmp.z);
      }
    }
```

```
    for (n = 0; n < nd->mNumChildren; ++n) {
      get_bounding_box_for_node(nd-> mChildren[n],min,max,trafo);
    }
    *trafo = prev;
  }
```

The resulting bounding box allows us to calculate the scaling factor and recenter the object coordinate to fit within the viewable screen.

In the `main.cpp` file, we integrate the code by first inserting the header file:

```
#include <ObjLoader.h>
```

Then, we create the `ObjLoader` object and load the model with the given filename in the main function:

```
ObjLoader *obj_loader = new ObjLoader();
int result = 0;
if(argc > 1){
  result = obj_loader->loadAsset(argv[1]);
}
else{
  result = obj_loader-> loadAsset("dragon.obj");
}
if(result){
  fprintf(stderr, "Final to Load the 3D file\n");
  glfwTerminate();
  exit(EXIT_FAILURE);
}
```

The `ObjLoader` contains an algorithm that recursively examines each mesh and computes the bounding box and the number of vertices in the scene. Then, we dynamically allocate the vertex buffer based on the number of vertices and load the vertices into the buffer:

```
GLfloat *g_vertex_buffer_data = (GLfloat*)
malloc (obj_loader->getNumVertices()*sizeof(GLfloat));
//load the scene data to the vertex buffer
obj_loader->loadVertices(g_vertex_buffer_data);
```

Now, we have all the necessary vertex information for display with our custom shader program written in OpenGL.

How it works...

Assimp provides the mechanism to load and parse the 3D data format efficiently. The key feature we utilized is the hierarchical way to import 3D objects, which allows us to unify our rendering pipeline regardless of the 3D format. The `aiImportFile` function reads the given file and returns its content in the `aiScene` structure. The second parameter of this function specifies the optional postprocessing steps to be executed after a successful import. The `aiProcessPreset_TargetRealtime_MaxQuality` flag is a predefined variable, which combines the following set of parameters:

```
( \
  aiProcessPreset_TargetRealtime_Quality | \
  aiProcess_FindInstances | \
  aiProcess_ValidateDataStructure | \
  aiProcess_OptimizeMeshes | \
  aiProcess_Debone | \
0 )
```

These postprocessing options are described in further detail at `http://assimp.sourceforge.net/lib_html/postprocess_8h.html#a64795260b95f5a4b3f3dc1be4f52e410`. Advanced users can look into each option and understand whether these functions need to be enabled or disabled based on the content.

At this point, we have a simple mechanism to load graphics into the Assimp `aiScene` object, present the bounding box size, as well as extract the number of vertices required to render the scene. Next, we will create a simple shader program as well as various drawing functions to visualize the content with different styles. In short, by integrating this with the OpenGL graphics rendering engine, we now have a flexible way to visualize 3D models using the various tools we developed in the previous chapters.

Rendering 3D models with points, lines, and triangles

The next step after importing the 3D model is to display the content on the screen using an intuitive and aesthetically pleasing way. Many complex scenes consist of multiple surfaces (meshes) and many vertices. In the previous chapter, we implemented a simple shader program to visualize the point cloud at various depth values based on a heat map. In this section, we will utilize very simple primitives (points, lines, and triangles) with transparency to create skeleton-like rendering effects.

How to do it...

We will continue the implementation of the ObjLoader class to support loading vertices and draw the graphics for each mesh in the scene.

In the source file of ObjLoader.cpp, we add a recursive function to extract all vertices from the scene and store them in a single vertex buffer array. This allows us to reduce the number of vertex buffers to be managed, thus reducing the complexity of the code:

```
void ObjLoader::loadVertices(GLfloat *g_vertex_buffer_data)
{
  recursiveVertexLoading(scene->mRootNode, g_vertex_buffer_data,
    0);
}
unsigned int ObjLoader::recursiveVertexLoading (const struct
  aiNode *nd, GLfloat *g_vertex_buffer_data, unsigned int
    v_counter)
{
  unsigned int i;
  unsigned int n = 0, t;
  /* save all data to the vertex array, perform offset and scaling
    to reduce the computation */
  for (; n < nd->mNumMeshes; ++n) {
    const struct aiMesh* mesh = scene-> mMeshes[nd->mMeshes[n]];
    for (t = 0; t < mesh->mNumFaces; ++t) {
      const struct aiFace* face = &mesh->mFaces[t];
      for(i = 0; i < face->mNumIndices; i++) {
        int index = face->mIndices[i];
        g_vertex_buffer_data[v_counter]=
          (mesh->mVertices[index].x-scene_center.x)*g_scale;
        g_vertex_buffer_data[v_counter+1]=
          (mesh->mVertices[index].y-scene_center.y)*g_scale;
        g_vertex_buffer_data[v_counter+2]=
          (mesh->mVertices[index].z-scene_center.z)*g_scale;
        v_counter+=3;
      }
    }
  }
  //traverse all children nodes
  for (n = 0; n < nd->mNumChildren; ++n) {
    v_counter = recursiveVertexLoading(nd-> mChildren[n],
      g_vertex_buffer_data, v_counter);
  }
  return v_counter;
}
```

To draw the graphics, we traverse the `aiScene` object from the root node and draw the meshes one piece at a time:

```
void ObjLoader::draw(const GLenum draw_mode){
  recursiveDrawing(scene->mRootNode, 0, draw_mode);
}
unsigned int ObjLoader::recursiveDrawing(const struct aiNode* nd,
  unsigned int v_counter, const GLenum draw_mode){
  /* break up the drawing, and shift the pointer to draw different
    parts of the scene */
  unsigned int i;
  unsigned int n = 0, t;
  unsigned int total_count = v_counter;
  // draw all meshes assigned to this node
  for (; n < nd->mNumMeshes; ++n) {
    unsigned int count=0;
    const struct aiMesh* mesh = scene-> mMeshes[nd->mMeshes[n]];
    for (t = 0; t < mesh->mNumFaces; ++t) {
      const struct aiFace* face = &mesh-> mFaces[t];
      count+=3*face->mNumIndices;
    }
    glDrawArrays(draw_mode, total_count, count);
      total_count+=count;
  }
  v_counter = total_count;
  // draw all children nodes recursively
  for (n = 0; n < nd->mNumChildren; ++n) {
    v_counter = recursiveDrawing(nd-> mChildren[n], v_counter,
      draw_mode);
  }
  return v_counter;
}
```

In the vertex shader, `pointcloud.vert`, we compute the color of vertices based on their positions in space. The remapping algorithm creates a heat map representation of the object in space, and it serves as an important depth cue for the human eye (depth perception):

```
#version 150 core
// Input
in vec3 vertexPosition_modelspace;
// Output
out vec4 color_based_on_position;
// Uniform/constant variable.
uniform mat4 MVP;
//heat map generator
```

```
vec4 heatMap(float v, float vmin, float vmax){
  float dv;
  float r=1.0f, g=1.0f, b=1.0f;
  if (v < vmin)
    v = vmin;
  if (v > vmax)
    v = vmax;
  dv = vmax - vmin;
  if (v < (vmin + 0.25f * dv)) {
    r = 0.0f;
    g = 4.0f * (v - vmin) / dv;
  } else if (v < (vmin + 0.5f * dv)) {
    r = 0.0f;
    b = 1.0f + 4.0f * (vmin + 0.25f * dv - v) / dv;
  } else if (v < (vmin + 0.75f * dv)) {
    r = 4.0f * (v - vmin - 0.5f * dv) / dv;
    b = 0.0f;
  } else {
    g = 1.0f + 4.0f * (vmin + 0.75f * dv - v) / dv;
    b = 0.0f;
  }
  //with 0.2 transparency - can be dynamic if we pass in variables
  return vec4(r, g, b, 0.2f);
}

void main () {
  // Output position of the vertex, in clip space : MVP * position
  gl_Position =  MVP * vec4(vertexPosition_modelspace, 1.0f);
  // remapping the color based on the depth (z) value.
  color_based_on_position = heatMap(vertexPosition_modelspace.z,
    -1.0f, 1.0f);
}
```

The vertex shader passes the heat-mapped color information along to the fragment shader through the `color_based_on_position` variable. Then, the final color is returned through the fragment shader (`pointcloud.frag`) directly without further processing. The implementation of such a simple pipeline is shown as follows:

```
#version 150 core
out vec4 color;
in vec4 color_based_on_position;
void main(){
  color = color_based_on_position;
}
```

Finally, we draw the scene with various styles: lines, points, and triangles with transparency. The following is the code snippet inside the drawing loop:

```
//draw the left eye (but full screen)
glViewport(0, 0, width, height);
//compute the MVP matrix from the IOD and virtual image plane distance
computeStereoViewProjectionMatrices(g_window, IOD, depthZ, true);
//get the View and Model Matrix and apply to the rendering
glm::mat4 projection_matrix = getProjectionMatrix();
glm::mat4 view_matrix = getViewMatrix();
glm::mat4 model_matrix = glm::mat4(1.0);
model_matrix = glm::translate(model_matrix, glm::vec3(0.0f, 0.0f,
  -depthZ));
model_matrix = glm::rotate(model_matrix,
glm::pi<float>()*rotateY, glm::vec3(0.0f, 1.0f, 0.0f));
model_matrix = glm::rotate(model_matrix,
glm::pi<float>()*rotateX, glm::vec3(1.0f, 0.0f, 0.0f));
glm::mat4 mvp = projection_matrix * view_matrix * model_matrix;
//send our transformation to the currently bound shader,
//in the "MVP" uniform variable
glUniformMatrix4fv(matrix_id, 1, GL_FALSE, &mvp[0][0]);
/* render scene with different modes that can be enabled separately
  to get different effects */
obj_loader->draw(GL_TRIANGLES);
if(drawPoints)
  obj_loader->draw(GL_POINTS);
if(drawLines)
  obj_loader->draw(GL_LINES);
```

The series of screenshots that follow illustrate the aesthetically pleasing results we can achieve with our custom shader. The color mapping based on the depth position using the heat map shader provides a strong depth perception that helps us understand the 3D structure of the objects more easily. Furthermore, we can enable and disable various rendering options separately to achieve various effects. For example, the same object can be rendered with different styles: points, lines, and triangles (surfaces) with transparency.

To demonstrate the effects, we will first render two objects with points only. The first example is a dragon model:

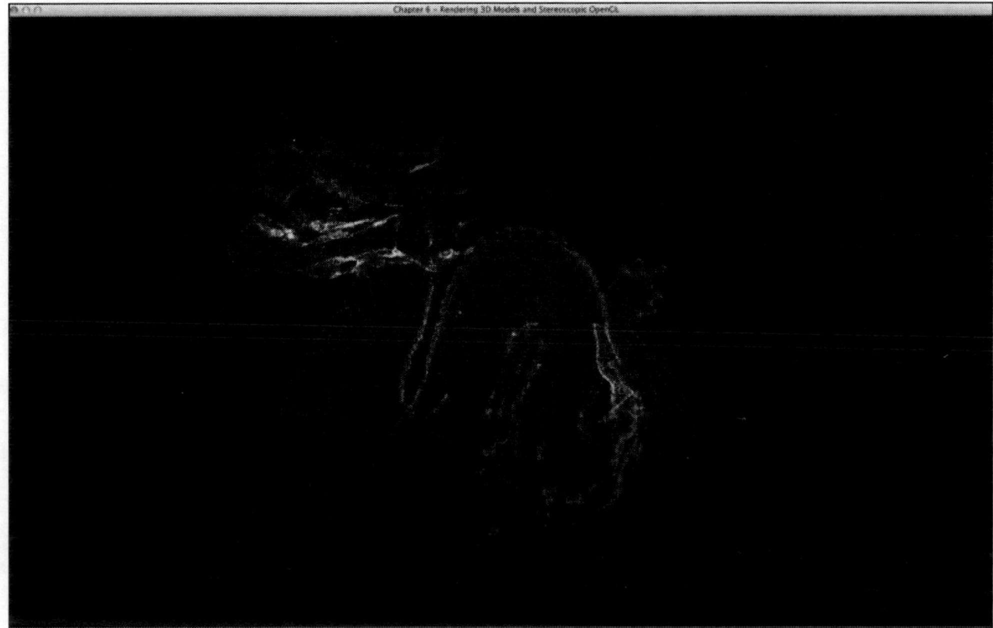

The second example is an architectural model:

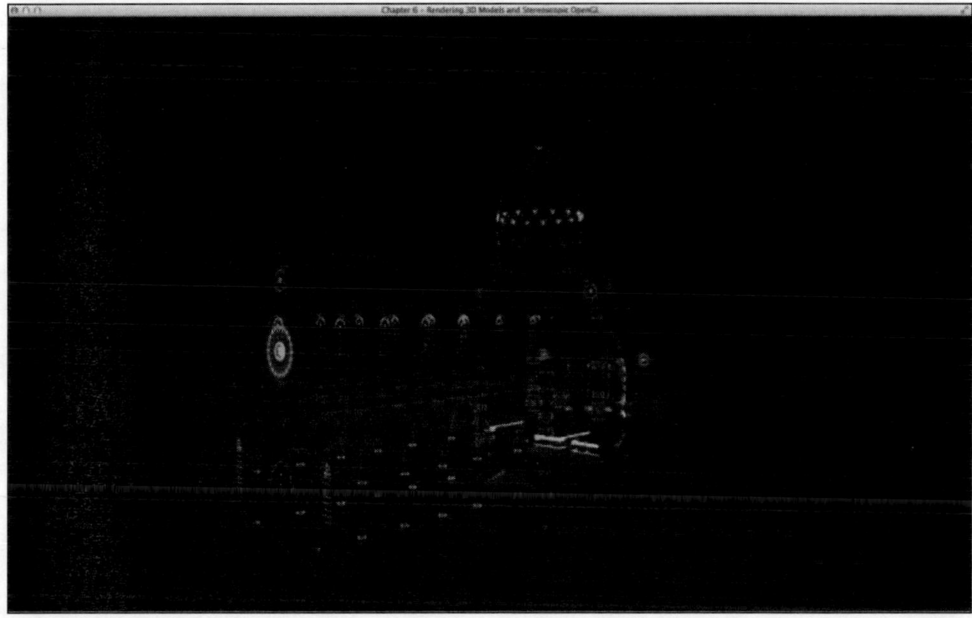

The point-based rendering style is great for visualizing a large dataset with unknown relations or distribution. Next, we will render the same objects with lines only:

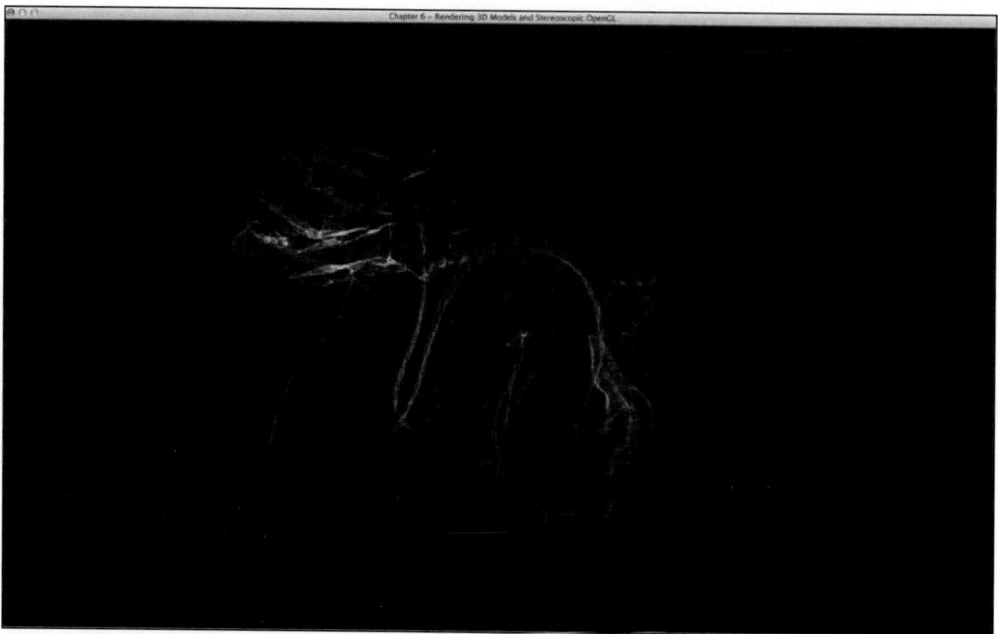

Here's the architectural model rendered with lines only:

With the lines, now we can see the structure of the object more easily. This rendering technique is great for simple structures, such as architectural models and other well-defined models. In addition, we can render the scene with both points and lines enabled, as shown here:

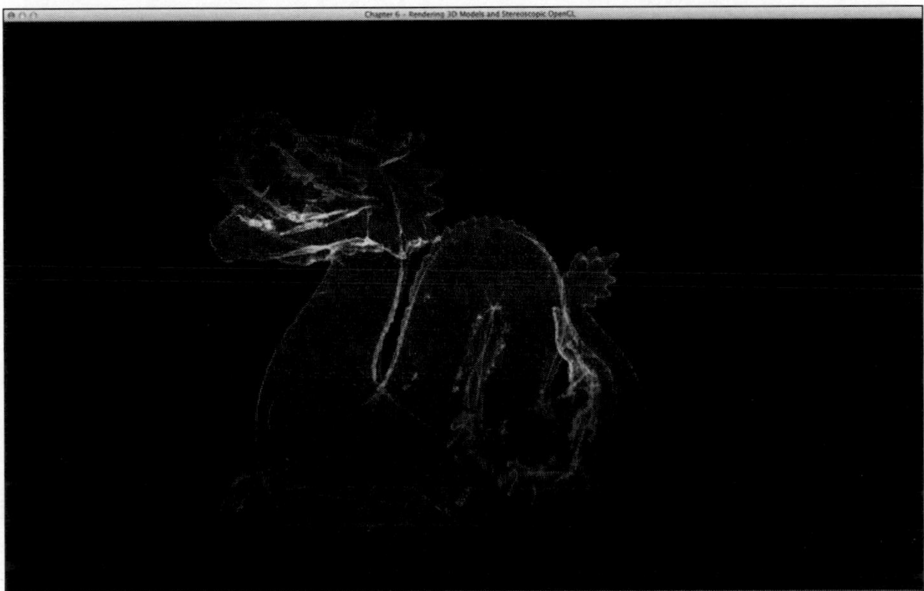

Here's the architectural model rendered with points and lines enabled:

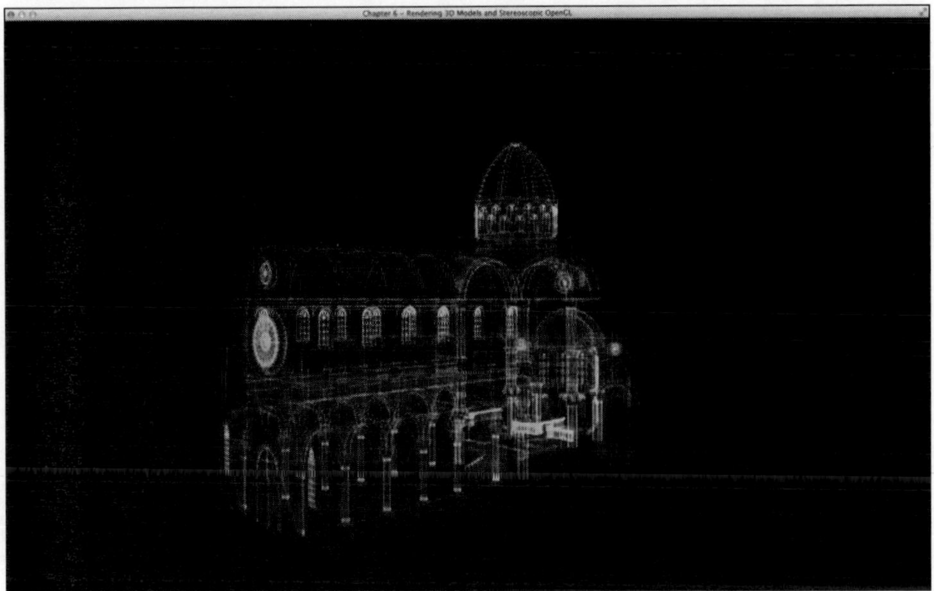

The combination of both points and lines provides additional visual cue to the structure of the object (that is, emphasis on the intersection points). Finally, we render the scene with all options enabled: points, lines, and triangles (surfaces) with transparency:

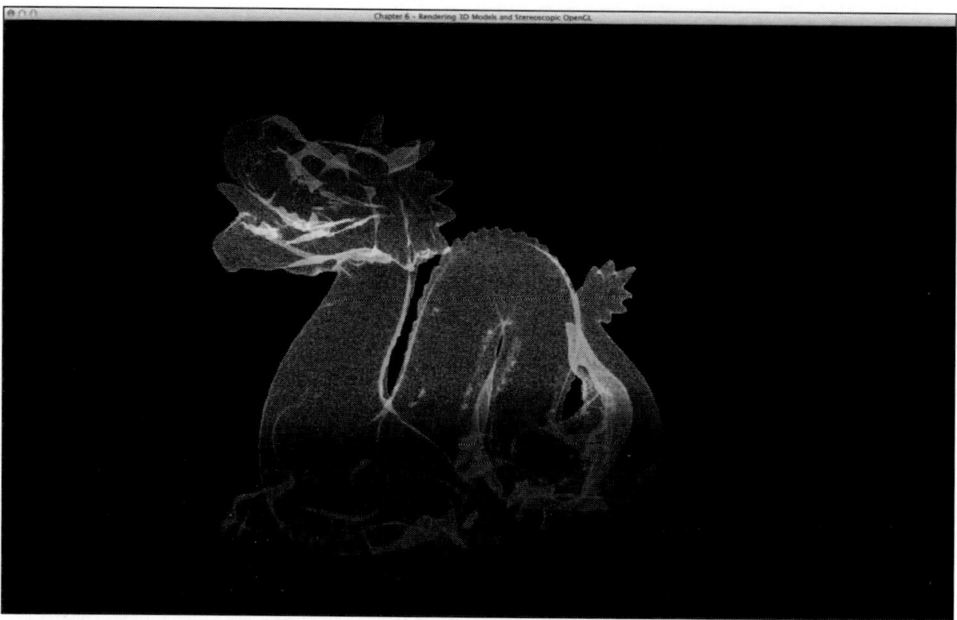

Here's the architectural model rendered using points, lines and triangles with transparency:

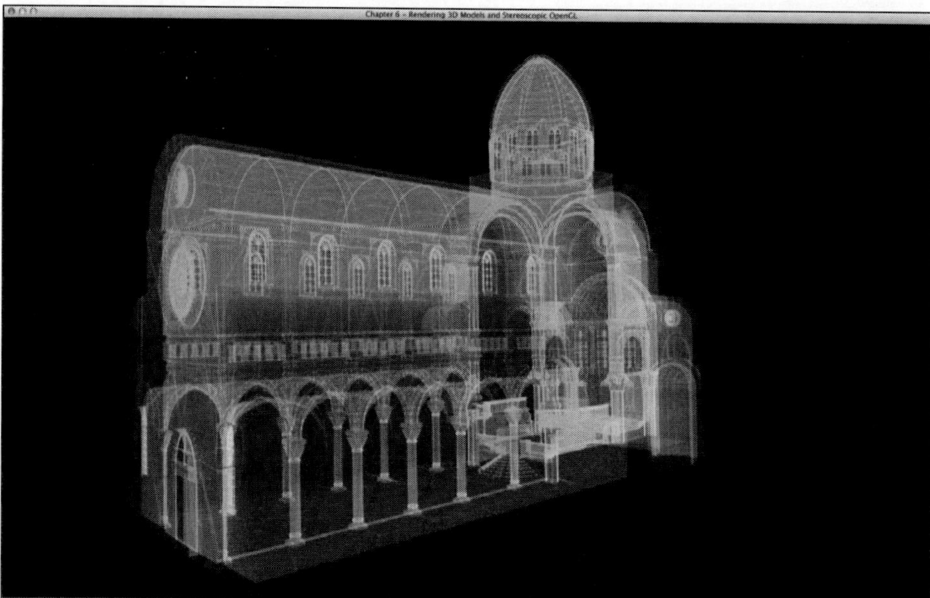

The final combination with all the options enabled provides an even more intuitive visualization of the volume of the object as well as the overall 3D structure. Alternatively, we can also enable the depth test and render the solid model with no transparency:

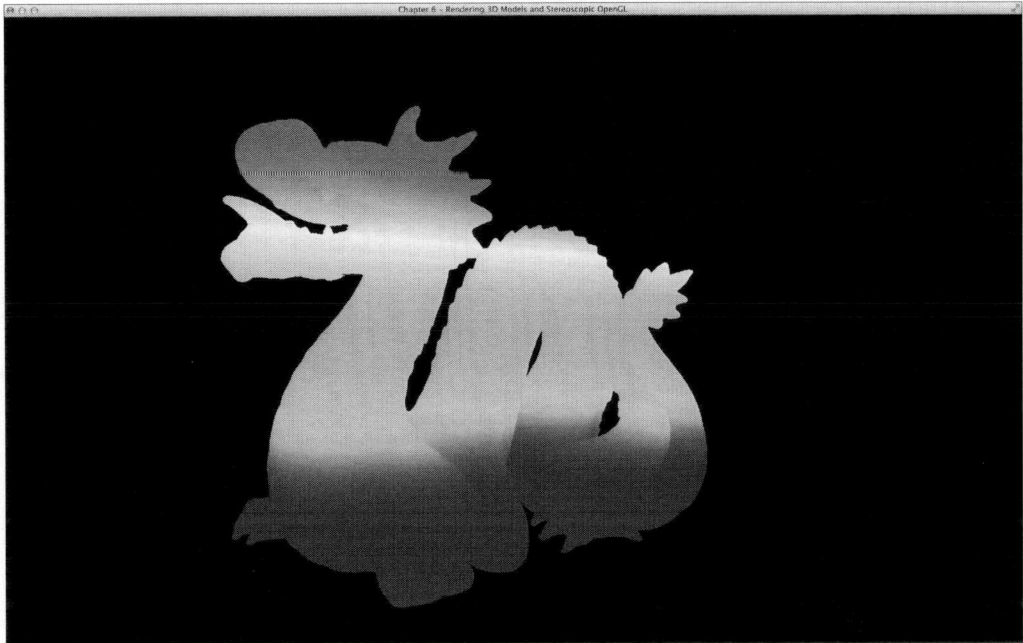

Instructions on how to enable/disable these options at runtime are documented in the source code.

How it works...

By combining the Assimp library and OpenGL, we can now dynamically load 3D models on the screen and create visually appealing 3D effects through an OpenGL-based interactive visualization tool.

In `ObjLoader.cpp`, the `loadVertices` function converts the scene into a single vertex buffer array to reduce the complexity of memory management. In particular, this approach reduces the number of OpenGL memory copies and the number of memory buffers on the rendering side (that is, `glBufferData` and `glGenBuffers`). In addition, the loading function handles the scaling and centering of vertices based on the bounding box. This step is critical as most 3D formats do not normalize their coordinate system.

Next, the `draw` function in `ObjLoader.cpp` traverses the `aiScene` object and draws each part of the scene with the vertex buffer. In the case of point-based rendering, we can skip this step and directly draw the entire array using `glDrawArray` because there is no dependency among the neighboring vertices.

The vertex shader (`pointcloud.vert`) contains the implementation of the heat map color generator. The `heatmap` function takes in three parameters: the input value (that is, the depth or *z* value), the minimum value, and maximum value. It returns the heat map color representation in the RGBA format.

Inside the drawing loop, the `computeStereoViewProjectionMatrices` function constructs the view and projection matrices. The details are explained in the next section.

Finally, we can mix and match various rendering techniques; for example, by enabling both points and lines only for skeleton-based rendering. Various depth visual cues, such as occlusion and motion parallax, can be easily added by supporting rotation or translation of the object. To further improve the result, other rendering techniques such as lighting or shading can be added based on the application requirements.

See also

The Assimp library also supports many file formats in addition to `.obj` files. For example, we can load `.stl` files into our system without changing the source code at all.

To download more 3D models, visit various 3D model-sharing websites such as *Makerbot ThingiVerse* (`http://www.thingiverse.com/`) or *Turbosquid* (`http://www.turbosquid.com/`):

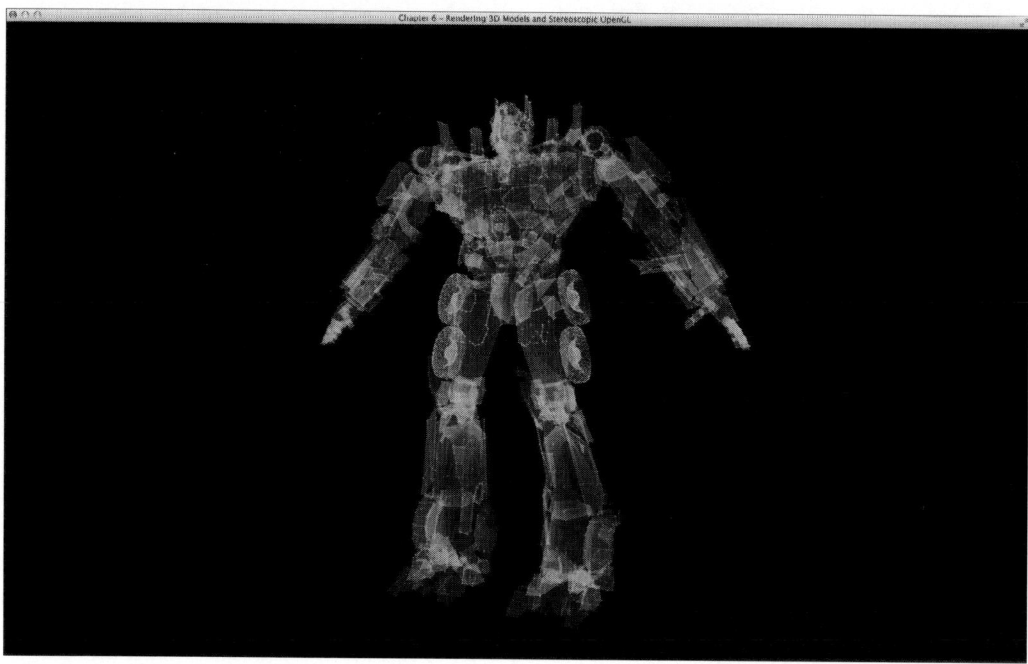

Stereoscopic 3D rendering

3D television and 3D glasses are becoming much more prevalent with the latest trends in consumer electronics and technological advances in wearable computing. In the market, there are currently many hardware options that allow us to visualize information with stereoscopic 3D technology. One common format is side-by-side 3D, which is supported by many 3D glasses as each eye sees an image of the same scene from a different perspective. In OpenGL, creating side-by-side 3D rendering requires asymmetric adjustment as well as viewport adjustment (that is, the area to be rendered) – asymmetric frustum parallel projection or equivalently to lens-shift in photography. This technique introduces no vertical parallax and widely adopted in the stereoscopic rendering. To illustrate this concept, the following diagram shows the geometry of the scene that a user sees from the right eye:

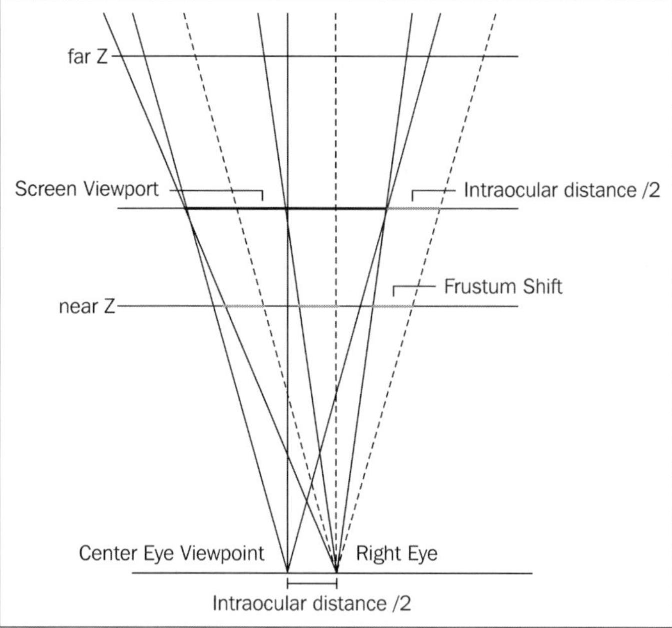

The **intraocular distance** (**IOD**) is the distance between two eyes. As we can see from the diagram, the **Frustum Shift** represents the amount of skew/shift for asymmetric frustrum adjustment. Similarly, for the left eye image, we perform the transformation with a mirrored setting. The implementation of this setup is described in the next section.

How to do it...

The following code illustrates the steps to construct the projection and view matrices for stereoscopic 3D visualization. The code uses the intraocular distance, the distance of the image plane, and the distance of the near clipping plane to compute the appropriate frustum shifts value. In the source file, `common/controls.cpp`, we add the implementation for the stereo 3D matrix setup:

```
void computeStereoViewProjectionMatrices(GLFWwindow* window,
  float IOD, float depthZ, bool left_eye){
  int width, height;
  glfwGetWindowSize(window, &width, &height);
  //up vector
  glm::vec3 up = glm::vec3(0,-1,0);
  glm::vec3 direction_z(0, 0, -1);
  //mirror the parameters with the right eye
  float left_right_direction = -1.0f;
  if(left_eye)
    left_right_direction = 1.0f;
  float aspect_ratio = (float)width/(float)height;
  float nearZ = 1.0f;
  float farZ = 100.0f;
  double frustumshift = (IOD/2)*nearZ/depthZ;
  float top = tan(g_initial_fov/2)*nearZ;
  float right =
aspect_ratio*top+frustumshift*left_right_direction;
//half screen
  float left =
    -aspect_ratio*top+frustumshift*left_right_direction;
  float bottom = -top;
  g_projection_matrix = glm::frustum(left, right, bottom, top,
    nearZ, farZ);
  // update the view matrix
 g_view_matrix =
 glm::lookAt(
   g_position-direction_z+
     glm::vec3(left_right_direction*IOD/2, 0, 0),
     //eye position
   g_position+
     glm::vec3(left_right_direction*IOD/2, 0, 0),
     //centre position
   up //up direction
 );
```

In the rendering loop in `main.cpp`, we define the viewports for each eye (*left* and *right*) and set up the projection and view matrices accordingly. For each eye, we translate our camera position by half of the intraocular distance, as illustrated in the previous figure:

```
if(stereo){
  //draw the LEFT eye, left half of the screen
  glViewport(0, 0, width/2, height);
  //computes the MVP matrix from the IOD and virtual image plane distance
  computeStereoViewProjectionMatrices(g_window, IOD, depthZ, true);
  //gets the View and Model Matrix and apply to the rendering
  glm::mat4 projection_matrix = getProjectionMatrix();
  glm::mat4 view_matrix = getViewMatrix();
  glm::mat4 model_matrix = glm::mat4(1.0);
  model_matrix = glm::translate(model_matrix, glm::vec3(0.0f,
    0.0f, -depthZ));
  model_matrix = glm::rotate(model_matrix, glm::pi<float>() *
    rotateY, glm::vec3(0.0f, 1.0f, 0.0f));
  model_matrix = glm::rotate(model_matrix, glm::pi<float>() *
    rotateX, glm::vec3(1.0f, 0.0f, 0.0f));
  glm::mat4 mvp = projection_matrix * view_matrix * model_matrix;
  //sends our transformation to the currently bound shader,
  //in the "MVP" uniform variable
  glUniformMatrix4fv(matrix_id, 1, GL_FALSE, &mvp[0][0]);
  //render scene, with different drawing modes

  if(drawTriangles)
  obj_loader->draw(GL_TRIANGLES);

  if(drawPoints)
    obj_loader->draw(GL_POINTS);

  if(drawLines)
    obj_loader->draw(GL_LINES);
  //Draw the RIGHT eye, right half of the screen
  glViewport(width/2, 0, width/2, height);
  computeStereoViewProjectionMatrices(g_window, IOD, depthZ,
    false);
  projection_matrix = getProjectionMatrix();
  view_matrix = getViewMatrix();
  model_matrix = glm::mat4(1.0);
  model_matrix = glm::translate(model_matrix, glm::vec3(0.0f,
    0.0f, -depthZ));
  model_matrix = glm::rotate(model_matrix, glm::pi<float>() *
    rotateY, glm::vec3(0.0f, 1.0f, 0.0f));
```

```
    model_matrix = glm::rotate(model_matrix, glm::pi<float>() *
      rotateX, glm::vec3(1.0f, 0.0f, 0.0f));
    mvp = projection_matrix * view_matrix * model_matrix;
    glUniformMatrix4fv(matrix_id, 1, GL_FALSE, &mvp[0][0]);
    if(drawTriangles)
      obj_loader->draw(GL_TRIANGLES);
    if(drawPoints)
      obj_loader->draw(GL_POINTS);
    if(drawLines)
      obj_loader->draw(GL_LINES);
}
```

The final rendering result consists of two separate images on each side of the display, and note that each image is compressed horizontally by a scaling factor of two. For some display systems, each side of the display is required to preserve the same aspect ratio depending on the specifications of the display.

Here are the final screenshots of the same models in true 3D using stereoscopic 3D rendering:

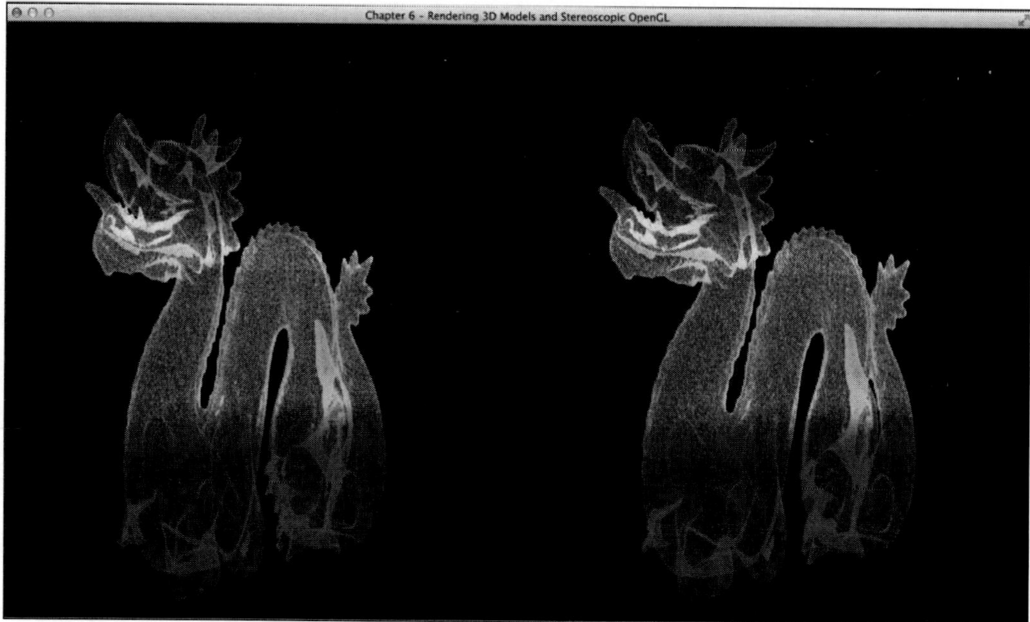

Here's the rendering of the architectural model in stereoscopic 3D:

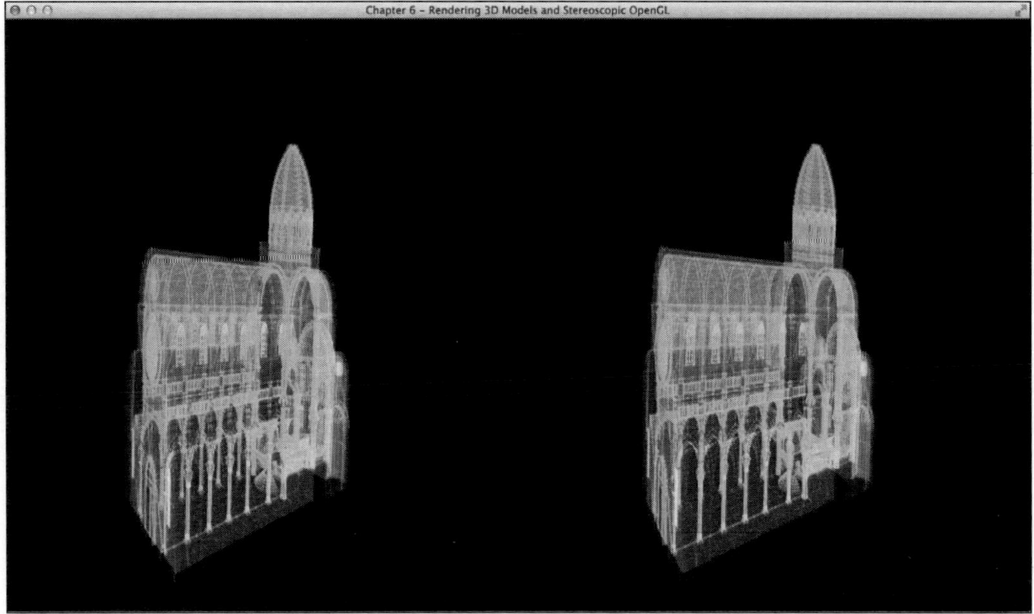

How it works...

The stereoscopic 3D rendering technique is based on the parallel axis and asymmetric frustum perspective projection principle. In simpler terms, we rendered a separate image for each eye as if the object was seen at a different eye position but viewed on the same plane. Parameters such as the intraocular distance and frustum shift can be dynamically adjusted to provide the desired 3D stereo effects.

For example, by increasing or decreasing the frustum asymmetry parameter, the object will appear to be moved in front or behind the plane of the screen. By default, the zero parallax plane is set to the middle of the view volume. That is, the object is set up so that the center position of the object is positioned at the screen level, and some parts of the object will appear in front of or behind the screen. By increasing the frustum asymmetry (that is, positive parallax), the scene will appear to be pushed behind the screen. Likewise, by decreasing the frustum asymmetry (that is, negative parallax), the scene will appear to be pulled in front of the screen.

The `glm::frustum` function sets up the projection matrix, and we implemented the asymmetric frustum projection concept illustrated in the drawing. Then, we use the `glm::lookAt` function to adjust the eye position based on the IOP value we have selected.

To project the images side by side, we use the `glViewport` function to constrain the area within which the graphics can be rendered. The function basically performs an affine transformation (that is, scale and translation) which maps the normalized device coordinate to the window coordinate. Note that the final result is a side-by-side image in which the graphic is scaled by a factor of two vertically (or compressed horizontally). Depending on the hardware configuration, we may need to adjust the aspect ratio.

The current implementation supports side-by-side 3D, which is commonly used in most wearable **Augmented Reality** (**AR**) or **Virtual Reality** (**VR**) glasses. Fundamentally, the rendering technique, namely the asymmetric frustum perspective projection described in our chapter, is platform-independent. For example, we have successfully tested our implementation on the Meta 1 Developer Kit (`https://www.getameta.com/products`) and rendered the final results on the optical see-through stereoscopic 3D display:

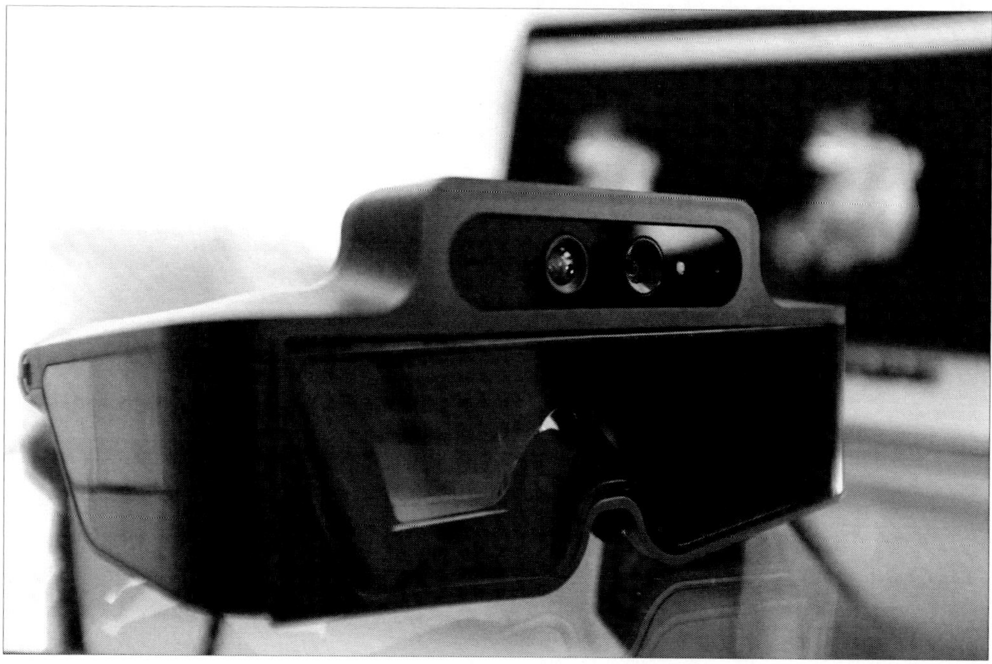

Here is the front view of the Meta 1 Developer Kit, showing the optical see-through stereoscopic 3D display and 3D range-sensing camera (introduced in *Chapter 5, Rendering of Point Cloud Data for 3D Range-sensing Cameras*):

The result is shown as follows, with the stereoscopic 3D graphics rendered onto the real world (which forms the basis of augmented reality):

In the upcoming chapters, we will transition to the increasingly powerful and ubiquitous mobile platform and introduce how to use OpenGL to visualize data in interesting ways using built-in motion sensors on mobile devices. Further details on implementing augmented reality applications will be covered in *Chapter 9, Augmented reality-based visualization on mobile or wearable platforms*.

See also

In addition, we can easily extend our code to support shutter glasses-based 3D monitors by utilizing the Quad Buffered OpenGL APIs (refer to the `GL_BACK_RIGHT` and `GL_BACK_LEFT` flags in the `glDrawBuffer` function). Unfortunately, such 3D formats require specific hardware synchronization and often require higher frame rate display (for example, 120Hz) as well as a professional graphics card. Further information on how to implement stereoscopic 3D in your application can be found at `http://www.nvidia.com/content/GTC-2010/pdfs/2010_GTC2010.pdf`.

7

An Introduction to Real-time Graphics Rendering on a Mobile Platform using OpenGL ES 3.0

In this chapter, we will cover the following topics:

- Setting up the Android SDK
- Setting up the **Android Native Development Kit** (**NDK**)
- Developing a basic framework to integrate the Android NDK
- Creating your first Android application with OpenGL ES 3.0

Introduction

In this chapter, we will transition to an increasingly powerful and ubiquitous computing platform by demonstrating how to visualize data on the latest mobile devices, from smart phones to tablets, using **OpenGL for Embedded Systems** (**OpenGL ES**). As mobile devices become more ubiquitous and with their increasing computing capability, we now have an unprecedented opportunity to develop novel interactive data visualization tools using high-performance graphics hardware directly integrated into modern mobile devices.

OpenGL ES plays an important role in standardizing the 2D and 3D graphics APIs to allow the large-scale deployment of mobile applications on embedded systems with various hardware settings. Among the various mobile platforms (predominantly Google Android, Apple iOS, and Microsoft Windows Phone), the Android mobile operating system is currently one of the most popular ones. Therefore, in this chapter, we will focus primarily on the development of an Android-based application (API 18 and higher) using OpenGL ES 3.0, which provides a newer version of GLSL support (including full support for integer and 32-bit floating point operations) and enhanced texture rendering support. Nevertheless, OpenGL ES 3.0 is also supported on other mobile platforms, such as Apple iOS and Microsoft Phone.

Here, we will first introduce how to set up the Android development platform, including the SDK that provides the essential tools to build mobile applications, and the NDK, which enables the use of native-code languages (C/C++) for high-performance scientific computing and simulations by exploiting direct hardware acceleration. We will provide a script to simplify the process of deploying your first Android-based application on your mobile device.

Setting up the Android SDK

The Google Android OS website provides a standalone package for Android application development called the **Android SDK**. It contains all the necessary compilation and debugging tools to develop an Android application (except native code support, which is provided by the Android NDK). The upcoming steps explain the installation procedure in Mac OS X or, similarly, in Linux, with minor modifications to the script and binary packages required.

How to do it...

To install the Android SDK, follow these steps:

1. Download the standalone package from the Android Developers website at `http://dl.google.com/android/android-sdk_r24.3.3-macosx.zip`.
2. Create a new directory called `3rd_party/android` and move the setup file into this folder:

   ```
   mkdir 3rd_party/android
   mv android-sdk_r24.3.3-macosx.zip 3rd_party/android
   ```

3. Unzip the package:

   ```
   cd 3rd_party/android && unzip android-sdk_r24.3.3-macosx.zip
   ```

4. Execute the Android SDK Manager:

   ```
   ./android-sdk-macosx/tools/android
   ```

5. Select **Android 4.3.1 (API 18)** from the list of packages in addition to the default options. Deselect **Android M (API22, MBC preview)** and **Android 5.1.1 (API 22)**. Press the **Install 9 packages...** button on the **Android SDK Manager** screen, as shown here:

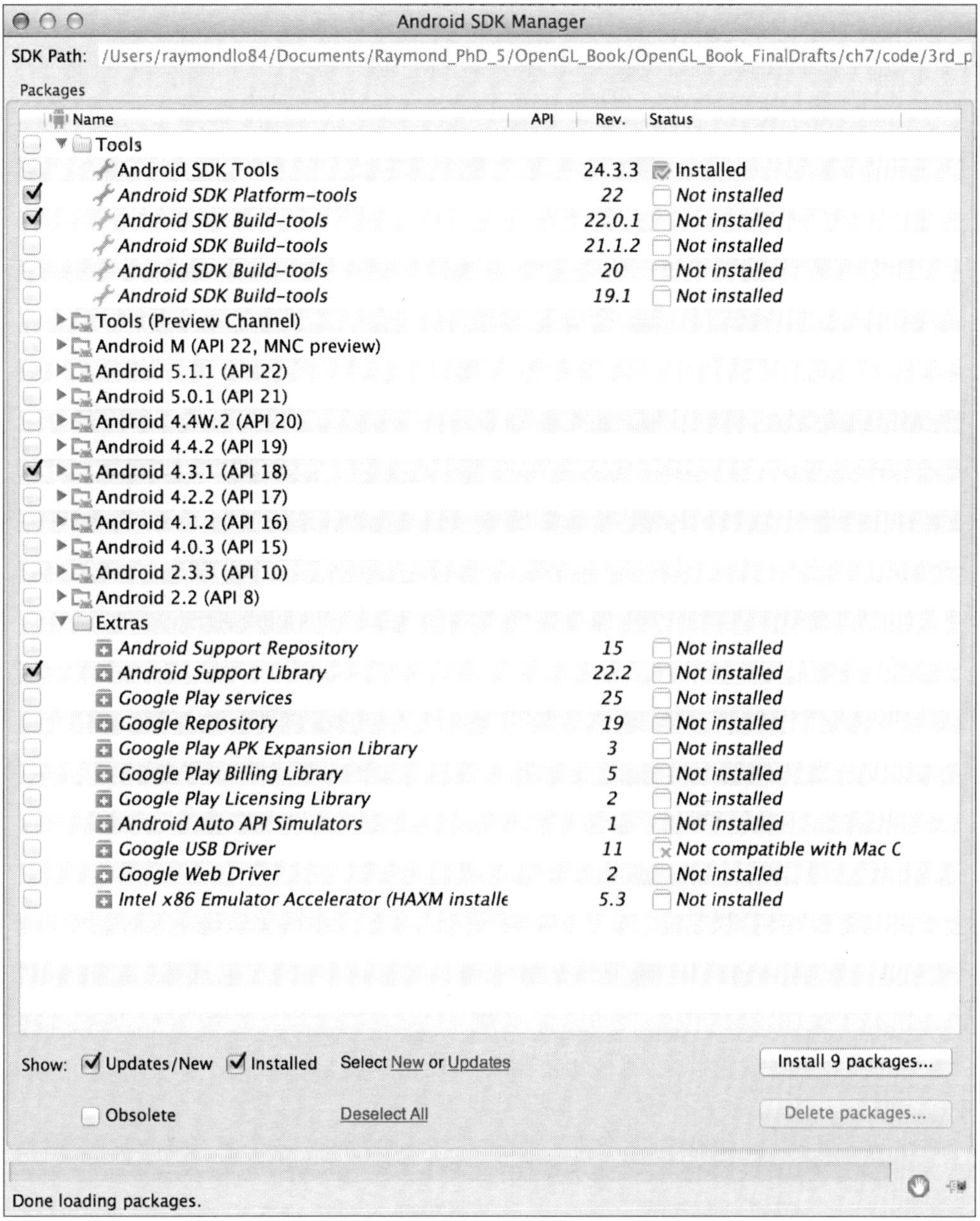

Android SDK Manager

SDK Path: /Users/raymondlo84/Documents/Raymond_PhD_5/OpenGL_Book/OpenGL_Book_FinalDrafts/ch7/code/3rd_p

Packages

	Name	API	Rev.	Status
	Tools			
	Android SDK Tools		24.3.3	Installed
✓	Android SDK Platform-tools		22	Not installed
✓	Android SDK Build-tools		22.0.1	Not installed
	Android SDK Build-tools		21.1.2	Not installed
	Android SDK Build-tools		20	Not installed
	Android SDK Build-tools		19.1	Not installed
	Tools (Preview Channel)			
	Android M (API 22, MNC preview)			
	Android 5.1.1 (API 22)			
	Android 5.0.1 (API 21)			
	Android 4.4W.2 (API 20)			
	Android 4.4.2 (API 19)			
✓	Android 4.3.1 (API 18)			
	Android 4.2.2 (API 17)			
	Android 4.1.2 (API 16)			
	Android 4.0.3 (API 15)			
	Android 2.3.3 (API 10)			
	Android 2.2 (API 8)			
	Extras			
	Android Support Repository		15	Not installed
✓	Android Support Library		22.2	Not installed
	Google Play services		25	Not installed
	Google Repository		19	Not installed
	Google Play APK Expansion Library		3	Not installed
	Google Play Billing Library		5	Not installed
	Google Play Licensing Library		2	Not installed
	Android Auto API Simulators		1	Not installed
	Google USB Driver		11	Not compatible with Mac C
	Google Web Driver		2	Not installed
	Intel x86 Emulator Accelerator (HAXM installe		5.3	Not installed

Show: ✓ Updates/New ✓ Installed Select New or Updates [Install 9 packages...]

Obsolete Deselect All [Delete packages...]

Done loading packages.

6. Select **Accept License** and click on the **Install** button:

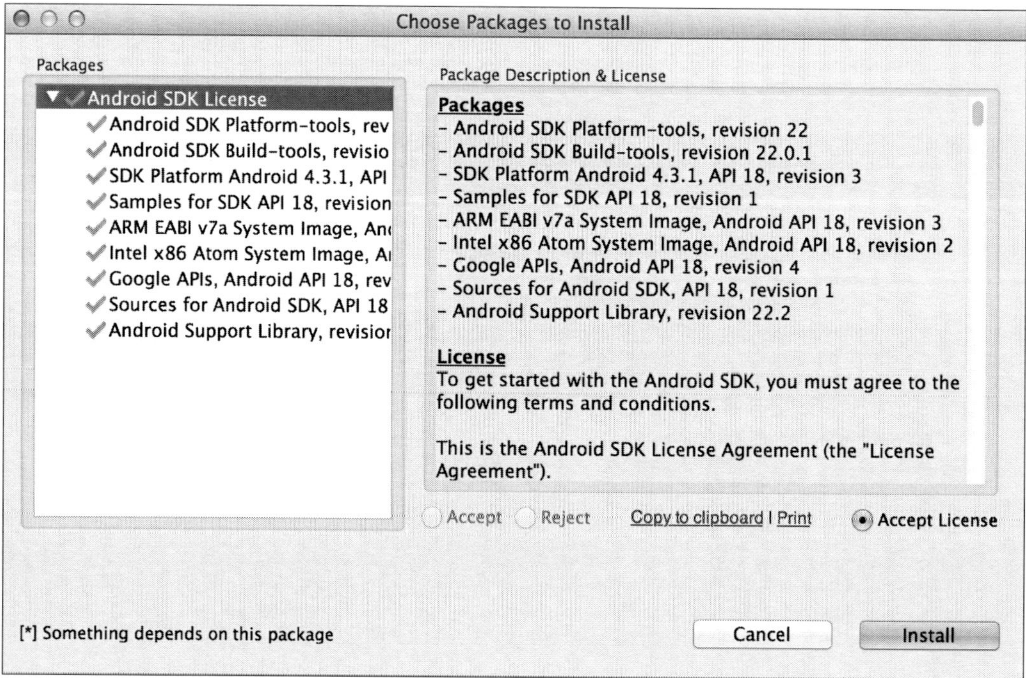

7. To verify the installation, type the following command into the terminal:

```
./android-sdk-macosx/tools/android list
```

8. This is an example that illustrates the successful installation of the Android 4.3.1 platform:

```
Available Android targets:
----------
id: 1 or "android-18"
Name: Android 4.3.1
Type: Platform
API level: 18
Revision: 3
Skins: HVGA, QVGA, WQVGA400, WQVGA432, WSVGA, WVGA800
  (default), WVGA854, WXGA720, WXGA800, WXGA800-7in
Tag/ABIs : default/armeabi-v7a, default/x86
...
```

9. Finally, we will install Apache Ant to automate the software build process for Android application development. We can easily obtain the Apache Ant package by using MacPort with the command line or from its official website at `http://ant.apache.org/`:

   ```
   sudo port install apache-ant
   ```

See also

To install the Android SDK in Linux or Windows, download the corresponding installation files and follow the instructions on the Android developer website at `https://developer.android.com/sdk/index.html`.

The setup procedures to set up the Android SDK in Linux are essentially identical using the command-line interface, except that a different standalone package should be downloaded using this link: `http://dl.google.com/android/android-sdk_r24.3.3-linux.tgz`.

In addition, for Windows users, the standalone package can be obtained using this link: `http://dl.google.com/android/installer_r24.3.3-windows.exe`.

To verify that your mobile phone has proper OpenGL ES 3.0 support, consult the Android documentation on how to check the OpenGL ES version at runtime: `http://developer.android.com/guide/topics/graphics/opengl.html#version-check`.

Setting up the Android Native Development Kit (NDK)

The Android NDK environment is essential for native-code language development. Here, we will outline the setup steps for the Mac OS X platform again.

How to do it...

To install the Android NDK, follow these steps:

1. Download the NDK installation package from the Android developer website at `http://dl.google.com/android/ndk/android-ndk-r10e-darwin-x86_64.bin`.
2. Move the setup file into the same installation folder:

   ```
   mv android-ndk-r10e-darwin-x86_64.bin 3rd_party/android
   ```

3. Set the permission of the file to be an executable:

   ```
   cd 3rd_party/android && chmod +x android-ndk-r10e-darwin-
     x86_64.bin
   ```

4. Run the NDK installation package:

```
./android-ndk-r10e-darwin-x86_64.bin
```

5. The installation process is fully automated and the following output confirms the successful installation of the Android NDK:

```
...
Extracting  android-ndk-r10e/build/tools
Extracting  android-ndk-r10e/build/gmsl
Extracting  android-ndk-r10e/build/core
Extracting  android-ndk-r10e/build/awk
Extracting  android-ndk-r10e/build
Extracting  android-ndk-r10e

Everything is Ok
```

See also

To install the Android NDK on Linux or Windows, download the corresponding installation files and follow the instructions on the Android developer website at `https://developer.android.com/tools/sdk/ndk/index.html`.

Developing a basic framework to integrate the Android NDK

Now that we have successfully installed the Android SDK and NDK, we will demonstrate how to develop a basic framework to integrate native C/C++ code into a Java-based Android application. Here, we describe the general mechanism to create high-performance code for deployment on mobile devices using OpenGL ES 3.0.

OpenGL ES 3.0 supports both Java and C/C++ interfaces. Depending on the specific requirements of the application, you may choose to implement the solution in Java due to its flexibility and portability. For high-performance computing and applications that require a high memory bandwidth, it is preferable that you use the NDK for fine-grain optimization and memory management. In addition, we can port our existing libraries, such as OpenCV with Android NDK, using static library linking. The cross-platform compilation capability opens up many possibilities for real-time image and signal processing on a mobile platform with minimal development effort.

Here, we introduce a basic framework that consists of three classes: `GL3JNIActivity`, `GL3JNIView`, and `GL3JNIActivity`. We show a simplified class diagram in the following figure, illustrating the relationship between the classes. The native code (C/C++) is implemented separately and will be described in detail in the next section:

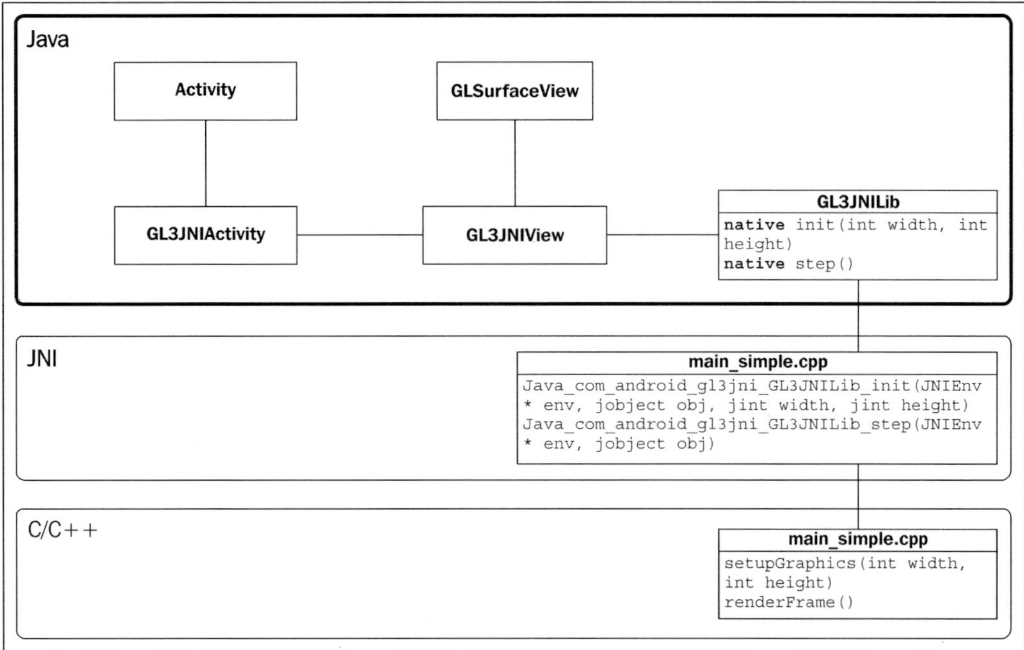

How to do it...

First, we will create the core Java source files that are essential to an Android application. These files serve as a wrapper for our OpenGL ES 3.0 native code:

1. In the project directory, create a folder named `src/com/android/gl3jni` with the following command:

   `mkdir src/com/android/gl3jni`

2. Create the first class, `GL3JNIActivity`, in the Java source file, `GL3JNIActivity.java`, within the new folder, `src/com/android/gl3jni/`:

```
package com.android.gl3jni;

import android.app.Activity;
import android.os.Bundle;
/**
 * Main application for Android
 */
public class GL3JNIActivity extends Activity {

  GL3JNIView mView;
```

```
    @Override protected void onCreate(Bundle icicle) {
      super.onCreate(icicle);
      mView = new GL3JNIView(getApplication());
      setContentView(mView);
    }

    @Override protected void onPause() {
      super.onPause();
      mView.onPause();
    }

    @Override protected void onResume() {
      super.onResume();
      mView.onResume();
    }
  }
```

3. Next, implement the `GL3JNIView` class, which handles the OpenGL rendering setup in the `GL3JNIView.java` source file inside `src/com/android/gl3jni/`:

```
package com.android.gl3jni;

import android.content.Context;
import android.opengl.GLSurfaceView;
import javax.microedition.khronos.egl.EGLConfig;
import javax.microedition.khronos.opengles.GL10;

/**
* A simple application that uses OpenGL ES3 and GLSurface
*/
class GL3JNIView extends GLSurfaceView {
  public GL3JNIView(Context context) {
    super(context);
     /* Pick an EGLConfig with RGB8 color, 16-bit depth,
     no stencil, supporting OpenGL ES 3.0 or later */
    setEGLConfigChooser(8, 8, 8, 0, 16, 0);
    setEGLContextClientVersion(3);
    setRenderer(new Renderer());
  }
  private static class Renderer implements
    GLSurfaceView.Renderer {
    public void onDrawFrame(GL10 gl) {
```

```
        GL3JNILib.step();
      }

      public void onSurfaceChanged(GL10 gl, int width,
        int height) {
        GL3JNILib.init(width, height);
      }
      public void onSurfaceCreated(GL10 gl, EGLConfig
        config) {
      }
    }
  }
```

4. Finally, create the `GL3JNILib` class to handle native library loading and calling in `GL3JNILib.java` inside `src/com/android/gl3jni`:

```
package com.android.gl3jni;

public class GL3JNILib {
  static {
    System.loadLibrary("gl3jni");
  }

  public static native void init(int width, int height);
  public static native void step();
}
```

5. Now, in the project directory of the project, add the `AndroidManifest.xml` file, which contains all the essential information about your application on the Android system:

```
<?xml version="1.0" encoding="utf-8"?>
<manifest xmlns:android=
  "http://schemas.android.com/apk/res/android"
  package="com.android.gl3jni">
    <application android:label=
    "@string/gl3jni_activity">
      <activity android:name="GL3JNIActivity"
android:theme=
      "@android:style/Theme.NoTitleBar.Fullscreen"
      android:launchMode="singleTask"
android:configChanges=
      "orientation|keyboardHidden">
```

```
                <intent-filter>
                    <action android:name=
                "android.intent.action.MAIN" />
                    <category android:name=
                      "android.intent.category.LAUNCHER" />
                </intent-filter>
            </activity>
        </application>
        <uses-feature android:glEsVersion="0x00030000"/>
        <uses-sdk android:minSdkVersion="18"/>
</manifest>
```

6. In the `res/values/` directory, add the `strings.xml` file, which saves our application's name:

```
<?xml version="1.0" encoding="utf-8"?>
<resources>
  <string name="gl3jni_activity">OpenGL ES Demo</string>
</resources>
```

How it works...

The following class diagram illustrates the core functions and relationships between the classes. Similar to all other Android applications with a user interface, we define the **Activity** class, which handles the core interactions. The implementation of `GL3JNIActivity` is straightforward. It captures the events from the Android application (for example, `onPause` and `onResume`) and also creates an instance of the `GL3JNIView` class, which handles graphics rendering. Instead of adding UI elements, such as textboxes or labels, we create a surface based on `GLSurfaceView`, which handles hardware-accelerated OpenGL rendering:

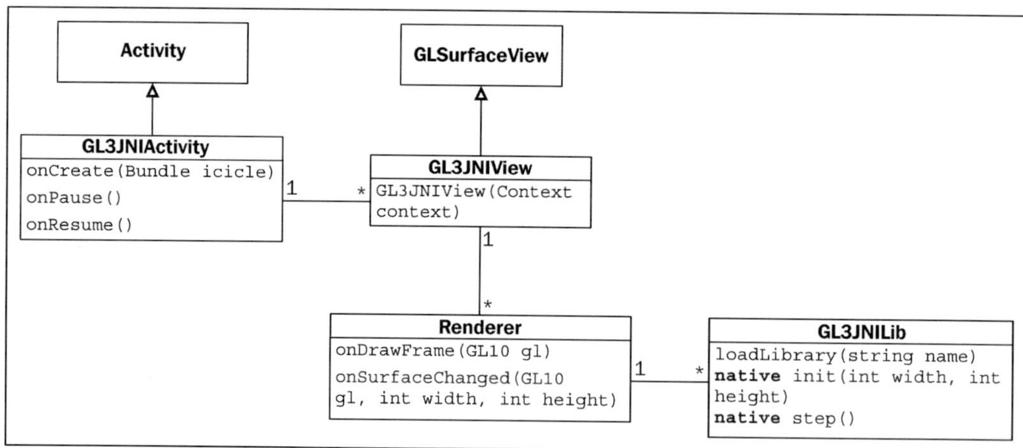

The `GL3JNIView` class is a subclass of the `GLSurfaceView` class, which provides a dedicated surface for OpenGL rendering. We choose the RGB8 color mode, a 16-bit depth buffer, and no stencil with the `setEGLConfigChooser` function and ensure that the environment is set up for OpenGL ES 3.0 by using the `setEGLContextClientVersion` function. The `setRenderer` function then registers the custom `Renderer` class, which is responsible for the actual OpenGL rendering.

The `Renderer` class implements the key event functions—`onDrawFrame`, `onSurfaceChanged`, and `onSurfaceCreated`—in the rendering loop. These functions connect to the native implementation (C/C++) portion of the code that is handled by the `GL3JNILib` class.

Finally, the `GL3JNILib` class creates the interface to communicate with the native code functions. First, it loads the native library named `gl3jni`, which contains the actual OpenGL ES 3.0 implementation. The function prototypes, `step` and `init`, are used to interface with the native code, which will be defined separately in the next section. Note that we can also pass in the canvas width and height values to the native functions as parameters.

The `AndroidManifest.xml` and `strings.xml` files are the configuration files required by the Android application, and they must be stored in the root directory of the project in the XML format. The `AndroidManifest.xml` file defines all the essential information including the name of the Java package and the declaration of permission requirements (for example, file read/write access), as well as the minimum version of the Android API that the application requires.

See also

For further information on Android application development, the Android Developers website provides detailed documentation on the API at `http://developer.android.com/guide/index.html`.

For further information on using OpenGL ES within an Android application, the Android programming guide describes the programming workflow in detail and provides useful examples at `http://developer.android.com/training/graphics/opengl/environment.html`.

Creating your first Android application with OpenGL ES 3.0

In this section, we will complete our implementation with native code in C/C++ to create the first Android application with OpenGL ES 3.0. As illustrated in the simplified class diagram, the Java code only provides the basic interface on the mobile device. Now, on the C/C++ side, we implement all the functionalities previously defined on the Java side and also include all the required libraries from OpenGL ES 3.0 (inside the `main_simple.cpp` file). The `main_simple.cpp` file also defines the key interface between the C/C++ and Java side by using the **Java Native Interface** (**JNI**):

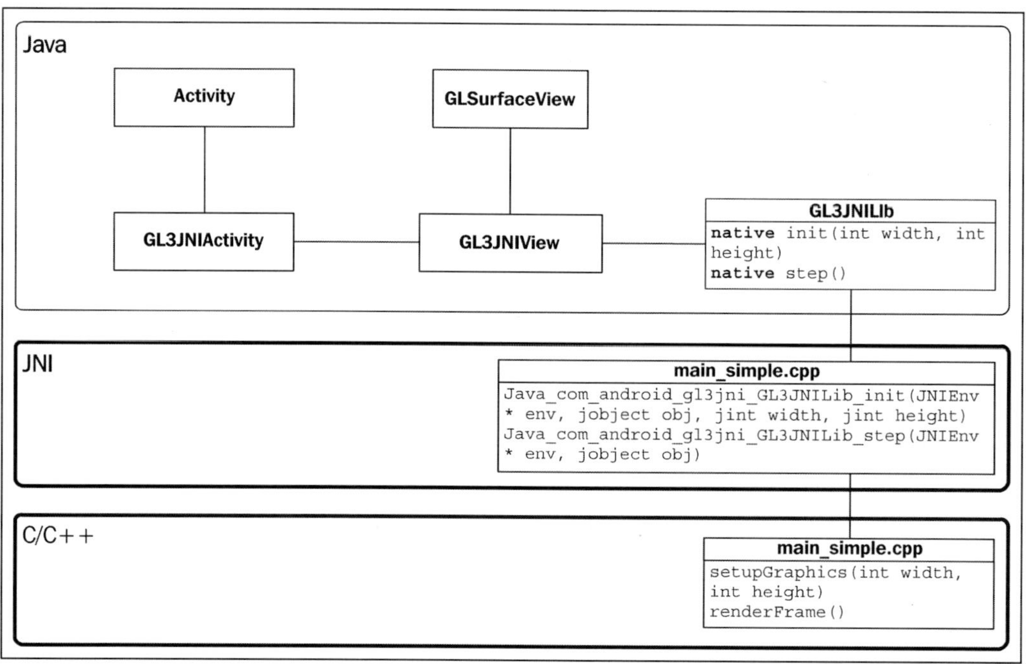

Getting ready

We assume that you have installed all the prerequisite tools from the Android SDK and NDK in addition to setting up the basic framework introduced in the previous section. Also, you should review the basics of shader programming, introduced in earlier chapters, before you proceed.

How to do it...

Here, we describe the implementation of the OpenGL ES 3.0 native code to complete the demo application:

1. In the project directory, create a folder named `jni` by using the following command:

   mkdir jni

2. Create a file named `main_simple.cpp` and store it inside the `jni` directory.
3. Include all necessary header files for JNI and OpenGL ES 3.0:

```
//header for JNI
#include <jni.h>

//header for the OpenGL ES3 library
#include <GLES3/gl3.h>
```

4. Include the logging header and define the macros to show the debug messages:

```
#include <android/log.h>
#include <stdio.h>
#include <stdlib.h>
#include <math.h>

//android error log interface
#define  LOG_TAG    "libgl3jni"
#define  LOGI(...)  __android_log_print(ANDROID_LOG_INFO,LOG_
TAG,__VA_ARGS__)
#define  LOGE(...)  __android_log_print(ANDROID_LOG_ERROR,LOG_
TAG,__VA_ARGS__)
```

5. Declare the shader program variables for our demo application:

```
GLuint gProgram;
GLuint gvPositionHandle;
GLuint gvColorHandle;

int width = 1280;
int height = 720;
```

6. Define the shader program code for the vertex shader and the fragment shader:

```
// Vertex shader source code
static const char g_vshader_code[] =
  "#version 300 es\n"
    "in vec4 vPosition;\n"
```

```
    "in vec4 vColor;\n"
      "out vec4 color;\n"
      "void main() {\n"
        "  gl_Position = vPosition;\n"
        "  color = vColor;\n"
    "}\n";

// fragment shader source code
static const char g_fshader_code[] =
  "#version 300 es\n"
    "precision mediump float;\n"
  "in vec4 color;\n"
    "out vec4 color_out;\n"
    "void main() {\n"
      "  color_out = color;\n"
  "}\n";
```

7. Implement the error call handlers for OpenGL ES, using the Android log:

```
/**
 * Print out the error string from OpenGL
 */
static void printGLString(const char *name, GLenum s) {
  const char *v = (const char *) glGetString(s);
  LOGI("GL %s = %s\n", name, v);
}

/**
* Error checking with OpenGL calls
*/
static void checkGlError(const char* op) {
  for (GLint error = glGetError(); error; error
  = glGetError()) {
    LOGI("After %s() glError (0x%x)\n", op, error);
  }
}
```

8. Implement the vertex or fragment program-loading mechanisms. The warning and error messages are redirected to the Android log output:

```
GLuint loadShader(GLenum shader_type, const char* p_source) {
  GLuint shader = glCreateShader(shader_type);
  if (shader) {
    glShaderSource(shader, 1, &p_source, 0);
    glCompileShader(shader);
```

```
    GLint compiled = 0;
    glGetShaderiv(shader, GL_COMPILE_STATUS, &compiled);

    //Report error and delete the shader
    if (!compiled) {
      GLint infoLen = 0;
      glGetShaderiv(shader, GL_INFO_LOG_LENGTH, &infoLen);
      if (infoLen) {
        char* buf = (char*) malloc(infoLen);
        if (buf) {
          glGetShaderInfoLog(shader, infoLen, 0, buf);
          LOGE("Could not compile shader %d:\n%s\n",
            shader_type, buf);
          free(buf);
        }
        glDeleteShader(shader);
        shader = 0;
      }
    }
  }
  return shader;
}
```

9. Implement the shader program creation mechanism. The function also attaches and links the shader program:

```
GLuint createShaderProgram(const char *vertex_shader_code,
  const char *fragment_shader_code){
  //create the vertex and fragment shaders
  GLuint vertex_shader_id = loadShader(GL_VERTEX_SHADER,
    vertex_shader_code);
  if (!vertex_shader_id) {
    return 0;
  }

  GLuint fragment_shader_id =
    loadShader(GL_FRAGMENT_SHADER, fragment_shader_code);
  if (!fragment_shader_id) {
    return 0;
  }

  GLint result = GL_FALSE;
  //link the program
  GLuint program_id = glCreateProgram();
  glAttachShader(program_id, vertex_shader_id);
  checkGlError("glAttachShader");
```

```
    glAttachShader(program_id, fragment_shader_id);
    checkGlError("glAttachShader");
    glLinkProgram(program_id);

    //check the program and ensure that the program is linked properly
    glGetProgramiv(program_id, GL_LINK_STATUS, &result);
    if ( result != GL_TRUE ){
      //error handling with Android
      GLint bufLength = 0;
      glGetProgramiv(program_id, GL_INFO_LOG_LENGTH,
        &bufLength);
      if (bufLength) {
        char* buf = (char*) malloc(bufLength);
        if (buf) {
          glGetProgramInfoLog(program_id, bufLength, 0, buf);
          LOGE("Could not link program:\n%s\n",
            buf);
          free(buf);
        }
      }
      glDeleteProgram(program_id);
      program_id = 0;
    }
    else {
      LOGI("Linked program Successfully\n");
    }

    glDeleteShader(vertex_shader_id);
    glDeleteShader(fragment_shader_id);

    return program_id;
  }
```

10. Create a function to handle the initialization. This function is a helper function that handles requests from the Java side:

```
bool setupGraphics(int w, int h) {
  printGLString("Version", GL_VERSION);
  printGLString("Vendor", GL_VENDOR);
  printGLString("Renderer", GL_RENDERER);
  printGLString("Extensions", GL_EXTENSIONS);

  LOGI("setupGraphics(%d, %d)", w, h);
  gProgram = createShaderProgram(g_vshader_code,
    g_fshader_code);
  if (!gProgram) {
    LOGE("Could not create program.");
    return false;
  }
```

```
    gvPositionHandle = glGetAttribLocation(gProgram,
      "vPosition");
    checkGlError("glGetAttribLocation");
    LOGI("glGetAttribLocation(\"vPosition\") = %d\n",
    gvPositionHandle);

    gvColorHandle = glGetAttribLocation(gProgram,
      "vColor");
    checkGlError("glGetAttribLocation");
    LOGI("glGetAttribLocation(\"vColor\") = %d\n",
    gvColorHandle);

    glViewport(0, 0, w, h);
    width = w;
    height = h;

    checkGlError("glViewport");

    return true;
  }
```

11. Set up the rendering function that draws a triangle on the screen with red, green, and blue vertices:

```
//vertices
GLfloat gTriangle[9]={-1.0f, -1.0f, 0.0f,
  1.0f, -1.0f, 0.0f,
  0.0f, 1.0f, 0.0f};
GLfloat gColor[9]={1.0f, 0.0f, 0.0f,
  0.0f, 1.0f, 0.0f,
  0.0f, 0.0f, 1.0f};

void renderFrame() {
  glClearColor(0.0f, 0.0f, 0.0f, 1.0f);
  checkGlError("glClearColor");

  glClear(GL_COLOR_BUFFER_BIT | GL_DEPTH_BUFFER_BIT);
  checkGlError("glClear");

  glUseProgram(gProgram);
  checkGlError("glUseProgram");

  glVertexAttribPointer(gvPositionHandle, 3, GL_FLOAT,
    GL_FALSE, 0, gTriangle);
  checkGlError("glVertexAttribPointer");

  glVertexAttribPointer(gvColorHandle, 3, GL_FLOAT,
    GL_FALSE, 0, gColor);
  checkGlError("glVertexAttribPointer");
```

```
    glEnableVertexAttribArray(gvPositionHandle);
    checkGlError("glEnableVertexAttribArray");

    glEnableVertexAttribArray(gvColorHandle);
    checkGlError("glEnableVertexAttribArray");

    glDrawArrays(GL_TRIANGLES, 0, 9);
    checkGlError("glDrawArrays");
}
```

12. Define the JNI prototypes that connect to the Java side. These calls are the interfaces to communicate between the Java code and the C/C++ native code:

```
//external calls for Java
extern "C" {
  JNIEXPORT void JNICALL
    Java_com_android_gl3jni_GL3JNILib_init(JNIEnv * env,
      jobject obj, jint width, jint height);
  JNIEXPORT void JNICALL
    Java_com_android_gl3jni_GL3JNILib_step(JNIEnv * env,
      jobject obj);
};
```

13. Set up the internal function calls with the helper functions:

```
//link to internal calls
JNIEXPORT void JNICALL
Java_com_android_gl3jni_GL3JNILib_init(JNIEnv * env,
  jobject obj, jint width, jint height)
{
  setupGraphics(width, height);
}

JNIEXPORT void JNICALL
  Java_com_android_gl3jni_GL3JNILib_step(JNIEnv * env,
    jobject obj)
{
  renderFrame();
}
//end of file
```

14. Now that we have completed the implementation of the native code, we must compile the code and link it to the Android application. To compile the code, create a `build` file that is similar to a `Makefile`, called `Android.mk`, in the `jni` folder:

```
LOCAL_PATH:= $(call my-dir)

include $(CLEAR_VARS)
```

```
LOCAL_MODULE     := libgl3jni
LOCAL_CFLAGS     := -Werror
#for simplified demo
LOCAL_SRC_FILES := main_simple.cpp
LOCAL_LDLIBS     := -llog -lGLESv3

include $(BUILD_SHARED_LIBRARY)
```

15. In addition, we must create an `Application.mk` file that provides information about the build type, such as the **Application Binary Interface** (**ABI**). The `Application.mk` file must be stored inside the `jni` directory:

```
APP_ABI := armeabi-v7a
#required for GLM and other static libraries
APP_STL := gnustl_static
```

16. At this point, we should have the following list of files in the root directory:

```
src/com/android/gl3jni/GL3JNIActivity.java
src/com/android/gl3jni/GL3JNILib.java
src/com/android/gl3jni/GL3JNIView.java
AndroidManifest.xml
res/value/strings.xml
jni/Android.mk
jni/Application.mk
jni/main_simple.cpp
```

To compile the native source code and deploy our application on a mobile phone, run the following `build` script in the terminal, which is shown as follows:

1. Set up our environment variables for the SDK and the NDK. (Note that the following relative paths assume that the SDK and NDK are installed 3 levels outside the current directory, where the `compile.sh` and `install.sh` scripts are executed in the code package. These paths should be modified to match your code directory structure as necessary.):

```
export ANDROID_SDK_PATH="../../../3rd_party/android/android-sdk-
macosx"
export ANDROID_NDK_PATH="../../../3rd_party/android/android-ndk-
r10e"
```

2. Initialize the project with the android `update` command for the first-time compilation. This will generate all the necessary files (such as the `build.xml` file) for later steps:

```
$ANDROID_SDK_PATH/tools/android update project -p . -s
  --target "android-18"
```

3. Compile the JNI native code with the `build` command:

```
$ANDROID_NDK_PATH/ndk-build
```

4. Run the `build` command. Apache Ant takes the `build.xml` script and builds the **Android Application Package** (**APK**) file that is ready for deployment:

   ```
   ant debug
   ```

5. Install the Android application by using the **Android Debug Bridge** (**adb**) command:

   ```
   $ANDROID_SDK_PATH/platform-tools/adb install -r
     bin/GL3JNIActivity-debug.apk
   ```

For this command to work, before connecting the mobile device through the USB port, ensure that the USB Debugging mode is enabled and accept any prompts for security-related warnings. On most devices, you can find this option by navigating to **Settings** | **Applications** | **Development** or **Settings** | **Developer**. However, on Android 4.2 or higher, this option is hidden by default and must be enabled by navigating to **Settings** | **About Phone** (or **About Tablet**) and tapping **Build Number** multiple times. For further details, follow the instructions provided on the official Android Developer website at `http://developer.android.com/tools/device.html`. Here is a sample screenshot of an Android phone with the USB debugging mode successfully configured:

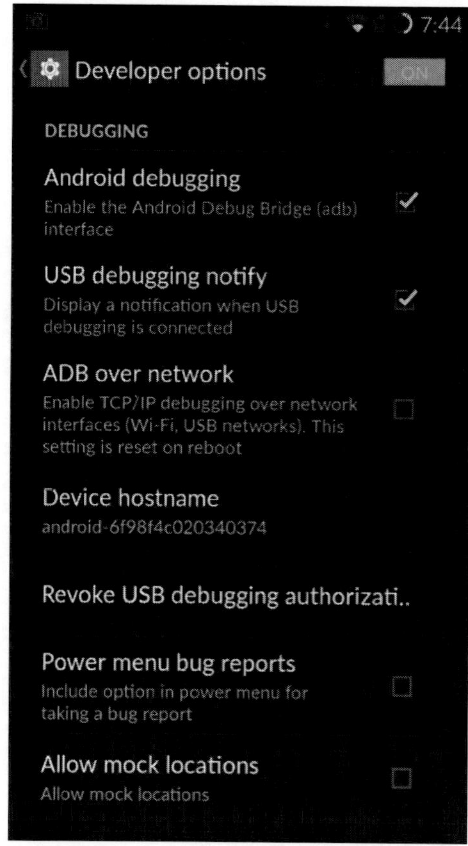

After the application is installed, we can execute the application as we normally do with any other Android application by opening it directly using the application icon on the phone, as shown here:

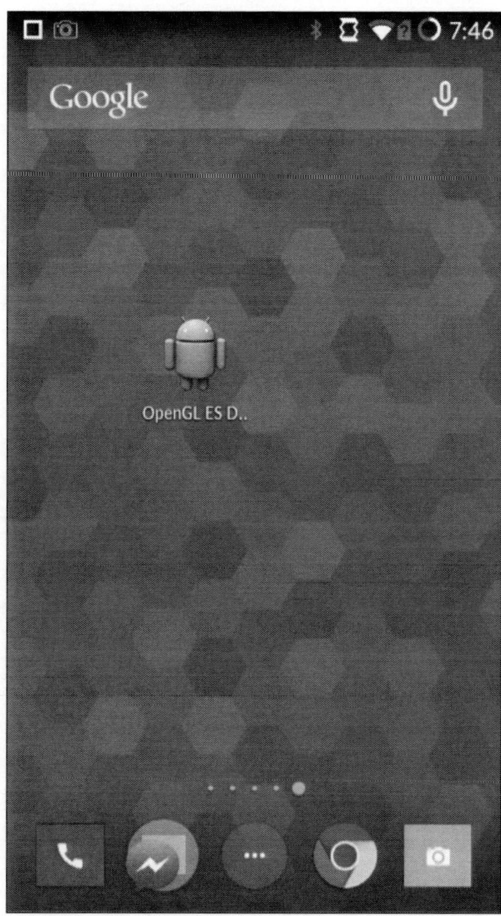

A screenshot after launching the application is shown next. Note that the CPU monitor has been enabled to show the CPU utilization. This is not enabled by default but can be found in **Developer Options**. The application supports both the portrait and landscape modes and the graphics automatically scale to the window size upon changing the frame buffer size:

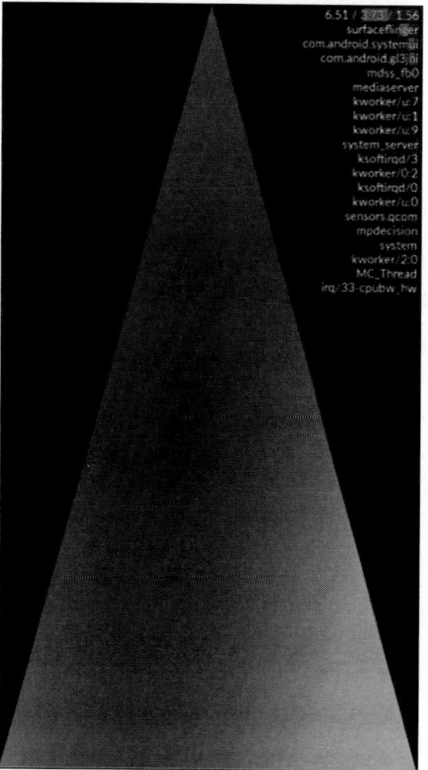

Here is another screenshot of the landscape mode:

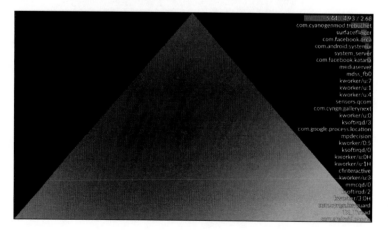

How it works...

This chapter demonstrates the portability of our approach in previous chapters. Essentially, the native code developed in this chapter resembles what we covered in previous chapters. In particular, the shader program's creation and loading mechanism is virtually identical, except that we have used a predefined string (`static char[]`) to simplify the complexity of loading files in Android. However, there are some subtle differences. Here, we will list the differences and new features.

In the fragment program and vertex program, we need to add the `#version 300 es` directive to ensure that the shader code can access the new features, such as uniform blocks and the full support of integer and floating point operations. For example, OpenGL ES 3.0 replaces the attribute and varying qualifiers with the **in** and **out** keywords. This standardization allows much faster code development of OpenGL on various platforms.

The other notable difference is that we have replaced the GLFW library completely with the EGL library, which comes as a standard library in Android, for context management. All event handling, such as Windows management and user inputs, are now handled through the Android API and the native code is only responsible for graphics rendering.

The Android log and error reporting system is now accessible through the Android `adb` program. The interaction is similar to a terminal output, and we can see the log in real time with the following command:

```
adb logcat
```

For example, our application reports the OpenGL ES version, as well as the extensions supported by the mobile device in the log. With the preceding command, we can extract the following information:

```
I/libgl3jni( 6681): GL Version = OpenGL ES 3.0 V@66.0
AU@04.04.02.048.042 LNXBUILD_AU_LINUX_ANDROID_LNX.LA.3.5.1_
RB1.04.04.02.048.042+PATCH[ES]_msm8974_LNX.LA.3.5.1_RB1__release_ENGG
(CL@)
I/libgl3jni( 6681): GL Vendor = Qualcomm
I/libgl3jni( 6681): GL Renderer = Adreno (TM) 330
I/libgl3jni( 6681): GL Extensions = GL_AMD_compressed_ATC_texture
GL_AMD_performance_monitor GL_AMD_program_binary_Z400 GL_EXT_debug_
label GL_EXT_debug_marker GL_EXT_discard_framebuffer GL_EXT_robustness
GL_EXT_texture_format_BGRA8888 GL_EXT_texture_type_2_10_10_10_REV
GL_NV_fence GL_OES_compressed_ETC1_RGB8_texture GL_OES_depth_texture
GL_OES_depth24 GL_OES_EGL_image GL_OES_EGL_image_external GL_OES_
element_index_uint GL_OES_fbo_render_mipmap GL_OES_fragment_precision_
high GL_OES_get_program_binary GL_OES_packed_depth_stencil GL_OES_
depth_texture_cube_map GL_OES_rgb8_rgba8 GL_OES_standard_derivatives
GL_OES_texture_3D GL_OES_texture_float GL_OES_texture_half_float
GL_OES_texture_half_float_linear GL_OES_texture_npot GL_OES_vertex_
half_float GL_OES_vertex_type_10_10_10_2 GL_OES_vertex_array_object
```

```
GL_QCOM_alpha_test GL_QCOM_binning_control GL_QCOM_driver_control
GL_QCOM_perfmon_global_mode GL_QCOM_extended_get GL_QCOM_extended_get2
GL_QCOM_tiled_rendering GL_QCOM_writeonly_rendering GL_EXT_sRGB GL_
EXT_sRGB_write_control GL_EXT_
I/libgl3jni( 6681): setupGraphics(1440, 2560)
```

The real-time log data is very useful for debugging and can allow developers to quickly analyze the problem.

One common question is how the Java and C/C++ elements communicate with each other. The JNI syntax is rather puzzling to understand in the first place, but we can decode it by carefully analyzing the following code snippet:

```
JNIEXPORT void JNICALL Java_com_android_gl3jni_GL3JNILib_init
(JNIEnv *env, jobject obj, jint width, jint height)
```

The `JNIEXPORT` and `JNICALL` tags allow the functions to be located in the shared library at runtime. The class name is specified by `com_android_gl3jni_GL3JNILib` (`com.android.gl3jni.GL3JNILib`), and `init` is the method name of the Java native function. As we can see, the period in the class name is replaced by an underscore. In addition, we have two additional parameters, namely the width and height of the frame buffer. More parameters can be simply appended to the end of the parameters' list in the function, as required.

In terms of backward compatibility, we can see that OpenGL 4.3 is a complete superset of OpenGL ES 3.0. In OpenGL 3.1 and higher, we can see that the embedded system version of OpenGL and the standard Desktop version of OpenGL are slowly converging, which reduces the underlying complexity in maintaining various versions of OpenGL in the application life cycle.

See also

A detailed description of the Android OS architecture is beyond the scope of this book. However, you are encouraged to consult the official developer workflow guide at `http://developer.android.com/tools/workflow/index.html`.

Further information on the OpenGL ES Shading Language can be found at `https://www.khronos.org/registry/gles/specs/3.0/GLSL_ES_Specification_3.00.3.pdf`.

8
Interactive Real-time Data Visualization on Mobile Devices

In this chapter, we will cover the following topics:

- Visualizing real-time data from built-in Inertial Measurement Units (IMUs)
- Part I – handling multi-touch interface and motion sensor inputs
- Part II – interactive, real-time data visualization with mobile GPUs

Introduction

In this chapter, we will demonstrate how to visualize data interactively using built-in motion sensors called **Inertial Measurement Units** (**IMUs**) and the multi-touch interface on mobile devices. We will further explore the use of shader programs to accelerate computationally intensive operations to enable real-time visualization of 3D data with mobile graphics hardware. We will assume familiarity with the basic framework for building an Android-based OpenGL ES 3.0 application introduced in the previous chapter and add significantly more complexity in the implementation in this chapter to achieve interactive, real-time 3D visualization of a Gaussian function using both motion sensors and the multi-touch gesture interface. The final demo is designed to work on any Android-based mobile device with proper sensor hardware support.

Here, we will first introduce how to extract data directly from the IMUs and plot the real-time data stream acquired on an Android device. We will divide the final demo into two parts given its complexity. In part I, we will demonstrate how to handle the multi-touch interface and motion sensor inputs on the Java side. In part II, we will demonstrate how to implement the shader program in OpenGL ES 3.0 and other components of the native code to finish our interactive demo.

Visualizing real-time data from built-in Inertial Measurement Units (IMUs)

Many modern mobile devices now integrate a plethora of built-in sensors including various motion and position sensors (such as an accelerometer, gyroscope, and magnetometer/digital compass) to enable novel forms of user interaction (such as complex gesture and motion control) as well as other environmental sensors, which can measure environmental conditions (such as an ambient light sensor and proximity sensor) to enable smart wearable applications. The Android Sensor Framework provides a comprehensive interface to access many types of sensors, which can be either hardware-based (physical sensors) or software-based (virtual sensors that derive inputs from hardware sensors). In general, there are three major categories of sensors—motion sensors, position sensors, and environmental sensors.

In this section, we will demonstrate how to utilize the Android Sensor Framework to communicate with the sensors available on your device, register sensor event listeners to monitor changes in the sensors, and acquire raw sensor data for display on your mobile device. To create this demo, we will implement the Java code and native code using the same framework design introduced in the previous chapter. The following block diagram illustrates the core functions and the relationship among the classes that will be implemented in this demo:

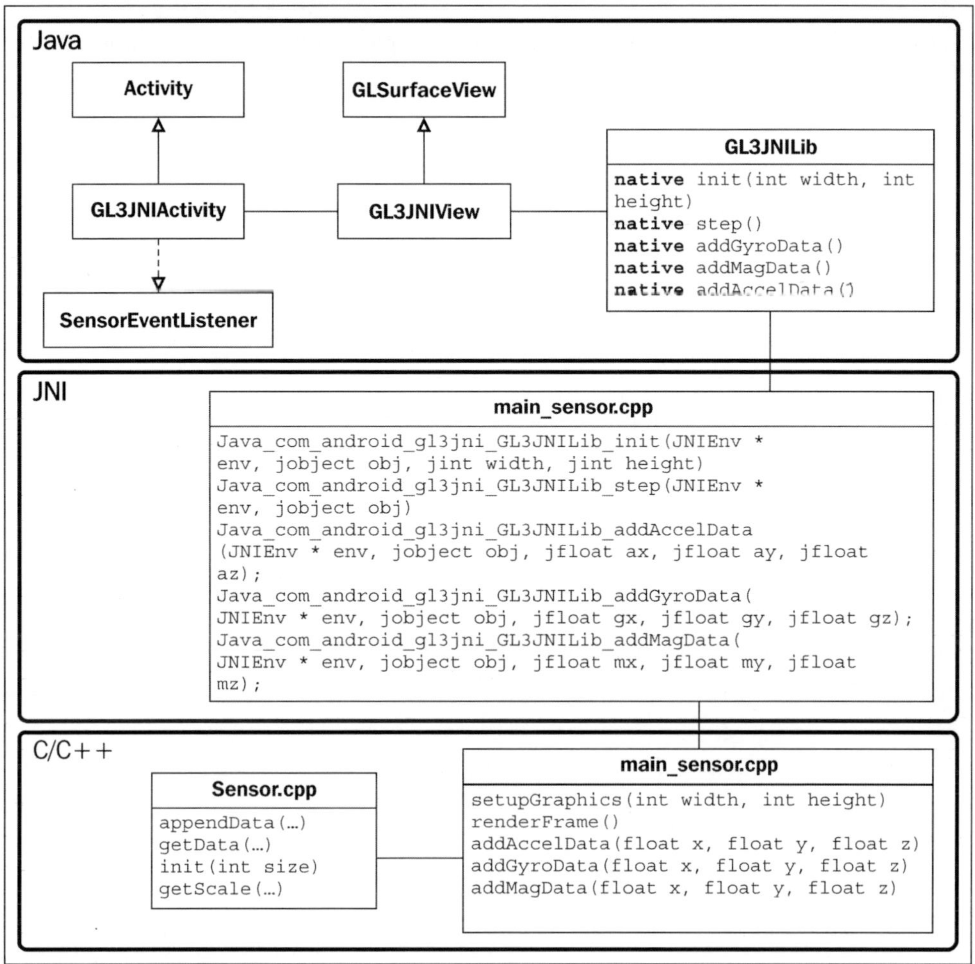

Getting ready

This demo requires an Android device with OpenGL ES 3.0 support as well as physical sensor hardware support. Unfortunately, at the moment these functions cannot be simulated with an emulator shipped with the Android SDK. Specifically, an Android mobile device with the following set of sensors, which are now commonly available, would be required to run this demo: an accelerometer, gyroscope, and magnetometer (digital compass).

In addition, we assume that the Android SDK and Android NDK are configured as discussed in *Chapter 7, An Introduction to Real-time Graphics Rendering on a Mobile Platform using OpenGL ES 3.0*.

How to do it...

First, we will create the core Java source files similar to the previous chapter. Since the majority of the code is similar, we will only discuss the new and significant elements that are introduced in the current code. The rest of the code is abbreviated with the "..." notation. Please download the complete source code from the official Packt Publishing website.

In the `GL3JNIActivity.java` file, we first integrate Android Sensor Manager, which allows us to read and parse sensor data. The following steps are required to complete the integration:

1. Import the classes for the Android Sensor Manager:

   ```
   package com.android.gl3jni;
   ...
   import android.hardware.Sensor;
   import android.hardware.SensorEvent;
   import android.hardware.SensorEventListener;
   import android.hardware.SensorManager;
   ...
   ```

2. Add the `SensorEventListener` interface to interact with the sensors:

   ```
   public class GL3JNIActivity extends Activity implements
   SensorEventListener{
   ```

3. Define the `SensorManager` and the `Sensor` variables to handle the data from the accelerometer, gyroscope, and magnetometer:

   ```
     ...
     private SensorManager mSensorManager;
     private Sensor mAccelerometer;
     private Sensor mGyro;
     private Sensor mMag;
   ```

4. Initialize the `SensorManager` as well as all other sensor services:

   ```
   @Override protected void onCreate(Bundle icicle) {
     super.onCreate(icicle);
     setRequestedOrientation(
       ActivityInfo.SCREEN_ORIENTATION_LANDSCAPE);

     mSensorManager =
       (SensorManager)getSystemService(SENSOR_SERVICE);
   ```

```
    mAccelerometer = mSensorManager.getDefaultSensor(
      Sensor.TYPE_ACCELEROMETER);
    mGyro = mSensorManager.getDefaultSensor(
      Sensor.TYPE_GYROSCOPE);
    mMag = mSensorManager.getDefaultSensor(
      Sensor.TYPE_MAGNETIC_FIELD);
    mView = new GL3JNIView(getApplication());
    setContentView(mView);
  }
```

5. Register the callback functions and start listening to these events:

```
@Override protected void onPause() {
  super.onPause();
  mView.onPause();
  //unregister accelerometer and other sensors
  mSensorManager.unregisterListener(this, mAccelerometer);
  mSensorManager.unregisterListener(this, mGyro);
  mSensorManager.unregisterListener(this, mMag);
}

@Override protected void onResume() {
  super.onResume();
  mView.onResume();
  /* register and activate the sensors. Start streaming
    data and handle with callback functions */
  mSensorManager.registerListener(this,
    mAccelerometer, SensorManager.SENSOR_DELAY_GAME);
  mSensorManager.registerListener(this,
    mGyro, SensorManager.SENSOR_DELAY_GAME);
  mSensorManager.registerListener(this,
    mMag, SensorManager.SENSOR_DELAY_GAME);
}
```

6. Handle the `sensor` events. The `onSensorChanged` and `onAccuracyChanged` functions capture any changes detected and the `SensorEvent` variable holds all the information about the sensor type, time-stamp, accuracy, and so on:

```
@Override
public void onAccuracyChanged(Sensor sensor, int
  accuracy) {
  //included for completeness
}
@Override
public void onSensorChanged(SensorEvent event) {
  //handle the accelerometer data
  //All values are in SI units (m/s^2)
```

```
        if (event.sensor.getType() ==
          Sensor.TYPE_ACCELEROMETER) {
          float ax, ay, az;
          ax = event.values[0];
          ay = event.values[1];
          az = event.values[2];
          GL3JNILib.addAccelData(ax, ay, az);
        }
        /* All values are in radians/second and measure the
          rate of rotation around the device's local X, Y,
          and Z axes */
        if (event.sensor.getType() ==
          Sensor.TYPE_GYROSCOPE) {
          float gx, gy, gz;
          //angular speed
          gx = event.values[0];
          gy = event.values[1];
          gz = event.values[2];
          GL3JNILib.addGyroData(gx, gy, gz);
        }
        //All values are in micro-Tesla (uT) and measure
          the ambient magnetic field in the X, Y and Z axes.
        if (event.sensor.getType() ==
          Sensor.TYPE_MAGNETIC_FIELD) {
          float mx, my, mz;
          mx = event.values[0];
          my = event.values[1];
          mz = event.values[2];
          GL3JNILib.addMagData(mx, my, mz);
        }
      }
```

Next implement the `GL3JNIView` class, which handles OpenGL rendering, in the `GL3JNIView.java` source file inside the `src/com/android/gl3jni/` directory. Since this implementation is identical to content in the *Chapter 7, An Introduction to Real-time Graphics Rendering on a Mobile Platform using OpenGL ES 3.0*, we will not discuss it again here.

Finally, integrate all the new features in the `GL3JNILib` class, which handles native library loading and calling, in the `GL3JNILib.java` file inside the `src/com/android/gl3jni` directory:

```
package com.android.gl3jni;

public class GL3JNILib {
  static {
```

```
        System.loadLibrary("gl3jni");
      }

      public static native void init(int width, int   height);
      public static native void step();

      public static native void addAccelData(float ax,
        float ay, float az);
      public static native void addGyroData(float gx,
        float gy, float gz);
      public static native void addMagData(float mx,
        float my, float mz);
    }
```

Now, on the JNI/C++ side, create a class called `Sensor` for managing the data buffer for each sensor, including the accelerometer, gyroscope, and magnetometer (digital compass). First, create a header file for the `Sensor` class called `Sensor.h`:

```
#ifndef SENSOR_H_
#define SENSOR_H_
#include <stdlib.h>
#include <jni.h>
#include <GLES3/gl3.h>
#include <math.h>

class Sensor {
  public:
    Sensor();
    Sensor(unsigned int size);
    virtual ~Sensor();

    //Resize buffer size dynamically with this function
    void init(unsigned int size);
    //Append new data to the buffer
    void appendAccelData(GLfloat x, GLfloat y,GLfloat z);
    void appendGyroData(GLfloat x, GLfloat y, GLfloat z);
    void appendMagData(GLfloat x, GLfloat y, GLfloat z);

    //Get sensor data buffer
    GLfloat *getAccelDataPtr(int channel);
    GLfloat *getGyroDataPtr(int channel);
    GLfloat *getMagDataPtr(int channel);
    GLfloat *getAxisPtr();
```

```
        //Auto rescale factors based on max and min
        GLfloat getAccScale();
        GLfloat getGyroScale();
        GLfloat getMagScale();

      unsigned int getBufferSize();

    private:
      unsigned int buffer_size;

      GLfloat **accel_data;
      GLfloat **gyro_data;
      GLfloat **mag_data;
      GLfloat *x_axis;

      GLfloat abs_max_acc;
      GLfloat abs_max_mag;
      GLfloat abs_max_gyro;

      void createBuffers(unsigned int size);
      void free_all();

      void findAbsMax(GLfloat *src, GLfloat *max);
      void appendData(GLfloat *src, GLfloat data);
      void setNormalizedAxis(GLfloat *data,
        unsigned int size, float min, float max);
    };

    #endif /* SENSOR_H_ */
```

Then, implement the `Sensor` class in the `Sensor.cpp` file with the following steps:

1. Implement the constructor and destructor for the `Sensor` class. Set the default size of the buffer to `256`:

    ```
    #include "Sensor.h"
    Sensor::Sensor() {
      //use default size
      init(256);
    }
    // Initialize with different buffer size
    Sensor::Sensor(unsigned int size) {
      init(size);
    }
    Sensor::~Sensor() {
      free_all();
    }
    ```

2. Add the initialization function, which sets all default parameters, and allocate and deallocate memory at runtime:

```
void Sensor::init(unsigned int size){
  buffer_size = size;
  //delete the old memory if already exist
  free_all();
  //allocate the memory for the buffer
  createBuffers(size);
  setNormalizedAxis(x_axis, size, -1.0f, 1.0f);
  abs_max_acc = 0;
  abs_max_gyro = 0;
  abs_max_mag = 0;
}
```

3. Implement the `createBuffers` function for memory allocation:

```
// Allocate memory for all sensor data buffers
void Sensor::createBuffers(unsigned int buffer_size){
  accel_data = (GLfloat**)malloc(3*sizeof(GLfloat*));
  gyro_data = (GLfloat**)malloc(3*sizeof(GLfloat*));
  mag_data = (GLfloat**)malloc(3*sizeof(GLfloat*));

  //3 channels for accelerometer
  accel_data[0] =
    (GLfloat*)calloc(buffer_size,sizeof(GLfloat));
  accel_data[1] =
    (GLfloat*)calloc(buffer_size,sizeof(GLfloat));
  accel_data[2] =
    (GLfloat*)calloc(buffer_size,sizeof(GLfloat));

  //3 channels for gyroscope
  gyro_data[0] =
    (GLfloat*)calloc(buffer_size,sizeof(GLfloat));
  gyro_data[1] =
    (GLfloat*)calloc(buffer_size,sizeof(GLfloat));
  gyro_data[2] =
    (GLfloat*)calloc(buffer_size,sizeof(GLfloat));

  //3 channels for digital compass
  mag_data[0] =
    (GLfloat*)calloc(buffer_size,sizeof(GLfloat));
  mag_data[1] =
    (GLfloat*)calloc(buffer_size,sizeof(GLfloat));
  mag_data[2] =
    (GLfloat*)calloc(buffer_size,sizeof(GLfloat));
```

```
    //x-axis precomputed
    x_axis = (GLfloat*)calloc(buffer_size,sizeof(GLfloat));
}
```

4. Implement the `free_all` function for deallocating memory:

```
// Deallocate all memory
void Sensor::free_all(){
  if(accel_data){
    free(accel_data[0]);
    free(accel_data[1]);
    free(accel_data[2]);
    free(accel_data);
  }
  if(gyro_data){
    free(gyro_data[0]);
    free(gyro_data[1]);
    free(gyro_data[2]);
    free(gyro_data);
  }
  if(mag_data){
    free(mag_data[0]);
    free(mag_data[1]);
    free(mag_data[2]);
    free(mag_data);
  }
  if(x_axis){
    free(x_axis);
  }
}
```

5. Create routines for appending data to the data buffer of each sensor:

```
// Append acceleration data to the buffer
void Sensor::appendAccelData(GLfloat x, GLfloat y, GLfloat z){
  abs_max_acc = 0;
  float data[3] = {x, y, z};
  for(int i=0; i<3; i++){
    appendData(accel_data[i], data[i]);
    findAbsMax(accel_data[i], &abs_max_acc);
  }
}

// Append the gyroscope data to the buffer
void Sensor::appendGyroData(GLfloat x, GLfloat y, GLfloat z){
```

```
    abs_max_gyro = 0;
    float data[3] = {x, y, z};
    for(int i=0; i<3; i++){
      appendData(gyro_data[i], data[i]);
      findAbsMax(gyro_data[i], &abs_max_gyro);
    }
  }

  // Append the magnetic field data to the buffer
  void Sensor::appendMagData(GLfloat x, GLfloat y, GLfloat z){
    abs_max_mag = 0;
    float data[3] = {x, y, z};
    for(int i=0; i<3; i++){
      appendData(mag_data[i], data[i]);
      findAbsMax(mag_data[i], &abs_max_mag);
    }
  }

  // Append Data to the end of the buffer
  void Sensor::appendData(GLfloat *src, GLfloat data){
    //shift the data by one
    int i;
    for(i=0; i<buffer_size-1; i++){
      src[i]=src[i+1];
    }
    //set the last element with the new data
    src[buffer_size-1]=data;
  }
```

6. Create routines for returning the pointer to the memory buffer of each sensor:

```
// Return the x-axis buffer
GLfloat* Sensor::getAxisPtr() {
  return x_axis;
}

// Get the acceleration data buffer
GLfloat* Sensor::getAccelDataPtr(int channel) {
  return accel_data[channel];
}

// Get the Gyroscope data buffer
GLfloat* Sensor::getGyroDataPtr(int channel) {
  return gyro_data[channel];
}
```

```
// Get the Magnetic field data buffer
GLfloat* Sensor::getMagDataPtr(int channel) {
  return mag_data[channel];
}
```

7. Implement methods for displaying/plotting the data stream properly from each sensor (for example, determining the maximum value of the data stream from each sensor to scale the data properly):

```
// Return buffer size
unsigned int Sensor::getBufferSize() {
  return buffer_size;
}

/* Return the global max for the acceleration data
  buffer (for rescaling and fitting purpose) */
GLfloat Sensor::getAccScale() {
  return abs_max_acc;
}

/* Return the global max for the gyroscope data
  buffer (for rescaling and fitting purpose) */
GLfloat Sensor::getGyroScale() {
  return abs_max_gyro;
}

/* Return the global max for the magnetic field data
  buffer (for rescaling and fitting purpose) */
GLfloat Sensor::getMagScale() {
  return abs_max_mag;
}

// Pre-compute the x-axis for the plot
void Sensor::setNormalizedAxis(GLfloat *data,
  unsigned int size, float min, float max){
  float step_size = (max - min)/(float)size;
  for(int i=0; i<size; i++){
    data[i]=min+step_size*i;
  }
}

// Find the absolute maximum from the buffer
void Sensor::findAbsMax(GLfloat *src, GLfloat *max){
  int i=0;
  for(i=0; i<buffer_size; i++){
    if(*max < fabs(src[i])){
```

```
            *max= fabs(src[i]);
          }
        }
      }
```

Finally, we describe the implementation of the OpenGL ES 3.0 native code to complete the demo application (`main_sensor.cpp`). The code is built upon the structure introduced in the previous chapter, so only new changes and modifications will be described in the following steps:

1. In the project directory, create a file named `main_sensor.cpp` and store it inside the `jni` directory.
2. Include all necessary header files, including `Sensor.h` at the beginning of the file:

   ```
   #include <Sensor.h>
   ...
   ```

3. Declare shader program handlers and variables for handling sensor data:

   ```
   GLuint gProgram;
   GLuint gxPositionHandle;
   GLuint gyPositionHandle;
   GLuint gColorHandle;
   GLuint gOffsetHandle;
   GLuint gScaleHandle;
   static Sensor g_sensor_data;
   ```

4. Define the shader program code for both the vertex shader and fragment shader to render points and lines:

   ```
   // Vertex shader source code
   static const char g_vshader_code[] =
     "#version 300 es\n"
     "in float yPosition;\n"
     "in float xPosition;\n"
     "uniform float scale;\n"
     "uniform float offset;\n"
     "void main() {\n"
       "  vec4 position = vec4(xPosition,
         yPosition*scale+offset, 0.0, 1.0);\n"
       "  gl_Position = position;\n"
     "}\n";

   // fragment shader source code
   static const char g_fshader_code[] =
     "#version 300 es\n"
     "precision mediump float;\n"
     "uniform vec4 color;\n"
   ```

```
"out vec4 color_out;\n"
"void main() {\n"
"  color_out = color;\n"
"}\n";
```

5. Set up all attribute variables in the `setupGraphics` function. These variables will be used to communicate with the shader programs:

```
bool setupGraphics(int w, int h) {

  ...

  gxPositionHandle = glGetAttribLocation(gProgram,
    "xPosition");
  checkGlError("glGetAttribLocation");
  LOGI("glGetAttribLocation(\"vPosition\") =
    %d\n", gxPositionHandle);

  gyPositionHandle = glGetAttribLocation(gProgram,    "yPosition");
  checkGlError("glGetAttribLocation");
  LOGI("glGetAttribLocation(\"vPosition\") = %d\n",
    gyPositionHandle);

  gColorHandle = glGetUniformLocation(gProgram,
    "color");
  checkGlError("glGetUniformLocation");
  LOGI("glGetUniformLocation(\"color\") = %d\n",
    gColorHandle);

  gOffsetHandle = glGetUniformLocation(gProgram,
    "offset");
  checkGlError("glGetUniformLocation");
  LOGI("glGetUniformLocation(\"offset\") = %d\n",
    gOffsetHandle);

  gScaleHandle = glGetUniformLocation(gProgram,
    "scale");
  checkGlError("glGetUniformLocation");
  LOGI("glGetUniformLocation(\"scale\") = %d\n",
    gScaleHandle);

  glViewport(0, 0, w, h);
  width = w;
  height = h;
```

```
    checkGlError("glViewport");

    return true;
  }
```

6. Create a function for drawing 2D plots to display real-time sensor data:

```
  void draw2DPlot(GLfloat *data, unsigned int size, GLfloat scale,
  GLfloat offset){
    glVertexAttribPointer(gyPositionHandle, 1, GL_FLOAT,
      GL_FALSE, 0, data);
    checkGlError("glVertexAttribPointer");

    glEnableVertexAttribArray(gyPositionHandle);
    checkGlError("glEnableVertexAttribArray");

    glUniform1f(gOffsetHandle, offset);
    checkGlError("glUniform1f");

    glUniform1f(gScaleHandle, scale);
    checkGlError("glUniform1f");

    glDrawArrays(GL_LINE_STRIP, 0,
      g_sensor_data.getBufferSize());
    checkGlError("glDrawArrays");
  }
```

7. Set up the rendering function which draws the various 2D time series with the data stream from the sensors:

```
  void renderFrame() {
    glClearColor(0.0f, 0.0f, 0.0f, 1.0f);
    checkGlError("glClearColor");

    glClear(GL_COLOR_BUFFER_BIT | GL_DEPTH_BUFFER_BIT);
    checkGlError("glClear");

    glUseProgram(gProgram);
    checkGlError("glUseProgram");

    glVertexAttribPointer(gxPositionHandle, 1, GL_FLOAT,
      GL_FALSE, 0, g_sensor_data.getAxisPtr());
    checkGlError("glVertexAttribPointer");

    glEnableVertexAttribArray(gxPositionHandle);
    checkGlError("glEnableVertexAttribArray");
```

```
    //Obtain the scaling factor based on the dataset
    //0.33f for 1/3 of the screen for each graph
    float acc_scale = 0.33f/g_sensor_data.getAccScale();
    float gyro_scale =
      0.33f/g_sensor_data.getGyroScale();
    float mag_scale = 0.33f/g_sensor_data.getMagScale();

    glLineWidth(4.0f);

    //set the rendering color
    glUniform4f(gColorHandle, 1.0f, 0.0f, 0.0f, 1.0f);
    checkGlError("glUniform1f");
    /* Render the accelerometer, gyro, and digital compass data.
As the vertex shader does not use any projection matrix, every
visible vertex has to be in the range of [-1, 1].  0.67f, 0.0f,
and -0.67f define the vertical positions of each graph */
    draw2DPlot(g_sensor_data.getAccelDataPtr(0),
      g_sensor_data.getBufferSize(), acc_scale, 0.67f);
    draw2DPlot(g_sensor_data.getGyroDataPtr(0),
      g_sensor_data.getBufferSize(), gyro_scale, 0.0f);
    draw2DPlot(g_sensor_data.getMagDataPtr(0),
      g_sensor_data.getBufferSize(), mag_scale, -0.67f);

    glUniform4f(gColorHandle, 0.0f, 1.0f, 0.0f, 1.0f);
    checkGlError("glUniform1f");
    draw2DPlot(g_sensor_data.getAccelDataPtr(1),
      g_sensor_data.getBufferSize(), acc_scale, 0.67f);
    draw2DPlot(g_sensor_data.getGyroDataPtr(1),
      g_sensor_data.getBufferSize(), gyro_scale, 0.0f);
    draw2DPlot(g_sensor_data.getMagDataPtr(1),
      g_sensor_data.getBufferSize(), mag_scale, -0.67f);

    glUniform4f(gColorHandle, 0.0f, 0.0f, 1.0f, 1.0f);
    checkGlError("glUniform1f");
    draw2DPlot(g_sensor_data.getAccelDataPtr(2),
      g_sensor_data.getBufferSize(), acc_scale, 0.67f);
    draw2DPlot(g_sensor_data.getGyroDataPtr(2),
      g_sensor_data.getBufferSize(), gyro_scale, 0.0f);
    draw2DPlot(g_sensor_data.getMagDataPtr(2),
      g_sensor_data.getBufferSize(), mag_scale, -0.67f);
}
```

8. Define the JNI prototypes that connect to the Java side. These calls are the interfaces for communicating between the Java code and C/C++ native code:

```
//external calls for Java
extern "C" {
  JNIEXPORT void JNICALL
    Java_com_android_gl3jni_GL3JNILib_init(JNIEnv *
    env, jobject obj, jint width, jint height);
  JNIEXPORT void JNICALL
    Java_com_android_gl3jni_GL3JNILib_step(JNIEnv *
    env, jobject obj);
  JNIEXPORT void JNICALL
    Java_com_android_gl3jni_GL3JNILib_addAccelData
   (JNIEnv * env, jobject obj, jfloat ax, jfloat ay, jfloat az);
  JNIEXPORT void JNICALL
    Java_com_android_gl3jni_GL3JNILib_addGyroData
    (JNIE nv * env, jobject obj, jfloat gx, jfloat
    gy, jfloat gz);
  JNIEXPORT void JNICALL
Java_com_android_gl3jni_GL3JNILib_addMagData
(JNIEnv * env, jobject obj, jfloat mx, jfloat my, jfloat mz)
{
  g_sensor_data.appendMagData(mx, my, mz);
}
};

//link to internal calls
JNIEXPORT void JNICALL Java_com_android_gl3jni_GL3JNILib_
init(JNIEnv * env, jobject obj,  jint width, jint height)
{
  setupGraphics(width, height);
}
JNIEXPORT void JNICALL Java_com_android_gl3jni_GL3JNILib_
step(JNIEnv * env, jobject obj)
{
  renderFrame();
}
JNIEXPORT void JNICALL Java_com_android_gl3jni_GL3JNILib_
addAccelData(JNIEnv * env, jobject obj,  jfloat ax, jfloat ay,
jfloat az){
  g_sensor_data.appendAccelData(ax, ay, az);
}
JNIEXPORT void JNICALL Java_com_android_gl3jni_GL3JNILib_
addGyroData(JNIEnv * env, jobject obj,  jfloat gx, jfloat gy,
jfloat gz){
  g_sensor_data.appendGyroData(gx, gy, gz);
}
```

```
JNIEXPORT void JNICALL Java_com_android_gl3jni_GL3JNILib_
addMagData(JNIEnv * env, jobject obj,  jfloat mx, jfloat my,
jfloat mz){
  g_sensor_data.appendMagData(mx, my, mz);
}
```

Finally, we need to compile and install the Android application with the same instructions as outlined in the previous chapter.

The following screenshots show the real-time sensor data stream from the accelerometer, gyroscope, and digital compass (top panel, middle panel, and bottom panel, respectively) on our Android device. Red, green, and blue are used to differentiate the channels from each sensor data stream. For example, the red plot in the top panel represents the acceleration value of the device along the *x* axis (the blue plot for the *y* axis and the green plot for the *z* axis). In the first example, we rotated the phone freely at various orientations and the plots show the corresponding changes in the sensor values. The visualizer also provides an auto-scale function, which automatically computes the maximum values to rescale the plots accordingly:

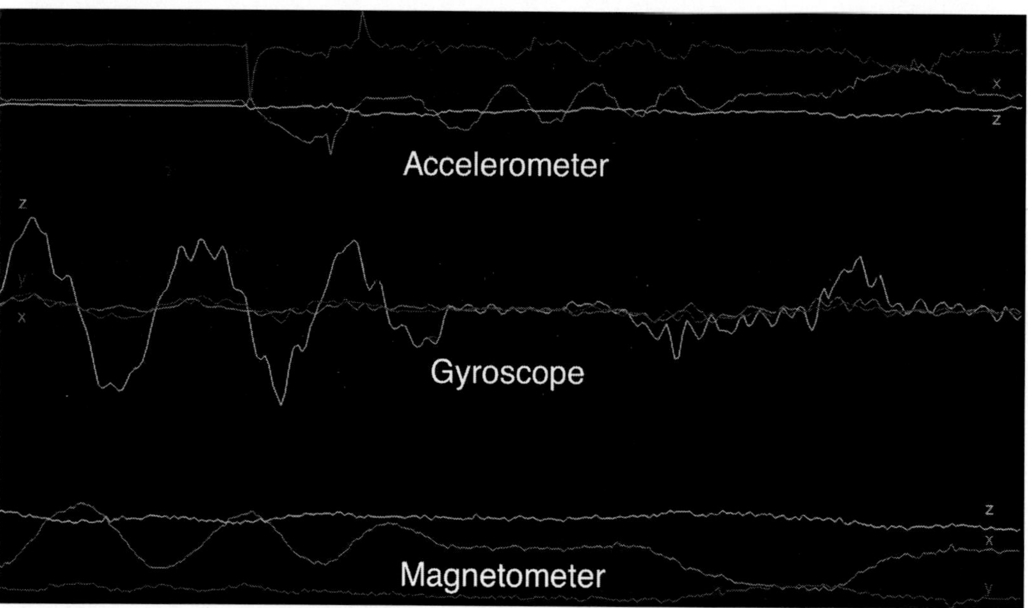

Next, we positioned the phone on a stationary surface and we plotted the values of the sensors. Instead of observing constant values over time, the time series plots show that there are some very small changes (jittering) in the sensor values due to sensor noise. Depending on the application, you will often need to apply filtering techniques to ensure that the user experience is jitter-free. One simple solution is to apply a low-pass filter to smooth out any high-frequency noise. More details on the implementation of such filters can be found at `http://developer.android.com/guide/topics/sensors/sensors_motion.html`.

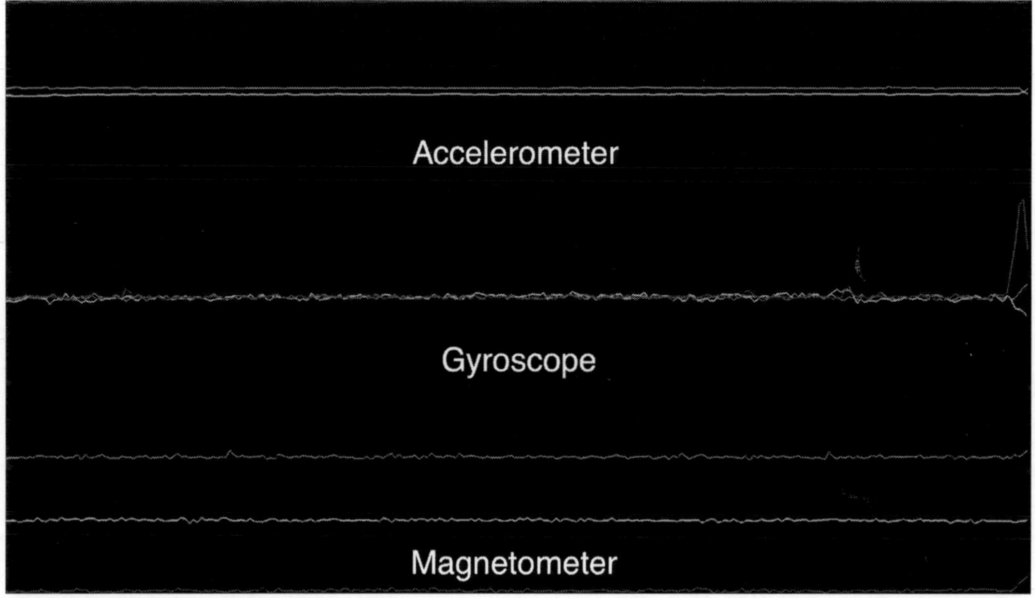

How it works...

The Android Sensor Framework allows users to access the raw data from various types of sensors on a mobile device. This framework is part of the `android.hardware` package and the sensor package includes a set of classes and interfaces for sensor-specific features.

The `SensorManager` class provides an interface and methods for accessing and listing the available sensors from the device. Some common hardware sensors include the accelerometer, gyroscope, proximity sensor, and the magnetometer (digital compass). These sensors are represented by constant variables (such as `TYPE_ACCELEROMETER` for the accelerometer, `TYPE_MAGNETIC_FIELD` for the magnetometer, and `TYPE_GYROSCOPE` for the gyroscope) and the `getDefaultSensor` function returns an instance of the `Sensor` object based on the type requested.

To enable data streaming, we must register the sensor to the `SensorEventListener` class such that the raw data is reported back to the application upon updates. The `registerListener` function then creates the callback to handle updates to the sensor value or sensor accuracy. The `SensorEvent` variable stores the name of the sensor, the timestamp and accuracy of the event, as well as the raw data.

The raw data stream from each sensor is reported back with the `onSensorChange` function. Since sensor data may be acquired and streamed at a high rate, it is important that we do not block callback function calls or perform any computationally intensive processes within the `onSensorChange` function. In addition, it is a good practice to reduce the data rate of the sensor based on your application requirements. In our case, we set the sensor to run at the optimal rate for gaming purposes by passing the constant preset variable `SENSOR_DELAY_GAME` to the `registerListener` function.

The `GL3JNILib` class then handles all the data passing to the native code using the new functions. For simplicity, we have created separate functions for each sensor type, which makes it easier for the reader to understand the data flow for each sensor.

At this point, we have created the interfaces that redirect data to the native side. However, to plot the sensor data on the screen, we need to create a simple buffering mechanism that stores the data points over some period of time. We have created a custom `Sensor` class in C++ to handle data creation, updates, and processing needed to manage these interactions. The implementation of the class is straightforward, and we preset the buffer size to store 256 data points by default.

On the OpenGL ES side, we create the 2D plot by appending the data stream to our vertex buffer. The scale of the data stream is adjusted dynamically based on the current values to ensure that the values fit on the screen. Notice that we have also performed all data scaling and translation on the vertex shader to reduce any overhead in the CPU computation.

See also

- For more information on the Android Sensor Framework, consult the documentation online at `http://developer.android.com/guide/topics/sensors/sensors_overview.html`.

Part I – handling multi-touch interface and motion sensor inputs

Now that we have introduced the basics of handling sensor inputs, we will develop an interactive, sensor-based data visualization tool. In addition to using motion sensors, we will introduce a multi-touch interface for user interaction. The following is a preview of the final application, integrating all the elements in this chapter:

In this section, we will focus solely on the Java side of the implementation and the native code will be described in part II. The following class diagram illustrates the various components of the Java code (part I) that provide the basic interface for user interaction on the mobile device and demonstrates how the native code (part II) completes the entire implementation:

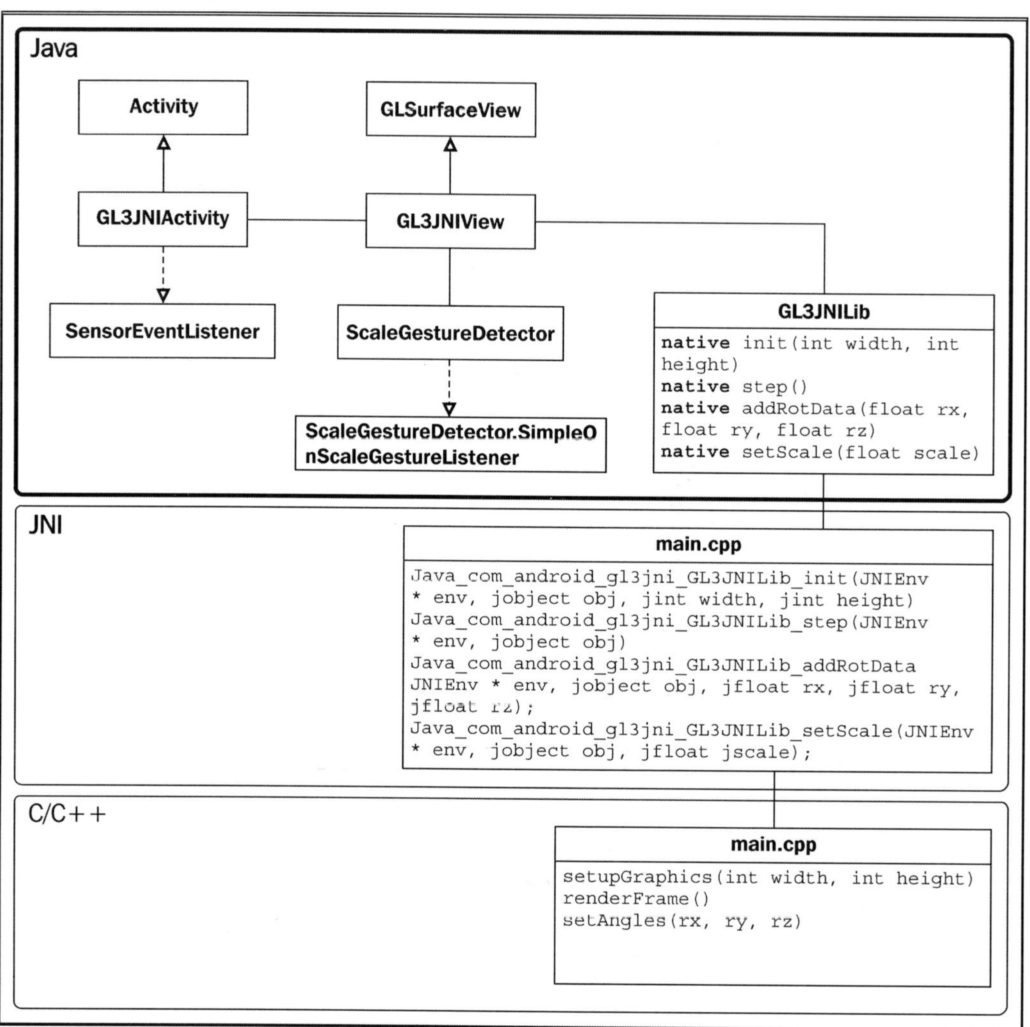

How to do it...

First, we will create the core Java source files that are essential to an Android application. These files serve as a wrapper for our OpenGL ES 3.0 native code. The code structure is based on the `gl3jni` package described in the previous section. Here we will highlight the major changes made to the code and discuss the interaction of these new components.

In the project directory, modify the `GL3JNIActivity` class in the `GL3JNIActivity.java` file within the `src/com/android/gl3jni` directory. Instead of using the raw sensor data, we will utilize the Android sensor fusion algorithm, which intelligently combines all sensor data to recover the orientation of the device as a rotation vector. The steps to enable this feature are described as follows:

1. In the `GL3JNIActivity` class, add the new variables for handling the rotation matrix and vector:

```
public class GL3JNIActivity extends Activity implements
SensorEventListener{
  GL3JNIView mView;
  private SensorManager mSensorManager;
  private Sensor mRotate;
  private float[] mRotationMatrix=new float[16];
  private float[] orientationVals=new float[3];
```

2. Initialize the `Sensor` variable with the `TYPE_ROTATION_VECTOR` type, which returns the device orientation as a rotation vector/matrix:

```
@Override protected void onCreate(Bundle icicle) {
  super.onCreate(icicle);
  //lock the screen orientation for this demo
  //otherwise the canvas will rotate
  setRequestedOrientation
    (ActivityInfo.SCREEN_ORIENTATION_LANDSCAPE);

  mSensorManager = (SensorManager)getSystemService
    (SENSOR_SERVICE);
    //TYPE_ROTATION_VECTOR for device orientation
    mRotate = mSensorManager.getDefaultSensor
      (Sensor.TYPE_ROTATION_VECTOR);

    mView = new GL3JNIView(getApplication());
    setContentView(mView);
}
```

3. Register the Sensor Manager object and set the sensor response rate to `SENSOR_DELAY_GAME`, which is used for gaming or real-time applications:

```
@Override protected void onResume() {
  super.onResume();
  mView.onResume();
  mSensorManager.registerListener(this, mRotate,
    SensorManager.SENSOR_DELAY_GAME);
}
```

4. Retrieve the device orientation and save the event data as a rotation matrix. Then convert the rotation matrix into Euler angles that are passed to the native code:

```
@Override
public void onSensorChanged(SensorEvent event) {
  if (event.sensor.getType() ==
    Sensor.TYPE_ROTATION_VECTOR){
    SensorManager.getRotationMatrixFromVector
      (mRotationMatrix,event.values);
    SensorManager.getOrientation (mRotationMatrix,
      orientationVals);
    GL3JNILib.addRotData(orientationVals[0],
      orientationVals[1],orientationVals[2]);
  }
}
```

Next, modify the `GL3JNIView` class, which handles OpenGL rendering, in the `GL3JNIView.java` file inside the `src/com/android/gl3jni/` directory. To make the application interactive, we also integrate the touch-based gesture detector that handles multi-touch events. Particularly, we add the `ScaleGestureDetector` class that enables the pinch gesture for scaling the 3D plot. To implement this feature, we make the following modifications to the `GL3JNIView.java` file:

1. Import the `MotionEvent` and `ScaleGestureDetector` classes:

```
package com.android.gl3jni;
...
import android.view.MotionEvent;
import android.view.ScaleGestureDetector;
...
```

2. Create a `ScaleGestureDetector` variable and initialize with `ScaleListener`:

```
class GL3JNIView extends GLSurfaceView {
  private ScaleGestureDetector mScaleDetector;
  ...

  public GL3JNIView(Context context) {
    super(context);
    ...
    //handle gesture input
    mScaleDetector = new ScaleGestureDetector
     (context, new ScaleListener());
  }
```

3. Pass the motion event to the gesture detector when a touch screen event occurs (`onTouchEvent`):

   ```
   @Override
   public boolean onTouchEvent(MotionEvent ev) {
     // Let ScaleGestureDetector inspect all events.
     mScaleDetector.onTouchEvent(ev);
     return true;
   }
   ```

4. Implement `SimpleOnScaleGestureListener` and handle the callback (`onScale`) on pinch gesture events:

   ```
   private class ScaleListener extends
     ScaleGestureDetector.SimpleOnScaleGestureListener {
     private float mScaleFactor = 1.f;
     @Override
     public boolean onScale(ScaleGestureDetector
       detector)
     {
       //scaling factor
       mScaleFactor *= detector.getScaleFactor();
       //Don't let the object get too small/too large.
       mScaleFactor = Math.max(0.1f,
         Math.min(mScaleFactor, 5.0f));
       invalidate();
       GL3JNILib.setScale(mScaleFactor);
       return true;
     }
   }
   ```

Finally, in the `GL3JNILib` class, we implement the functions to handle native library loading and calling in the `GL3JNILib.java` file inside the `src/com/android/gl3jni` directory:

```
package com.android.gl3jni;

public class GL3JNILib {
  static {
    System.loadLibrary("gl3jni");
  }

  public static native void init(int width, int height);
  public static native void step();
```

```
    /* pass the rotation angles and scaling factor to the
      native code */
    public static native void addRotData(float rx, float
      ry, float rz);
    public static native void setScale(float scale);
}
```

How it works...

Similar to the previous demo, we will use the Android Sensor Framework to handle the sensor inputs. Notice that, in this demo, we specify `TYPE_ROTATION_VECTOR` for the sensor type inside the `getDefaultSensor` function in `GL3JNIActivity.java`, which allows us to detect the device orientation. This is a software type sensor in which all IMUs data (from the accelerometer, gyroscope, and magnetometer) are fused together to create the rotation vector. The device orientation data is first stored in the rotation matrix `mRotationMatrix` using the `getRotationMatrixFromVector` function and the azimuth, pitch, and roll angles (rotation around the *x*, *y*, and *z* axes, respectively) are retrieved using the `getOrientation` function. Finally, we pass the three orientation angles to the native code portion of the implementation using the `GL3JNILib.addRotData` call. This allows us to control 3D graphics based on the device's orientation.

Next we will explain how the multi-touch interface works. Inside the `GL3JNIView` class, you will notice that we have created an instance (`mScaleDetector`) of a new class called `ScaleGestureDetector`. The `ScaleGestureDetector` class detects scaling transformation gestures (pinching with two fingers) using the `MotionEvent` class from the multi-touch screen. The algorithm returns the scale factor that can be redirected to the OpenGL pipeline to update the graphics in real time. The `SimpleOnScaleGestureListener` class provides a callback function for the `onScale` event and we pass the scale factor (`mScaleFactor`) to the native code using the `GL3JNILib.setScale` call.

See also

- For further information on the Android multi-touch interface, see the detailed documentation at `http://developer.android.com/training/gestures/index.html`.

Part II – interactive, real-time data visualization with mobile GPUs

Now we will complete our demo with the native code implementation to create our highly interactive Android-based data visualization application with OpenGL ES 3.0 as well as the Android sensor and gesture control interface.

The following class diagram highlights what remains to be implemented on the C/C++ side:

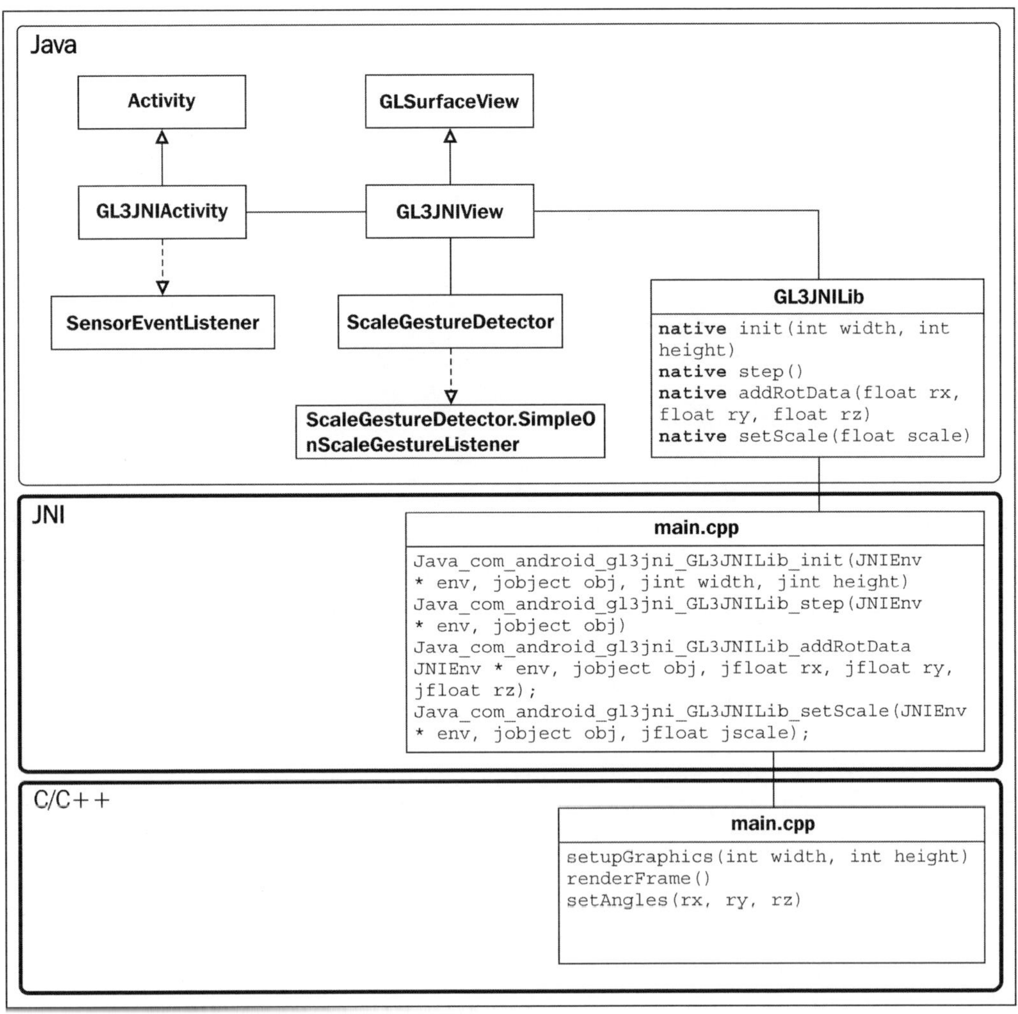

How to do it...

Here, we describe the implementation of the OpenGL ES 3.0 native code to complete the demo application. We will preserve the same code structure from *Chapter 7, An Introduction to Real-time Graphics Rendering on a Mobile Platform using OpenGL ES 3.0*. In the following steps, only the new codes are highlighted, and all changes are implemented in the `main.cpp` file inside the `jni` folder:

1. Include all necessary header files, including `JNI`, OpenGL ES 3.0, and the `GLM` library:

   ```
   #define GLM_FORCE_RADIANS

   //header for JNI
   #include <jni.h>
   ...

   //header for GLM library
   #include <glm/glm.hpp>
   #include <glm/gtc/matrix_transform.hpp>
   ```

2. Declare the shader program variables:

   ```
   //shader program handlers
   GLuint gProgram;
   GLuint gvPositionHandle;
   GLuint matrixHandle;
   GLuint sigmaHandle;
   GLuint scaleHandle;
   ```

3. Declare variables for setting up the camera as well as other relevant variables such as the rotation angles and grid:

   ```
   //the view matrix and projection matrix
   glm::mat4 g_view_matrix;
   glm::mat4 g_projection_matrix;

   //initial position of the camera
   glm::vec3 g_position = glm::vec3( 0, 0, 4 );

   //FOV of the camera
   float g_initial_fov = glm::pi<float>()*0.25f;
   //rotation angles, set by sensors or by touch screen
   float rx, ry, rz;
   float scale=1.0f;
   //vertices for the grid
   const unsigned int GRID_SIZE=400;
   GLfloat gGrid[GRID_SIZE*GRID_SIZE*3]={0};
   ```

4. Define the shader program code for both the vertex shader and fragment shader. Note the similarity in the heat map generation code between this implementation in OpenGL ES 3.0 and an earlier implementation in standard OpenGL (see chapters 4-6):

```
// Vertex shader source code
static const char g_vshader_code[] =
  "#version 300 es\n"
    "in vec4 vPosition;\n"
    "uniform mat4 MVP;\n"
  "uniform float sigma;\n"
  "uniform float scale;\n"
    "out vec4 color_based_on_position;\n"
    "// Heat map generator                \n"
    "vec4 heatMap(float v, float vmin, float vmax){\n"
    "    float dv;\n"
    "    float r=1.0, g=1.0, b=1.0;\n"
    "  if (v < vmin){\n"
    "    v = vmin;}\n"
    "  if (v > vmax){\n"
    "    v = vmax;}\n"
    "  dv = vmax - vmin;\n"
    "  if (v < (vmin + 0.25 * dv)) {\n"
    "    r = 0.0;\n"
    "    g = 4.0 * (v - vmin) / dv;\n"
    "  } else if (v < (vmin + 0.5 * dv)) {\n"
    "    r = 0.0;\n"
    "    b = 1.0 + 4.0 * (vmin + 0.25 * dv - v) /   dv;\n"
    "  } else if (v < (vmin + 0.75 * dv)) {\n"
    "    r = 4.0 * (v - vmin - 0.5 * dv) / dv;\n"
    "    b = 0.0;\n"
    "  } else {\n"
    "    g = 1.0 + 4.0 * (vmin + 0.75 * dv - v) /   dv;\n"
    "    b = 0.0;\n"
    "  }\n"
    "    return vec4(r, g, b, 0.1);\n"
    "}\n"
    "void main() {\n"
  "  //Simulation on GPU \n"
    "  float x_data = vPosition.x;\n"
    "  float y_data = vPosition.y;\n"
    "  float sigma2 = sigma*sigma;\n"
    "  float z = exp(-0.5*(x_data*x_data)/(sigma2)
    -0.5*(y_data*y_data)/(sigma2));\n"
    "  vec4 position = vPosition;\n"
```

```
    // scale the graphics based on user gesture input
    "  position.z = z*scale;\n"
    "  position.x = position.x*scale;\n"
    "  position.y = position.y*scale;\n"
    "  gl_Position = MVP*position;\n"
      "  color_based_on_position = heatMap(position.z, 0.0, 0.5);\n"
    "  gl_PointSize = 5.0*scale;\n"
      "}\n";

// fragment shader source code
static const char g_fshader_code[] =
  "#version 300 es\n"
    "precision mediump float;\n"
    "in vec4 color_based_on_position;\n"
  "out vec4 color;\n"
    "void main() {\n"
    "  color = color_based_on_position;\n"
    "}\n";
```

5. Initialize the grid pattern for data visualization:

```
void computeGrid(){
  float grid_x = GRID_SIZE;
  float grid_y = GRID_SIZE;
  unsigned int data_counter = 0;
  //define a grid ranging from -1 to +1
  for(float x = -grid_x/2.0f; x<grid_x/2.0f; x+=1.0f){
    for(float y = -grid_y/2.0f; y<grid_y/2.0f; y+=1.0f){
      float x_data = 2.0f*x/grid_x;
      float y_data = 2.0f*y/grid_y;
      gGrid[data_counter] = x_data;
      gGrid[data_counter+1] = y_data;
      gGrid[data_counter+2] = 0;
      data_counter+=3;
    }
  }
}
```

6. Set the rotation angles that are used to control the model viewing angles. These angles (device orientation) are passed from the Java side:

```
void setAngles(float irx, float iry, float irz){
  rx = irx;
  ry = iry;
  rz = irz;
}
```

7. Compute the projection and view matrices based on camera parameters:

```
void computeProjectionMatrices(){
  //direction vector for z
  glm::vec3 direction_z(0, 0, -1.0);
  //up vector
  glm::vec3 up = glm::vec3(0,-1,0);

  float aspect_ratio = (float)width/(float)height;
  float nearZ = 0.1f;
  float farZ = 100.0f;
  float top = tan(g_initial_fov/2*nearZ);
  float right = aspect_ratio*top;
  float left = -right;
  float bottom = -top;
  g_projection_matrix = glm::frustum(left, right,
    bottom, top, nearZ, farZ);

  // update the view matrix
  g_view_matrix = glm::lookAt(
    g_position,              // camera position
    g_position+direction_z, // view direction
    up                       // up direction
  );
}
```

8. Create a function for handling the initialization of all attribute variables for the shader program and other one-time setups, such as the memory allocation and initialization for the grid:

```
bool setupGraphics(int w, int h) {
  ...
  gvPositionHandle = glGetAttribLocation(gProgram,
    "vPosition");
  checkGlError("glGetAttribLocation");
  LOGI("glGetAttribLocation(\"vPosition\") = %d\n",
    gvPositionHandle);

  matrixHandle = glGetUniformLocation(gProgram, "MVP");
  checkGlError("glGetUniformLocation");
  LOGI("glGetUniformLocation(\"MVP\") = %d\n",
    matrixHandle);

  sigmaHandle = glGetUniformLocation(gProgram, "sigma");
  checkGlError("glGetUniformLocation");
```

```
    LOGI("glGetUniformLocation(\"sigma\") = %d\n",
      sigmaHandle);

    scaleHandle = glGetUniformLocation(gProgram,
      "scale");
    checkGlError("glGetUniformLocation");
    LOGI("glGetUniformLocation(\"scale\") = %d\n",
      scaleHandle);

    ...

    computeGrid();
    return true;
}
```

9. Set up the rendering function for the 3D plot of the Gaussian function:

```
void renderFrame() {
  glEnable(GL_BLEND);
  glBlendFunc(GL_SRC_ALPHA, GL_ONE_MINUS_SRC_ALPHA);

  static float sigma;

  //update the variables for animations
  sigma+=0.002f;
  if(sigma>0.5f){
    sigma = 0.002f;
  }

  /* gets the View and Model Matrix and apply to the
    rendering */
  computeProjectionMatrices();
  glm::mat4 projection_matrix = g_projection_matrix;
  glm::mat4 view_matrix = g_view_matrix;
  glm::mat4 model_matrix = glm::mat4(1.0);
  model_matrix = glm::rotate(model_matrix, rz,
    glm::vec3(-1.0f, 0.0f, 0.0f));
  model_matrix = glm::rotate(model_matrix, ry,
    glm::vec3(0.0f, -1.0f, 0.0f));
  model_matrix = glm::rotate(model_matrix, rx,
    glm::vec3(0.0f, 0.0f, 1.0f));
  glm::mat4 mvp = projection_matrix * view_matrix *
    model_matrix;
```

```
    glClearColor(0.0f, 0.0f, 0.0f, 1.0f);
    checkGlError("glClearColor");

    glClear(GL_COLOR_BUFFER_BIT | GL_DEPTH_BUFFER_BIT);
    checkGlError("glClear");

    glUseProgram(gProgram);
    checkGlError("glUseProgram");

    glUniformMatrix4fv(matrixHandle, 1, GL_FALSE,
      &mvp[0][0]);
    checkGlError("glUniformMatrix4fv");

    glUniform1f(sigmaHandle, sigma);
    checkGlError("glUniform1f");

    glUniform1f(scaleHandle, scale);
    checkGlError("glUniform1f");

    glVertexAttribPointer(gvPositionHandle, 3,
      GL_FLOAT, GL_FALSE, 0, gGrid);
    checkGlError("glVertexAttribPointer");

    glEnableVertexAttribArray(gvPositionHandle);
    checkGlError("glEnableVertexAttribArray");

    glDrawArrays(GL_POINTS, 0, GRID_SIZE*GRID_SIZE);
    checkGlError("glDrawArrays");
}
```

10. Define the JNI prototypes that connect to the Java side. These calls are the interfaces for communicating between the Java code and C/C++ native code:

```
extern "C" {
  JNIEXPORT void JNICALL
    Java_com_android_gl3jni_GL3JNILib_init(JNIEnv
    * env, jobject obj, jint width, jint height);
  JNIEXPORT void JNICALL
    Java_com_android_gl3jni_GL3JNILib_step(JNIEnv
    * env, jobject obj);
  JNIEXPORT void JNICALL
    Java_com_android_gl3jni_GL3JNILib_addRotData(JNIEnv
    * env, jobject obj, jfloat rx,
    jfloat ry, jfloat rz);
```

```
    JNIEXPORT void JNICALL
      Java_com_android_gl3jni_GL3JNILib_setScale(JNIEnv
      * env, jobject obj,  jfloat jscale);
};
```

11. Set up the internal function calls with the helper functions:

```
JNIEXPORT void JNICALL
  Java_com_android_gl3jni_GL3JNILib_init(JNIEnv
  * env, jobject obj,  jint width, jint height)
{
  setupGraphics(width, height);
}
JNIEXPORT void JNICALL
  Java_com_android_gl3jni_GL3JNILib_step(JNIEnv
  * env, jobject obj)
{
  renderFrame();
}
JNIEXPORT void JNICALL
  Java_com_android_gl3jni_GL3JNILib_addRotData(JNIEnv
  * env, jobject obj, jfloat rx, jfloat ry, jfloat rz)
{
  setAngles(rx, ry, rz);
}
JNIEXPORT void JNICALL
  Java_com_android_gl3jni_GL3JNILib_setScale(JNIEnv
  * env, jobject obj, jfloat jscale)
{
  scale = jscale;
  LOGI("Scale is %lf", scale);
}
```

Finally, in terms of the compilation steps, modify the build files `Android.mk` and `Application.mk` accordingly as follows:

1. Add in the GLM path to the `LOCAL_C_INCLUDES` variable in `Android.mk`:

```
LOCAL_PATH:= $(call my-dir)

include $(CLEAR_VARS)

LOCAL_MODULE    := libgl3jni
```

```
LOCAL_CFLAGS     := -Werror
LOCAL_SRC_FILES := main.cpp
LOCAL_LDLIBS     := -llog -lGLESv3
#The GLM library is installed in one of these two folders by default
LOCAL_C_INCLUDES := /opt/local/include /usr/local/include

include $(BUILD_SHARED_LIBRARY)
```

2. Add in `gnustl_static` to the `APP_STL` variable to use GNU STL as a static library. This allows for all runtime supports from C++, which is needed by the GLM library. See more at `http://www.kandroid.org/ndk/docs/CPLUSPLUS-SUPPORT.html`:

   ```
   APP_ABI := armeabi-v7a
   #required for GLM and other static libraries
   APP_STL := gnustl_static
   ```

3. Run the compilation script (this is similar to what we did in the previous chapter). Please note that the `ANDROID_SDK_PATH` and `ANDROID_NDK_PATH` variables should be changed to the correct directories based on the local environment setup:

   ```
   #!/bin/bash
   ANDROID_SDK_PATH="../../../3rd_party/android/android-sdk-macosx"
   ANDROID_NDK_PATH="../../../3rd_party/android/android-ndk-r10e"


   $ANDROID_SDK_PATH/tools/android update project -p . -s --target "android-18"
   $ANDROID_NDK_PATH/ndk-build
   ant debug
   ```

4. Install the **Android Application Package** (**APK**) on the Android phone, using the following commands in the terminal:

   ```
   ANDROID_SDK_PATH="../../../3rd_party/android/android-sdk-macosx"
   $ANDROID_SDK_PATH/platform-tools/adb install -r bin/GL3JNIActivity-debug.apk
   ```

The final results of our implementation are shown next. By changing the orientation of the phone, the Gaussian function can be viewed from different angles. This provides a very intuitive way to visualize 3D datasets. Here is a photo showing the Gaussian function when the device is oriented parallel to the ground:

Finally, we test our multi-touch gesture interface by pinching on the touch screen with 2 fingers. This provides an intuitive way to zoom into and out of the 3D data. Here is the first photo that shows the close-up view after zooming into the data:

Here is another photo that shows what the data looks like when you zoom out by pinching your fingers:

Finally, here is a screenshot of the demo application that shows a Gaussian distribution in 3D rendered in real-time with our OpenGL ES 3.0 shader program:

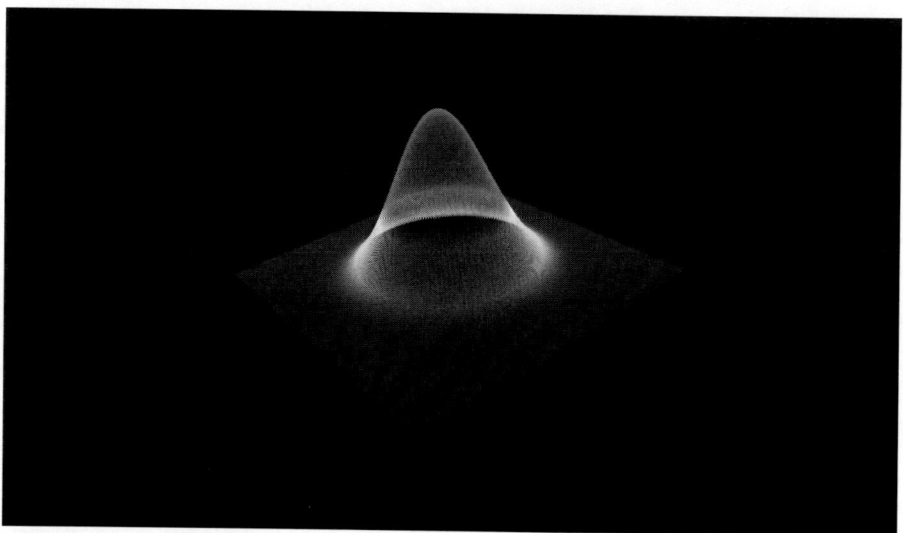

How it works...

In the second part of the demo, we demonstrated the use of a shader program written in OpenGL ES 3.0 to perform all the simulation and heat map-based 3D rendering steps to visualize a Gaussian distribution on a mobile GPU. Importantly, the shader code in OpenGL ES 3.0 is very similar to the code written in standard OpenGL 3.2 and above (see chapters 4 to 6). However, we recommend that you consult the specification to ensure that a particular feature of interest co-exists in both versions. More details on the OpenGL ES 3.0 specifications can be found at `https://www.khronos.org/registry/gles/specs/3.0/es_spec_3.0.0.pdf`.

The hardware-accelerated portion of the code is programmed within the vertex shader program and stored inside the `g_vshader_code` variable; then the fragment shade program passes the processed color information onto the screen's color buffer. The vertex program handles the computation related to the simulation (in our case, we have a Gaussian function with a time-varying sigma value as demonstrated in *Chapter 3, Interactive 3D Data Visualization*) in the graphics hardware. We pass in the sigma value as a uniform variable and it is used to compute the surface height. In addition, we also compute the heat map color value within the shader program based on the height value. With this approach, we have significantly improved the speed of the graphic rendering step by completely eliminating the use of the CPU cycles on these numerous floating point operations.

In addition, we have included the GLM library used in previous chapters into the Android platform by adding the headers as well as the GLM path in the build script `Android.mk`. The GLM library handles the view and projection matrix computation and also allows us to migrate most of our previous work, such as setting up 3D rendering, to the Android platform.

Finally, our Android-based application also utilizes the inputs from the multi-touch screen interface and the device orientation derived from the motion sensor data. These values are passed through the JNI directly to the shader program as uniform variables.

9
Augmented Reality-based Visualization on Mobile or Wearable Platforms

In this chapter, we will cover the following topics:

- Getting started I: Setting up OpenCV on Android
- Getting started II: Accessing the camera live feed using OpenCV
- Displaying real-time video processing with texture mapping
- Augmented reality-based data visualization over real-world scenes

Introduction

The field of digital graphics has traditionally been living within its own virtual world since computers were invented. Often, computer-generated content has no awareness of the user and how the information is relevant to the user in the real world. The application is always simply waiting for a user command such as the mouse or keyboard input. One major limiting factor in the early design of computer applications is that computers are typically sitting on a desk in an office or in a home environment. The lack of mobility and the inability to interact with its environment or user ultimately limited the development of real-world interactive visualization applications.

Today, with the evolution of mobile computing, we have redefined many of our daily interactions with the world—for example, through applications that enable navigation with GPS using a mobile phone. However, instead of enabling users to seamlessly interact with the world, mobile devices still draw users away from the real world. In particular, as in previous generations of desktop computing, users are still required to look away from the real world into a virtual world (in many cases, just a tiny mobile screen).

The notion of **Augmented Reality** (**AR**) is a step towards reconnecting the user with the real world through the fusion of the virtual world (generated by the computer) with the real world. This is distinctly different from virtual reality, in which the user is immersed into the virtual world and detached from the real world. For example, a typical embodiment of AR involves the use of a video see-through display in which virtual content (such as a computer-generated map) is combined with a real-world scene (captured continuously with a built-in camera). Now, the user is engaged with the real world—a step closer to a truly human-centric application.

Ultimately, the emergence of AR-enabled wearable computing devices (such as Meta's AR eyeglasses, which features the world's first holographic interface with 3D gesture detection and 3D stereoscopic display) will create a new era of computing that will greatly revolutionize the way humans interact with computers. Developers interested in data visualization now have another set of tools that are significantly more human-centric and intuitive. Such a design, needless to say, truly connects human, machine, and the real world together. Having information directly overlaid onto the real world (for example, by overlaying a virtual guidance map for navigation) is so much more powerful and meaningful.

This final chapter introduces the fundamental building blocks for creating your first AR-based application on a commodity Android-based mobile device: OpenCV for computer vision, OpenGL for graphics rendering, as well as Android's sensor framework for interaction. With these tools, the graphics rendering capability that used to only exist in Hollywood movie production can now be made available at everyone's fingertips. While we will only focus on the use of an Android-based mobile device in this chapter, the conceptual framework for AR-based data visualization introduced in this chapter can be similarly extended to state-of-the-art wearable computing platforms, such as Meta's AR eyeglasses.

Getting started I: Setting up OpenCV on Android

In this section, we will outline the steps to set up the OpenCV library on the Android platform, which is needed to enable access to the live camera stream central to any Augmented Reality applications.

Getting ready

We assume that the Android SDK and NDK are configured exactly as discussed in *Chapter 7, An Introduction to Real-time Graphics Rendering on a Mobile Platform Using OpenGL ES 3.0*. Here, we add in the support of OpenCV for Android. We will import and integrate the OpenCV library into our existing code structure from the previous chapter.

How to do it...

Here, we describe the major steps for setting up the OpenCV library, mainly path setup and pre-configuration of the Java SDK project setup:

1. Download the OpenCV for Android SDK package, Version 3.0.0 (`OpenCV-3.0.0-android-sdk-1.zip`) at `http://sourceforge.net/projects/opencvlibrary/files/opencv-android/3.0.0/OpenCV-3.0.0-android-sdk-1.zip`.
2. Move the package (`OpenCV-3.0.0-android-sdk-1.zip`) to the `3rd_party/android` folder created in *Chapter 7, An Introduction to Real-time Graphics Rendering on a Mobile Platform Using OpenGL ES 3.0*.
3. Unzip the package with the following commands

   ```
   cd 3rd_party/android && unzip OpenCV-3.0.0-android-sdk-1.zip
   ```

4. Then in the project folder (for example `ch9/code/opencv_demo_1`), run the following script to initialize the project for Android. Note that the `3rd_party` folder is assumed to be in the same top-level directory as in previous chapters:

   ```
   #!/bin/bash
   ANDROID_SDK_PATH="../../../3rd_party/android/android-sdk-macosx"
   OPENCV_SDK_PATH="../../../3rd_party/android/OpenCV-android-sdk"

   #initialize the SDK Java library
   $ANDROID_SDK_PATH/tools/android update project -p $OPENCV_SDK_
   PATH/sdk/java -s --target "android-18"
   $ANDROID_SDK_PATH/tools/android update project -p . -s --target
   "android-18" --library $OPENCV_SDK_PATH/sdk/java
   ```

5. Finally, include the OpenCV path in the build script `jni/Android.mk`.

```
LOCAL_PATH:= $(call my-dir)
#build the OpenGL + OpenCV code in JNI
include $(CLEAR_VARS)
#including OpenCV SDK
include ../../../3rd_party/android/OpenCV-android-sdk/sdk/native/
jni/OpenCV.mk
```

Now, the project is linked to the OpenCV library, both from the Java side as well as from the native side.

Next we must install the OpenCV Manager on the mobile phone. The OpenCV Manager allows us to create applications without statically linking all the required libraries, and it is recommended. To install the package, we can execute the following `adb` command from the same project folder (`ch9/code/opencv_demo_1`). Again, note the relative location of the `3rd_party` folder. You can also execute this command within the Android SDK folder and modify the relative path of the `3rd_party` folder accordingly.

```
$ANDROID_SDK_PATH/platform-tools/adb install ../../../3rd_party/
android/OpenCV-android-sdk/apk/OpenCV_3.0.0_Manager_3.00_armeabi-v7a.
apk
```

After we have successfully completed the setup, we are ready to create our first OpenCV Android application on the phone.

See also

Windows users should consult the following tutorials on Android development with OpenCV for setup instructions: `http://docs.opencv.org/doc/tutorials/introduction/android_binary_package/android_dev_intro.html` and `http://docs.opencv.org/doc/tutorials/introduction/android_binary_package/dev_with_OCV_on_Android.html#native-c`.

For further information on using OpenCV in an Android application, consult the online documentation at `http://opencv.org/platforms/android.html`.

Getting started II: Accessing the camera live feed using OpenCV

Next we need to demonstrate how to integrate OpenCV into our Android-based development framework. The following block diagram illustrates the core functions and relationship among the classes that will be implemented in this chapter (only the functions or classes relevant to the introduction of OpenCV will be discussed in this section):

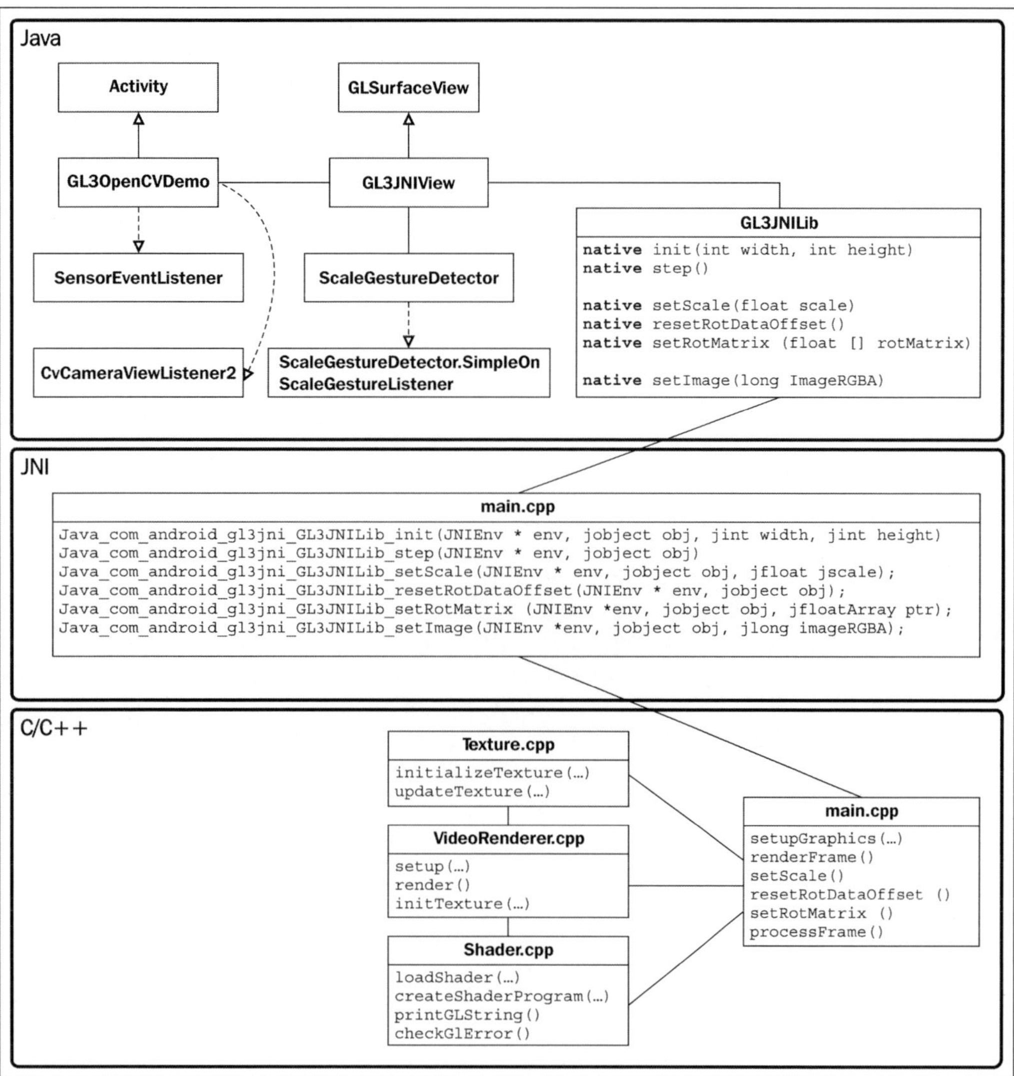

In particular, we will demonstrate how to extract an image frame from the camera video stream for further image processing steps. The OpenCV library provides camera support for accessing the live camera feed (the raw data buffer of the video data stream) as well as controlling the camera parameters. This feature allows us to get the raw frame data from the live preview camera with optimal resolution, frame rate, and image format.

Getting ready

The demos in this chapter build upon the basic structure introduced in the sample code of *Chapter 8, Interactive Real-time Data Visualization on Mobile Devices* which utilizes the multi-touch interface and motion sensor inputs to enable interactive real-time data visualization on mobile devices. The major changes that are made to support OpenCV will be highlighted. For the complete code, download the code package from the Packt Publishing website.

How to do it...

First, we will highlight the changes to the Java source files required to enable the use of OpenCV and the OpenCV camera module. Rename `GL3JNIActivity.java` (`src/com/android/gl3jni/`) as `GL3OpenCVDemo.java` and modify the code as follows:

1. Include the packages for the OpenCV library:

```
package com.android.gl3jni;
...
import org.opencv.android.BaseLoaderCallback;
import org.opencv.android.LoaderCallbackInterface;
import org.opencv.android.OpenCVLoader;
import org.opencv.android.CameraBridgeViewBase;
import org.opencv.android.CameraBridgeViewBase.CvCameraViewFrame;
import org.opencv.android.CameraBridgeViewBase.
CvCameraViewListener2;
import org.opencv.core.CvType;
import org.opencv.core.Mat;

import android.widget.RelativeLayout;
import android.view.SurfaceView;
```

2. Add the `CvCameraViewListener2` interface to the `GL3OpenCVDemo` class:

```
public class GL3OpenCVDemo extends Activity implements
  SensorEventListener, CvCameraViewListener2{
```

3. Create the variables to handle the camera view:

```
  private GL3JNIView mView=null;
  ...
  private boolean gl3_loaded = false;
  private CameraBridgeViewBase mOpenCvCameraView;
  private RelativeLayout l_layout;
```

4. Implement the `BaseLoaderCallback` function for `OpenCVLoader`:

```
private BaseLoaderCallback mLoaderCallback = new
  BaseLoaderCallback(this) {
@Override
public void onManagerConnected(int status) {
  switch (status) {
    case LoaderCallbackInterface.SUCCESS:{
      Log.i("OpenCVDemo", "OpenCV loaded successfully");
      // load the library *AFTER* we have OpenCV lib ready!
      System.loadLibrary("gl3jni");
      gl3_loaded = true;

      //load the view as we have all JNI loaded
      mView = new GL3JNIView(getApplication());
      l_layout.addView(mView);
      setContentView(l_layout);

      /* enable the camera, and push the images to the
        OpenGL layer */
      mOpenCvCameraView.enableView();
    } break;
    default:{
      super.onManagerConnected(status);
    } break;
  }
 }
};
```

5. Implement the OpenCV camera callback functions and pass the image data to the JNI C/C++ side for processing and rendering:

```
public void onCameraViewStarted(int width, int height) {
}
public void onCameraViewStopped() {
}
public Mat onCameraFrame(CvCameraViewFrame inputFrame) {
  //Log.i("OpenCVDemo", "Got Frame\n");
  Mat input = inputFrame.rgba();
  if(gl3_loaded){
    GL3JNILib.setImage(input.nativeObj);
  }
  //don't show on the java side
  return null;
}
```

6. Initialize the camera in the `onCreate` function, upon starting the application:

```
@Override protected void onCreate(Bundle icicle) {
  super.onCreate(icicle);
  ...
  //setup the Java Camera with OpenCV
  setContentView(R.layout.ar);
  l_layout =
    (RelativeLayout)findViewById(R.id.linearLayoutRest);
  mOpenCvCameraView =
    (CameraBridgeViewBase)findViewById(R.id.opencv_camera_
      surface_view);
  mOpenCvCameraView.setVisibility( SurfaceView.VISIBLE );
  mOpenCvCameraView.setMaxFrameSize(1280, 720); /* cap it at
    720 for performance issue */
  mOpenCvCameraView.setCvCameraViewListener(this);
  mOpenCvCameraView.disableView();
}
```

7. Load the OpenCV library using the asynchronized initialization function called `initAsync` from the `OpenCVLoader` class. This event is captured by the `BaseLoaderCallback mLoaderCallback` function defined earlier:

```
@Override
protected void onResume() {
  super.onResume();
  OpenCVLoader.initAsync(OpenCVLoader.OPENCV_VERSION_3_0_0,
    this, mLoaderCallback);
  ...
}
```

8. Finally, handle the `onPause` event, which pauses the camera preview when the application is no longer running in the foreground:

```
@Override
protected void onPause() {
  super.onPause();
  mSensorManager.unregisterListener(this);
  //stop the camera
  if(mView!=null){
    mView.onPause();
  }
  if (mOpenCvCameraView != null)
    mOpenCvCameraView.disableView();
  gl3_loaded = false;
}
```

9. Now inside `GL3JNILib.java` (`src/com/android/gl3jni/`), add the native `setImage` function to pass the camera raw data. The entire source file is shown here, given its simplicity:

```
package com.android.gl3jni;

public class GL3JNILib {
  public static native void init(int width, int height);
  public static native void step();

  //pass the image to JNI C++ side
  public static native void setImage(long imageRGBA);

  //pass the device rotation angles and the scaling factor
  public static native void resetRotDataOffset();
  public static native void setRotMatrix(float[]
    rotMatrix);
  public static native void setScale(float scale);
}
```

10. Finally, the source code inside `GL3JNIView.java` is virtually identical except that we offer the option to reset the rotation data and call the `setZOrderOnTop` function to ensure that the OpenGL layer is on top of the Java layer:

```
class GL3JNIView extends GLSurfaceView {
  ...
  public GL3JNIView(Context context) {
    super(context);
    // Pick an EGLConfig with RGB8 color, 16-bit depth, no stencil
    setZOrderOnTop(true);
    setEGLConfigChooser(8, 8, 8, 8, 16, 0);
    setEGLContextClientVersion(3);
    getHolder().setFormat(PixelFormat.TRANSLUCENT);
    renderer = new Renderer();
    setRenderer(renderer);
    //handle gesture input
    mScaleDetector = new ScaleGestureDetector(context, new
      ScaleListener());
  }
  ...
  @Override
  public boolean onTouchEvent(MotionEvent ev) {
    mScaleDetector.onTouchEvent(ev);
    int action = ev.getActionMasked();
    switch (action) {
```

```
            case MotionEvent.ACTION_DOWN:
              GL3JNILib.resetRotDataOffset();
              break;
          }
          return true;
        }
        ...
      }
```

11. Finally, define the JNI prototypes to interface with the Java side in the `main.cpp` file that connects all components.

```
//external calls for Java
extern "C" {
  JNIEXPORT void JNICALL
  Java_com_android_gl3jni_GL3JNILib_setImage(JNIEnv * jenv,
    jobject, jlong imageRGBA);
};
JNIEXPORT void JNICALL
  Java_com_android_gl3jni_GL3JNILib_setImage(
    JNIEnv * jenv, jobject, jlong imageRGBA) {
      cv::Mat* image = (cv::Mat*) imageRGBA;
      /* use mutex lock to ensure the write/read operations
        are synced (to avoid corrupting the frame) */
      pthread_mutex_lock(&count_mutex);
      frame = image->clone();
      pthread_mutex_unlock(&count_mutex);
      //LOGI("Got Image: %dx%d\n", frame.rows, frame.cols);
}
```

12. To access the device camera, the following elements must be declared in the `AndroidManifest.xml` file to ensure we have the permission to control the camera. In our current example, we request access to the front and back cameras with autofocus support.

```
<uses-permission android:name="android.permission.CAMERA"/>
<uses-feature android:name="android.hardware.camera"
  android:required="false"/>
<uses-feature
  android:name="android.hardware.camera.autofocus"
    android:required="false"/>
<uses-feature android:name="android.hardware.camera.front"
  android:required="false"/>
<uses-feature
  android:name="android.hardware.camera.front.autofocus"
    android:required="false"/>
```

At this point, we have developed a full demo application that supports OpenCV and real-time camera feed. In the next section, we will connect the camera raw data stream to the OpenGL layer and perform real-time feature extraction with OpenCV in C/C++.

How it works...

On the Java side, we have integrated the OpenCV Manager (installed previously) to handle the dynamic loading of all libraries at runtime. Upon starting the application, we must call the `OpenCVLoader.initAsync` function; all OpenCV-related JNI libraries must only be called after the OpenCV libraries are successfully loaded. To synchronize these actions in our case, the `callback` function (`BaseLoaderCallback`) checks the status of the initialization of OpenCV, and we proceed with the `System.loadLibrary` function to initialize OpenGL and other components only if the OpenCV loader returns success (`LoaderCallbackInterface.SUCCESS`). For simplicity, we did not include the implementation to handle library loading exceptions in this demo.

On the sensor side, we have also changed the implementation for the `SensorManager` function to return the rotation matrix instead of the Euler angles to avoid the issue of Gimbal lock (refer to `http://en.wikipedia.org/wiki/Gimbal_lock`). We also remapped the coordinates (from device orientation to OpenGL camera orientation) using the `SensorManager.remapCoordinateSystem` function. Then the rotation matrix is directed to the OpenGL side with the native calls `GL3JNILib.setRotMatrix`. Also, we can allow the user to reset the default orientation by touching the screen. This is achieved by calling the `GL3JNILib.resetRotDataOffset` function, which resets the rotation matrix with the touch event.

Additionally, we have added the `OpenCV CvCameraViewListener2` interface and `CameraBridgeViewBase` class to enable native camera access. The `CameraBridgeViewBase` class is a basic class that handles the interaction with the Android Camera class and OpenCV library. It is responsible for controlling the camera, such as resolution, and processing the frame, such as changing the image format. The client implements `CvCameraViewListener` to receive callback events. In the current implementation, we manually set the resolution as 1280 x 720. However, we can increase or decrease the resolution based on the application needs. Finally, the color frame buffers are returned in RGBA format, and the data stream will be transferred to the JNI C/C++ side and rendered using texture mapping.

Displaying real-time video using texture mapping

Today, most mobile phones are equipped with cameras that are capable of capturing high-quality photos as well as videos. For example, the Samsung Galaxy Note 4 is equipped with a 16MP back-facing camera as well as a 3.7MP front-facing camera for video conferencing applications. With these built-in cameras, we can record high-definition videos with exceptional image quality in both outdoor and indoor environments. The ubiquity of these imaging sensors, as well as the increasing computational capability of mobile processors, now enable us to develop much more interactive applications such as real-time tracking of objects or faces.

By combining OpenGL with the OpenCV library, we can create interactive applications that perform real-time video processing of the real world to register and augment 3D virtual information onto real-world objects. Since both libraries are hardware-accelerated (GPU and CPU optimized), it is important that we explore the use of these libraries to obtain real-time performance.

In the previous section, we introduced the framework that provides access to the live camera feed. Here, we will create a full demo that displays real-time video using OpenGL-based texture mapping techniques (similar to those introduced in *Chapter 4, Rendering 2D Images and Videos with Texture Mapping* to *Chapter 6, Rendering Stereoscopic 3D Models using OpenGL*, except we will deploy OpenGL ES for mobile platforms), and processes the video stream to perform corner detection using OpenCV. To help readers understand the additional code needed to finalize the demo, here is an overview diagram of the implementation:

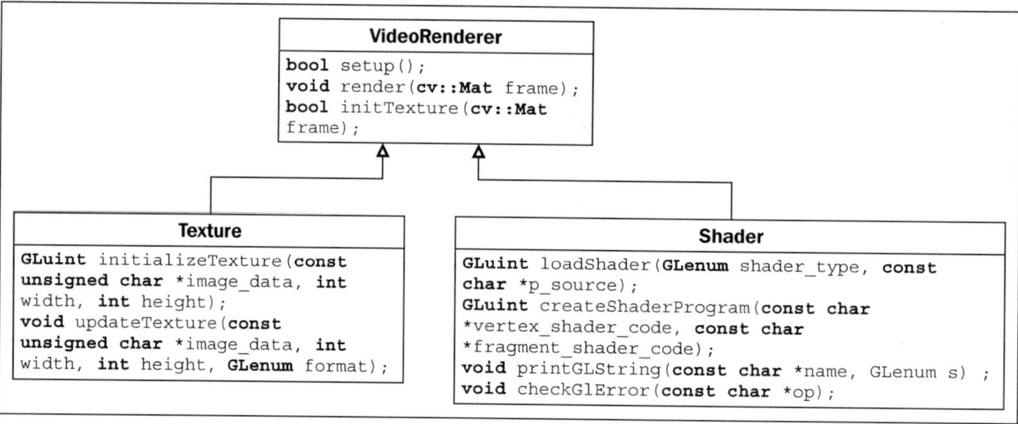

Getting ready

This demo requires the completion of all the *Getting ready* steps to enable the capture of the real-time video stream using OpenCV on an Android device. The implementation of the shader program and texture mapping code is based on the demos from *Chapter 8, Interactive Real-time Data Visualization on Mobile Devices*.

How to do it...

On the native code side, create two new files called `VideoRenderer.hpp` and `VideoRenderer.cpp`. These files contain the implementation to render the video using texture mapping. Also, we will import the `Texture.cpp` and `Texture.hpp` files from the previous chapter to handle texture creation.

Inside the `VideoRenderer.hpp` file, define the `VideoRenderer` class as follows (the details of each function will be discussed next):

```
#ifndef VIDEORENDERER_H_
#define VIDEORENDERER_H_
//The shader program and basic OpenGL calls
#include <Shader.hpp>
//for texture support
#include <Texture.hpp>
//opencv support
#include <opencv2/core/core.hpp>
#include <opencv2/imgproc/imgproc.hpp>
#include <opencv2/highgui/highgui.hpp>

class VideoRenderer {
  public:
    VideoRenderer();
    virtual ~VideoRenderer();
    //setup all shader program and texture mapping variables
    bool setup();
    bool initTexture(cv::Mat frame);
    //render the frame on screen
    void render(cv::Mat frame);

  private:
    //this handles the generic camera feed view
    GLuint gProgram;
    GLuint gvPositionHandle;
    GLuint vertexUVHandle;
    GLuint textureSamplerID;
```

```
    GLuint texture_id;
    Shader shader;
};

#endif /* VIDEORENDERER_H_ */
```

Inside the `VideoRenderer.cpp` file, we implement each of the three key member functions (`setup`, `initTexture`, and `render`). Here is the complete implementation:

1. Include the `VideoRenderer.hpp` header file, define functions to print debug messages, and define the constructor and destructor:

```
#include "VideoRenderer.hpp"

#define  LOG_TAG    "VideoRenderer"
#define  LOGI(...)
  __android_log_print(ANDROID_LOG_INFO,LOG_TAG,__VA_ARGS__)
#define  LOGE(...)
  __android_log_print(ANDROID_LOG_ERROR,LOG_TAG,__VA_ARGS__)

VideoRenderer::VideoRenderer() {
}

VideoRenderer::~VideoRenderer() {
}
```

2. Define the vertex and fragment shaders as well as associated configuration steps (similar to *Chapter 8, Interactive Real-time Data Visualization on Mobile Devices*):

```
bool VideoRenderer::setup(){
  // Vertex shader source code
  const char g_vshader_code[] =
  "#version 300 es\n"
  "layout(location = 1) in vec4 vPosition;\n"
  "layout(location = 2) in vec2 vertexUV;\n"
  "out vec2 UV;\n"
  "void main() {\n"
    "  gl_Position = vPosition;\n"
    "  UV=vertexUV;\n"
  "}\n";
  // fragment shader source code
  const char g_fshader_code[] =
  "#version 300 es\n"
  "precision mediump float;\n"
  "out vec4 color;\n"
  "uniform sampler2D textureSampler;\n"
  "in vec2 UV;\n"
```

```
    "void main() {\n"
      "  color = vec4(texture(textureSampler, UV).rgb,
        1.0);\n"
    "}\n";

    LOGI("setupVideoRenderer");
    gProgram =   shader.createShaderProgram(g_vshader_code,
      g_fshader_code);
    if (!gProgram) {
      LOGE("Could not create program.");
      return false;
    }

    gvPositionHandle = glGetAttribLocation(gProgram,
      "vPosition");
    shader.checkGlError("glGetAttribLocation");
    LOGI("glGetAttribLocation(\"vPosition\") = %d\n",
    gvPositionHandle);

    vertexUVHandle = glGetAttribLocation(gProgram,
      "vertexUV");
    shader.checkGlError("glGetAttribLocation");
    LOGI("glGetAttribLocation(\"vertexUV\") = %d\n",
    vertexUVHandle);

    textureSamplerID = glGetUniformLocation(gProgram,
      "textureSampler");
    shader.checkGlError("glGetUniformLocation");
    LOGI("glGetUniformLocation(\"textureSampler\") =   %d\n",
      textureSamplerID);

    return true;
  }
```

3. Initialize and bind the texture:

```
bool VideoRenderer::initTexture(cv::Mat frame){
  texture_id = initializeTexture(frame.data,
    frame.size().width, frame.size().height);
  //binds our texture in Texture Unit 0
  glActiveTexture(GL_TEXTURE0);
  glBindTexture(GL_TEXTURE_2D, texture_id);
  glUniform1i(textureSamplerID, 0);

  return true;
}
```

4. Render the camera feed on the screen with texture mapping:

```
void VideoRenderer::render(cv::Mat frame){
  //our vertices
  const GLfloat g_vertex_buffer_data[] = {
    1.0f,1.0f,0.0f,
    -1.0f,1.0f,0.0f,
    -1.0f,-1.0f,0.0f,
    1.0f,1.0f
    ,0.0f,
    -1.0f,-1.0f,0.0f,
    1.0f,-1.0f,0.0f
  };
  //UV map for the vertices
  const GLfloat g_uv_buffer_data[] = {
    1.0f, 0.0f,
    0.0f, 0.0f,
    0.0f, 1.0f,
    1.0f, 0.0f,
    0.0f, 1.0f,
    1.0f, 1.0f
  };

  glUseProgram(gProgram);
  shader.checkGlError("glUseProgram");

  glEnableVertexAttribArray(gvPositionHandle);
  shader.checkGlError("glEnableVertexAttribArray");

  glEnableVertexAttribArray(vertexUVHandle);
  shader.checkGlError("glEnableVertexAttribArray");

  glVertexAttribPointer(gvPositionHandle, 3, GL_FLOAT,
    GL_FALSE, 0, g_vertex_buffer_data);
  shader.checkGlError("glVertexAttribPointer");

  glVertexAttribPointer(vertexUVHandle, 2, GL_FLOAT,
    GL_FALSE, 0, g_uv_buffer_data);
  shader.checkGlError("glVertexAttribPointer");

  updateTexture(frame.data, frame.size().width,
    frame.size().height, GL_RGBA);
```

```
        //draw the camera feed on the screen
        glDrawArrays(GL_TRIANGLES, 0, 6);
        shader.checkGlError("glDrawArrays");

        glDisableVertexAttribArray(gvPositionHandle);
        glDisableVertexAttribArray(vertexUVHandle);
    }
```

To further enhance the readability of the code, we encapsulate the handling of the shader program and texture mapping inside `Shader.hpp` (`Shader.cpp`) and `Texture.hpp` (`Texture.cpp`), respectively. We will only show the header files here for completeness and refer readers to the code package on the Packt Publishing website for the detailed implementation of each function.

Here is the `Shader.hpp` file:

```
#ifndef SHADER_H_
#define SHADER_H_

#define GLM_FORCE_RADIANS
#include <jni.h>
#include <android/log.h>
#include <stdio.h>
#include <stdlib.h>
#include <math.h>
#include <GLES3/gl3.h>
#include <glm/glm.hpp>
#include <glm/gtc/matrix_transform.hpp>

class Shader {
  public:
  Shader();
  virtual ~Shader();
  GLuint loadShader(GLenum shader_type, const char*p_source);
  GLuint createShaderProgram(const char*vertex_shader_code,
    const char*fragment_shader_code);
  void printGLString(const char *name, GLenum s) ;
  void checkGlError(const char* op);
};

#endif /* SHADER_H_ */
```

The `Texture.hpp` file should read:

```
#ifndef TEXTURE_HPP
#define TEXTURE_HPP

#include <GLES3/gl3.h>

class Texture {
  public:
    Texture();
    virtual ~Texture();
    GLuint initializeTexture(const unsigned char *image_data,
      int width, int height);
    void updateTexture(const unsigned char *image_data, int width,
      int height, GLenum format);
};

#endif
```

Finally, we integrate everything inside the `main.cpp` file with the following steps:

1. Include all headers. In particular, include `pthread.h` to handle synchronization and OpenCV libraries for image processing.

   ```
   ...
   #include <pthread.h>
   #include <Texture.hpp>
   #include <Shader.hpp>
   #include <VideoRenderer.hpp>

   //including opencv headers
   #include <opencv2/core/core.hpp>
   #include <opencv2/imgproc/imgproc.hpp>
   #include <opencv2/highgui/highgui.hpp>
   #include <opencv2/features2d/features2d.hpp>
   ...
   ```

2. Define the `VideoRenderer` and `Shader` objects, as well as the `pthread_mutex_t` lock variable to handle synchronization for data copying using a mutex lock.

   ```
   //mutex lock for data copying
   pthread_mutex_t count_mutex;
   ...
   //pre-set image size.
   const int IMAGE_WIDTH = 1280;
   const int IMAGE_HEIGHT = 720;
   ```

```
bool enable_process = true;
//main camera feed from the Java side
cv::Mat frame;
//all shader related code
Shader shader;
//for video rendering
VideoRenderer videorenderer;
```

3. Set up the `VideoRenderer` object in the `setupGraphics` function and initialize the texture.

```
bool setupGraphics(int w, int h) {
  ...
  videorenderer.setup();
  //template for the first texture
  cv::Mat frameM(IMAGE_HEIGHT, IMAGE_WIDTH, CV_8UC4,
    cv::Scalar(0,0,0,255));
  videorenderer.initTexture(frameM);
  frame = frameM;
  ...
  return true;
}
```

4. Create a `processFrame` helper function to handle feature extraction with the OpenCV `goodFeaturesToTrack` function. The function also draws the result directly on the frame for visualization.

```
void processFrame(cv::Mat *frame_local){
  int maxCorners = 1000;
  if( maxCorners < 1 ) { maxCorners = 1; }
  cv::RNG rng(12345);
  // Parameters for Shi-Tomasi algorithm
  std::vector<cv::Point2f> corners;
  double qualityLevel = 0.05;
  double minDistance = 10;
  int blockSize = 3;
  bool useHarrisDetector = false;
  double k = 0.04;

  // Copy the source image
  cv::Mat src_gray;
  cv::Mat frame_small;
  cv::resize(*frame_local, frame_small, cv::Size(), 0.5,
    0.5, CV_INTER_AREA);
  cv::cvtColor(frame_small, src_gray, CV_RGB2GRAY );
```

```
    // Apply feature extraction
    cv::goodFeaturesToTrack( src_gray, corners, maxCorners,
      qualityLevel, minDistance, cv::Mat(), blockSize,
        useHarrisDetector, k );

    // Draw corners detected on the image
    int r = 10;
    for( int i = 0; i < corners.size(); i++ )
    {
      cv::circle(*frame_local, 2*corners[i], r,
        cv::Scalar(rng.uniform(0,255),
      rng.uniform(0,255), rng.uniform(0,255), 255), -1, 8, 0
        );
    }
    //LOGI("Found %d features", corners.size());
}
```

5. Implement frame copying with mutex lock synchronization (to avoid frame corruption due to shared memory and race condition) in the `renderFrame` function. Process the frame with the OpenCV library and render the result using OpenGL texture-mapping techniques.

```
void renderFrame() {
  shader.checkGlError("glClearColor");
  glClearColor(0.0f, 0.0f, 0.0f, 0.0f);
  glClear(GL_COLOR_BUFFER_BIT | GL_DEPTH_BUFFER_BIT);

  shader.checkGlError("glClear");

  pthread_mutex_lock(&count_mutex);
  cv::Mat frame_local = frame.clone();
  pthread_mutex_unlock(&count_mutex);

  if(enable_process)
    processFrame(&frame_local);
```

```
    //render the video feed on screen
    videorenderer.render(frame_local);
    //LOGI("Rendering OpenGL Graphics");
  }
```

6. Define the JNI prototypes and implement the `setImage` function, which receives the raw camera image data from the Java side using a mutex lock to ensure data copying is protected. Also, implement the `toggleFeatures` function to turn feature tracking on and off upon touching the screen.

```
extern "C" {
..
  JNIEXPORT void JNICALL
    Java_com_android_gl3jni_GL3JNILib_setImage(JNIEnv *
      jenv, jobject, jlong imageRGBA);
  //toggle features
  JNIEXPORT void JNICALL
    Java_com_android_gl3jni_GL3JNILib_toggleFeatures(JNIEnv
      * jenv, jobject);
};

JNIEXPORT void JNICALL
  Java_com_android_gl3jni_GL3JNILib_toggleFeatures(JNIEnv *
    env, jobject obj){
  //toggle the processing on/off
  enable_process = !enable_process;
}
JNIEXPORT void JNICALL
  Java_com_android_gl3jni_GL3JNILib_setImage(
  JNIEnv * jenv, jobject, jlong imageRGBA) {
  cv::Mat* image = (cv::Mat*) imageRGBA;
  /* use mutex lock to ensure the write/read operations
    are synced (to avoid corrupting the frame) */
  pthread_mutex_lock(&count_mutex);
```

```
        frame = image->clone();
        pthread_mutex_unlock(&count_mutex);
        //LOGI("Got Image: %dx%d\n", frame.rows, frame.cols);
    }
```

The resulting image is a post-processed frame from OpenCV. In addition to displaying the raw video frame, we demonstrate that our implementation can easily be extended to support real-time video processing with OpenCV. The `processFrame` function uses the OpenCV `goodFeaturesToTrack` corner detection function and we overlay all corners extracted from the scene on the image.

Image features are the fundamental elements for many tracking algorithms such as **Simultaneous localization and Mapping** (**SLAM**) as well as recognition algorithms such as image-based matching. For example, with the SLAM algorithm, we can construct a map of the environment and, at the same time, keep track of the position of the device in space. Such techniques are particularly useful in AR applications as we always need to align the virtual world with the real world. Next, we can see a feature extraction algorithm (corner detection) running in real-time on a mobile phone.

How it works...

The `VideoRenderer` class has two primary functions:

- Creating the shader program that handles texture mapping (`Shader.cpp` and `Texture.cpp`).
- Updating the texture memory with the OpenCV raw camera frame. Each time a new frame is retrieved from OpenCV, we call the render function, which updates the texture memory and also draws the frame on the screen.

The `main.cpp` file connects all the components of the implementation, and encapsulates all the logics for the interaction. It interfaces with the Java side (for example, `setImage`) and we offload all computationally intensive tasks to the C++ native side. For example, the `processFrame` function handles the OpenCV video processing pipeline, and we can efficiently handle memory I/O and parallelization. On the other hand, the `VideoRenderer` class accelerates rendering with OpenGL for real-time performance on the mobile platform.

One may notice that the implementations of OpenGL and OpenCV on Android are mostly identical to the desktop version. That's the key reason why we employ such cross-platform languages as we can easily extend our code to any future platform with minimal effort.

See also

On a mobile platform, computational resources are particularly limited and thus it is important to optimize the use of all available hardware resources. With OpenGL-based hardware acceleration, we can reduce most of our overhead in rendering graphics in 2D and 3D on the graphics processor. In the near future, especially with the emergence of mobile processors supporting GPGPU (for example, Nvidia's K1 mobile processor), we will enable more parallelized processing for computer vision algorithms and offer real-time performance for many applications on a mobile device. For example, Nvidia now officially supports CUDA for all its upcoming mobile processors, so we will see many more real-time image processing, machine learning (such as deep learning algorithms), and high-performance graphics emerging on the mobile platform. See the following website for more information: `https://developer.nvidia.com/embedded-computing`.

Augmented reality-based data visualization over real-world scenes

In our ultimate demo, we will introduce the basic framework for AR-based data visualization by overlaying 3D data on real-world objects and scenes. We apply the same GPU-accelerated simulation model and register it to the world with a sensor-based tracking approach. The following diagram illustrates the final architecture of the implementation in this chapter:

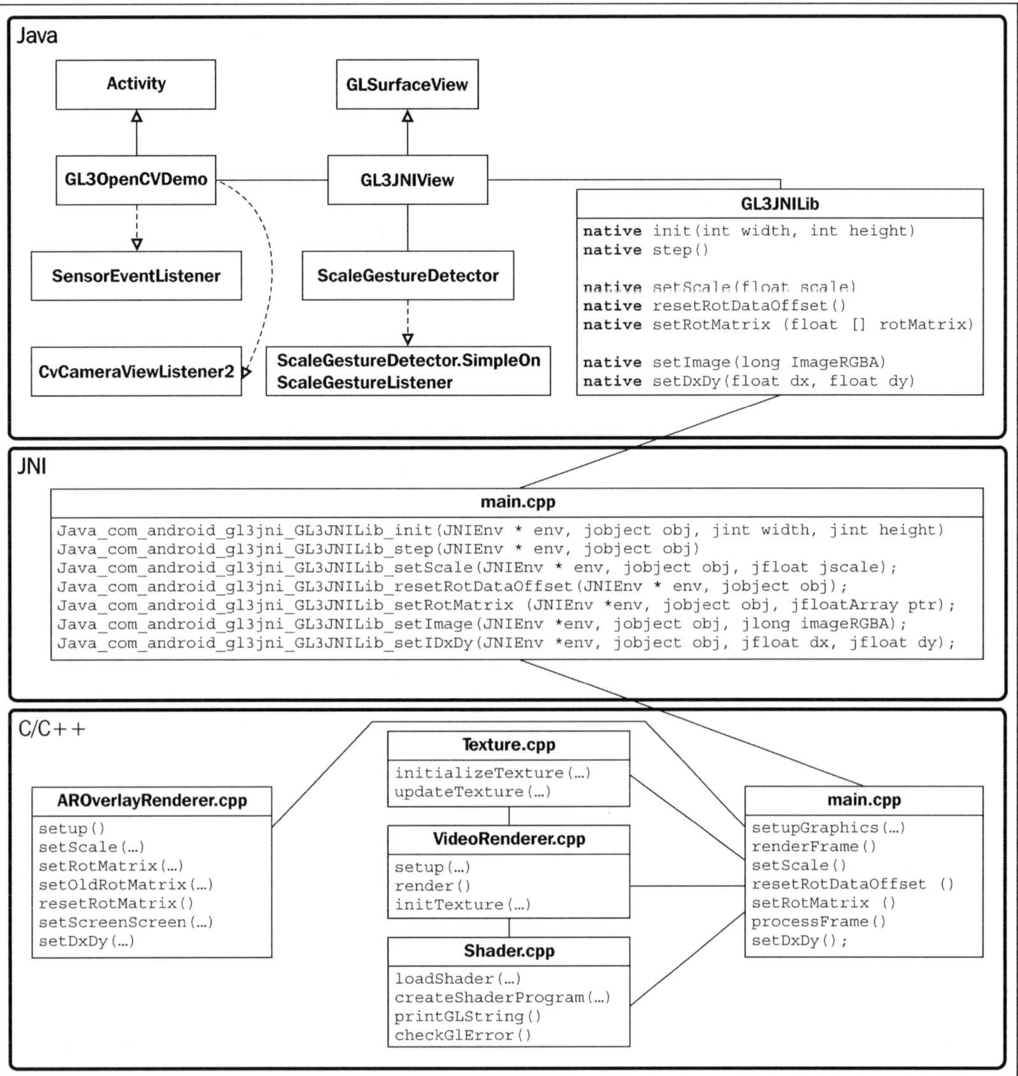

Getting ready

This final demo integrates together all the concepts previously introduced in this chapter and requires the capture (and possibly processing) of a real-time video stream using OpenCV on an Android-based phone. To reduce the complexity of the code, we have created the Augmented Reality layer (`AROverlayRenderer`) and we can improve the registration, alignment, and calibration of the layer with more advanced algorithms in the future.

How to do it...

Let's define a new class called `AROverlayRenderer` inside the `AROverlayRenderer.hpp` file:

```
#ifndef AROVERLAYRENDERER_H_
#define AROVERLAYRENDERER_H_

#include<Shader.hpp>

class AROverlayRenderer {
  public:
    AROverlayRenderer();
    virtual ~AROverlayRenderer();
    void render();
    bool setup();
    void setScale(float s);

    void setOldRotMatrix(glm::mat4 r_matrix);
    void setRotMatrix(glm::mat4 r_matrix);
    void resetRotMatrix();
    void setScreenSize(int width, int height);
    void setDxDy (float dx, float dy);
  private:
    //this renders the overlay view
    GLuint gProgramOverlay;
    GLuint gvOverlayPositionHandle;
    GLuint gvOverlayColorHandle;
    GLuint matrixHandle;
    GLuint sigmaHandle;
    GLuint scaleHandle;

  //vertices for the grid
  int grid_size;
  GLfloat *gGrid;
  GLfloat sigma;

  //for handling the object rotation from user
  GLfloat dx, dy;
  GLfloat rotX, rotY;

  //the view matrix and projection matrix
  glm::mat4 g_view_matrix;
```

```
    glm::mat4 g_projection_matrix;

    //initial position of the camera
    glm::vec3 g_position;
    //FOV of the virtual camera in OpenGL
    float g_initial_fov;

    glm::mat4 rotMatrix;
    glm::mat4 old_rotMatrix;

    float scale;
    int width;
    int height;

    Shader shader;
    void computeProjectionMatrices();
    void computeGrid();
};

#endif /* AROVERLAYRENDERER_H_ */
```

Now implement the `AROverlayRenderer` member functions inside the `AROverlayRenderer.cpp` file:

1. Include the `AROverlayRenderer.hpp` header file and define functions to print messages as well as the constructor and destructor:

```
#include "AROverlayRenderer.hpp"

#define  LOG_TAG    "AROverlayRenderer"
#define  LOGI(...)
  __android_log_print(ANDROID_LOG_INFO,LOG_TAG,__VA_ARGS__)
#define  LOGE(...)
  __android_log_print(ANDROID_LOG_ERROR,LOG_TAG,__VA_ARGS__)

AROverlayRenderer::AROverlayRenderer() {
  //initial position of the camera
  g_position = glm::vec3( 0.0f, 0.0f, 0.0f );

  //FOV of the virtual camera in OpenGL
  //45 degree FOV
  g_initial_fov = 45.0f*glm::pi<float>()/180.0f;

  /* scale for the panel and other objects, allow for
    zooming in with pinch. */
  scale = 1.0f;
```

```
    dx=0.0f; dy=0.0f;
    rotX=0.0f, rotY=0.0f;
    sigma = 0;

    grid_size = 400;
    //allocate memory for the grid
    gGrid = (GLfloat*)
      malloc(sizeof(GLfloat)*grid_size*grid_size*3);
  }

  AROverlayRenderer::~AROverlayRenderer() {
    //delete all dynamically allocated objects here
    free(gGrid);
  }
```

2. Initialize the grid pattern for the simulation:

```
void AROverlayRenderer::computeGrid(){
  float grid_x = grid_size;
  float grid_y = grid_size;
  unsigned int data_counter = 0;
  //define a grid ranging from -1 to +1
  for(float x = -grid_x/2.0f; x<grid_x/2.0f; x+=1.0f){
    for(float y = -grid_y/2.0f; y<grid_y/2.0f; y+=1.0f){
      float x_data = x/grid_x;
      float y_data = y/grid_y;
      gGrid[data_counter] = x_data;
      gGrid[data_counter+1] = y_data;
      gGrid[data_counter+2] = 0;
      data_counter+=3;
    }
  }
}
```

3. Set up the shader program to overlay graphics:

```
bool AROverlayRenderer::setup(){
  // Vertex shader source code
  static const char g_vshader_code_overlay[] =
    "#version 300 es\n"
    "in vec4 vPosition;\n"
    "uniform mat4 MVP;\n"
    "uniform float sigma;\n"
    "uniform float scale;\n"
    "out vec4 color_based_on_position;\n"
    "// Heat map generator                    \n"
```

```
  "vec4 heatMap(float v, float vmin, float vmax){\n"
  "    float dv;\n"
  "    float r=1.0, g=1.0, b=1.0;\n"
  "  if (v < vmin){\n"
  "    v = vmin;}\n"
  "  if (v > vmax){\n"
  "    v = vmax;}\n"
  "  dv = vmax - vmin;\n"
  "  if (v < (vmin + 0.25 * dv)) {\n"
    "    r = 0.0;\n"
    "    g = 4.0 * (v - vmin) / dv;\n"
  "  } else if (v < (vmin + 0.5 * dv)) {\n"
    "    r = 0.0;\n"
    "    b = 1.0 + 4.0 * (vmin + 0.25 * dv - v) / dv;\n"
  "  } else if (v < (vmin + 0.75 * dv)) {\n"
    "    r = 4.0 * (v - vmin - 0.5 * dv) / dv;\n"
    "    b = 0.0;\n"
  "  } else {\n"
    "    g = 1.0 + 4.0 * (vmin + 0.75 * dv - v) / dv;\n"
    "    b = 0.0;\n"
  "  }\n"
  "    return vec4(r, g, b, 0.1);\n"
"}\n"
"void main() {\n"
  "  //Simulation on GPU \n"
  "  float x_data = vPosition.x;\n"
  "  float y_data = vPosition.y;\n"
  "  float sigma2 = sigma*sigma;\n"
  "  float z = exp(-0.5*(x_data*x_data)/(sigma2)-
    0.5*(y_data*y_data)/(sigma2));\n"
  "  vec4 position = vPosition;\n"
  "  position.z = z*scale;\n"
  "  position.x = position.x*scale;\n"
  "  position.y = position.y*scale;\n"
  "  gl_Position = MVP*position;\n"
  "  color_based_on_position = heatMap(position.z, 0.0,
    0.5);\n"
  "  gl_PointSize = 5.0*scale;\n"
"}\n";

// fragment shader source code
static const char g_fshader_code_overlay[] =
  "#version 300 es\n"
    "precision mediump float;\n"
```

```
    "in vec4 color_based_on_position;\n"
    "out vec4 color;\n"
    "void main() {\n"
      "  color = color_based_on_position;\n"
    "}\n";

    //setup the shader for the overlay
    gProgramOverlay =
      shader.createShaderProgram(g_vshader_code_overlay,
        g_fshader_code_overlay);
  if (!gProgramOverlay) {
    LOGE("Could not create program for overlay.");
    return false;
  }
  //get handlers for the overlay side
  matrixHandle = glGetUniformLocation(gProgramOverlay, "MVP");
  shader.checkGlError("glGetUniformLocation");
  LOGI("glGetUniformLocation(\"MVP\") = %d\n",
      matrixHandle);

  gvOverlayPositionHandle = glGetAttribLocation(gProgramOverlay,
"vPosition");
  shader.checkGlError("glGetAttribLocation");
  LOGI("glGetAttribLocation(\"vPosition\") = %d\n",
      gvOverlayPositionHandle);

  sigmaHandle = glGetUniformLocation(gProgramOverlay,
    "sigma");
  shader.checkGlError("glGetUniformLocation");
  LOGI("glGetUniformLocation(\"sigma\") = %d\n",
      sigmaHandle);

  scaleHandle = glGetUniformLocation(gProgramOverlay,
    "scale");
  shader.checkGlError("glGetUniformLocation");
  LOGI("glGetUniformLocation(\"scale\") = %d\n",
    scaleHandle);

  computeGrid();
}
```

4. Create helper functions to set the scale, screen size, and rotation variables from the touch interface:

```
void AROverlayRenderer::setScale(float s) {
  scale = s;
}

void AROverlayRenderer::setScreenSize(int w, int h) {
  width = w;
  height = h;
}

void AROverlayRenderer::setRotMatrix(glm::mat4 r_matrix){
  rotMatrix= r_matrix;
}

void AROverlayRenderer::setOldRotMatrix(glm::mat4
  r_matrix){
  old_rotMatrix = r_matrix;
}

void AROverlayRenderer::resetRotMatrix(){
  old_rotMatrix = rotMatrix;
}

void AROverlayRenderer::setDxDy(float dx, float dy){
  //update the angle of rotation for each
  rotX += dx/width;
  rotY += dy/height;
}
```

5. Compute the projection and view matrices based on the camera parameters:

```
void AROverlayRenderer::computeProjectionMatrices(){
  //direction vector for z
  glm::vec3 direction_z(0.0, 0.0, -1.0);
  //up vector
  glm::vec3 up = glm::vec3(0.0, -1.0, 0.0);

  float aspect_ratio = (float)width/(float)height;
  float nearZ = 0.01f;
  float farZ = 50.0f;
  float top = tan(g_initial_fov/2*nearZ);
  float right = aspect_ratio*top;
  float left = -right;
  float bottom = -top;
```

```
  g_projection_matrix = glm::frustum(left, right, bottom, top,
    nearZ, farZ);

  g_view_matrix = glm::lookAt(
    g_position,           // camera position
    g_position+direction_z, //viewing direction
    up                   // up direction
  );
}
```

6. Render the graphics on the screen:

```
void AROverlayRenderer::render(){
  //update the variables for animations
  sigma+=0.002f;
  if(sigma>0.5f){
    sigma = 0.002f;
  }
  glUseProgram(gProgramOverlay);
  /* Retrieve the View and Model matrices and apply them to
    the rendering */
  computeProjectionMatrices();
  glm::mat4 projection_matrix = g_projection_matrix;
  glm::mat4 view_matrix = g_view_matrix;
  glm::mat4 model_matrix = glm::mat4(1.0);

  model_matrix = glm::translate(model_matrix,
    glm::vec3(0.0f, 0.0f, scale-5.0f));
  //X,Y reversed for the screen orientation
  model_matrix = glm::rotate(model_matrix,
    rotY*glm::pi<float>(), glm::vec3(-1.0f, 0.0f, 0.0f));
  model_matrix = glm::rotate(model_matrix,
    rotX*glm::pi<float>(), glm::vec3(0.0f, -1.0f, 0.0f));
  model_matrix = glm::rotate(model_matrix,
    90.0f*glm::pi<float>()/180.0f, glm::vec3(0.0f, 0.0f,
      1.0f));
  /* the inverse of rotational matrix is to counter-  rotate
    the graphics to the center. This allows us to reset the
      camera orientation since R*inv(R) = I. */
  view_matrix =
    rotMatrix*glm::inverse(old_rotMatrix)*view_matrix;

  //create the MVP (model view projection) matrix
  glm::mat4 mvp = projection_matrix * view_matrix *
    model_matrix;
  glUniformMatrix4fv(matrixHandle, 1, GL_FALSE,
    &mvp[0][0]);
```

```
    shader.checkGlError("glUniformMatrix4fv");
    glEnableVertexAttribArray(gvOverlayPositionHandle);
    shader.checkGlError("glEnableVertexAttribArray");
    glVertexAttribPointer(gvOverlayPositionHandle, 3,
      GL_FLOAT, GL_FALSE, 0, gGrid);
    shader.checkGlError("glVertexAttribPointer");
    glUniform1f(sigmaHandle, sigma);
    shader.checkGlError("glUniform1f");

    glUniform1f(scaleHandle, 1.0f);
    shader.checkGlError("glUniform1f");

    //draw the overlay graphics
    glDrawArrays(GL_POINTS, 0, grid_size*grid_size);
    shader.checkGlError("glDrawArrays");
    glDisableVertexAttribArray(gvOverlayPositionHandle);
  }
```

7. Finally, we only need to make minor modifications to the `main.cpp` file used in the previous demo to enable the AR overlay on top of the real-time video stream (real-world scene). Only the relevant code snippets that highlight the required modifications are shown here (download the complete code from the Packt Publishing website):

```
...
#include <AROverlayRenderer.hpp>
...
AROverlayRenderer aroverlayrenderer;
...
bool setupGraphics(int w, int h) {
  ...
  videorenderer.setup();
  aroverlayrenderer.setup();
  ...
  videorenderer.initTexture(frame);
  aroverlayrenderer.setScreenSize(width, height);
}

void renderFrame() {
  ...
  videorenderer.render(frame);
  aroverlayrenderer.render();
}
...
extern "C" {
  ...
```

```
    JNIEXPORT void JNICALL
      Java_com_android_gl3jni_GL3JNILib_setScale(JNIEnv *
        env, jobject obj,  jfloat jscale);
    JNIEXPORT void JNICALL
      Java_com_android_gl3jni_GL3JNILib_resetRotDataOffset(JNIEnv
        * env, jobject obj);
    JNIEXPORT void JNICALL
      Java_com_android_gl3jni_GL3JNILib_setRotMatrix (JNIEnv
        *env, jobject obj, jfloatArray ptr);
    JNIEXPORT void JNICALL
      Java_com_android_gl3jni_GL3JNILib_setDxDy(JNIEnv *env,
        jobject obj,  jfloat dx,  jfloat dy);
};
...
JNIEXPORT void JNICALL
  Java_com_android_gl3jni_GL3JNILib_resetRotDataOffset
    (JNIEnv * env, jobject obj){
  aroverlayrenderer.resetRotMatrix();
}
JNIEXPORT void JNICALL
  Java_com_android_gl3jni_GL3JNILib_setScale (JNIEnv * env,
    jobject obj, jfloat jscale)
{
  aroverlayrenderer.setScale(jscale);
  LOGI("Scale is %lf", scale);
}
JNIEXPORT void JNICALL
  Java_com_android_gl3jni_GL3JNILib_resetRotDataOffset
    (JNIEnv * env, jobject obj){
  aroverlayrenderer.resetRotMatrix();
}
JNIEXPORT void JNICALL
  Java_com_android_gl3jni_GL3JNILib_setRotMatrix
    (JNIEnv *env, jobject obj, jfloatArray ptr) {
  jsize len = env->GetArrayLength(ptr);
  jfloat *body = env->GetFloatArrayElements(ptr,0);
  //should be 16 elements from the rotation matrix
  glm::mat4 rotMatrix(1.0f);
  int count = 0;
  for(int i = 0; i<4; i++){
    for(int j=0; j<4; j++){
      rotMatrix[i][j] = body[count];
      count++;
    }
  }
  env->ReleaseFloatArrayElements(ptr, body, 0);
  aroverlayrenderer.setRotMatrix(rotMatrix);
}
```

```
JNIEXPORT void JNICALL
  Java_com_android_gl3jni_GL3JNILib_setDxDy(JNIEnv * env,
    jobject obj, jfloat dx, jfloat dy){
  aroverlayrenderer.setDxDy(dx, dy);
}
```

With this framework, one can overlay virtually any dataset on different real-world objects or surfaces and enable truly interactive applications, using the built-in sensors and gesture interface on mobile devices and emerging state-of-the-art wearable AR eyeglasses. Following are the results demonstrating a real-time, interactive, AR-based visualization of a 3-D dataset (in this case, a Gaussian distribution) overlaid on real-world scenes:

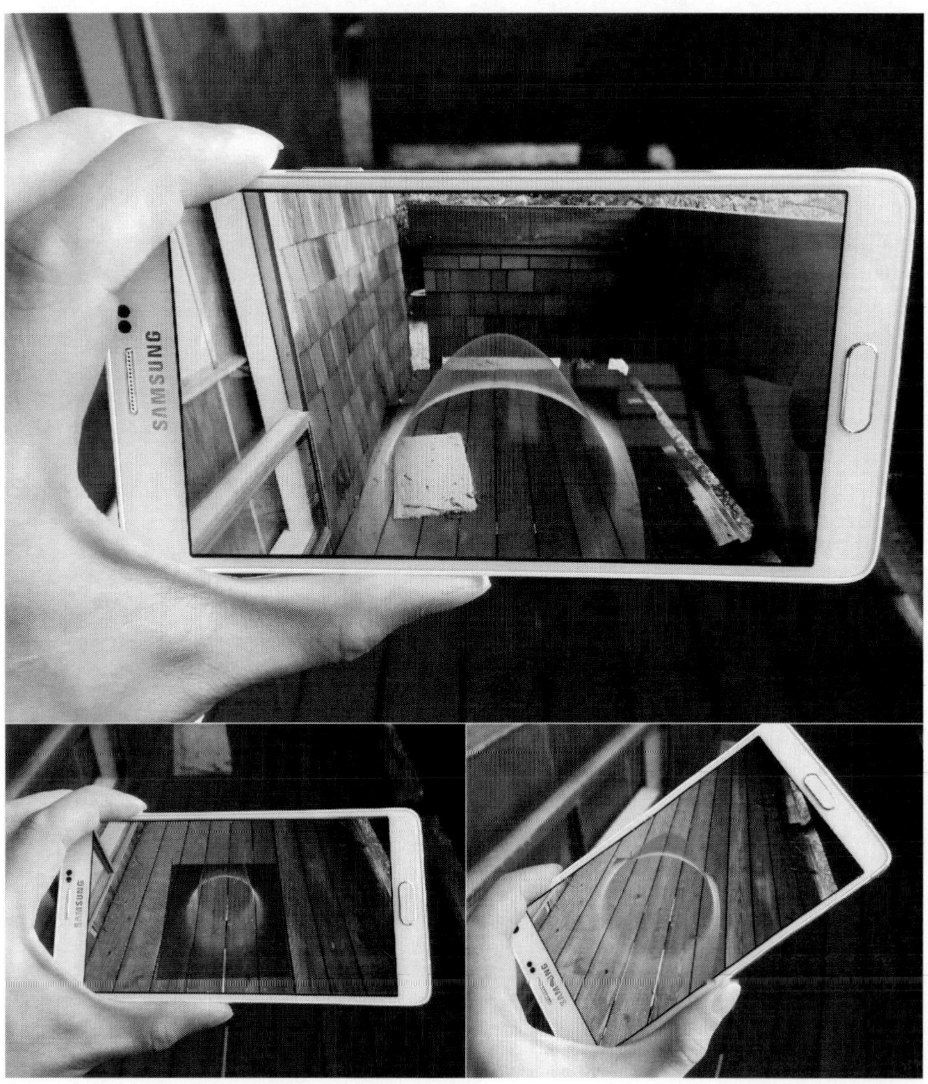

How it works...

The key element for enabling an AR application is the ability is overlay information onto the real world. The `AROverlayRenderer` class implements the core functions essential to all AR applications. First, we create a virtual camera that matches the parameters of the actual camera on the mobile phone. Parameters such as the **field of view** (**FOV**) and aspect ratio of the camera are currently hard-coded, but we can easily modify them in the `computeProjectionMatrices` function. Then, to perform the registration between the real world and virtual world, we control the orientation of the virtual camera based on the orientation of the device. The orientation values are fed through the rotation matrix passed from the Java side (the `setRotMatrix` function) and we apply this directly to the OpenGL camera view matrix (`view_matrix`). Also, we use the multi-touch interface of the mobile phone to reset the default orientation of the rotation matrix. This is achieved by storing the rotational matrix value upon the touch event (the `resetRotDataOffset` function) and we apply the inverse to the rotational matrix to the view matrix (this is equivalent to rotating the camera in the opposite direction).

In terms of user interaction, we have enabled the pinch and drag option to support dynamic interaction with the virtual object. Upon the pinch event, we take the scale factor and we position the rendered object at a farther distance by applying the `glm::translate` function on the `model_matrix` variable. In addition, we rotate the virtual object by capturing the dragging action from the Java side (the `setDxDy` function). The user can control the orientation of the virtual object by dragging a finger across the screen. Together, these multi-touch gestures enable a highly interactive application interface that allows users to change the perspective of the rendered object intuitively.

Due to the underlying complexity of the calibration process, we will not cover these details here. However, advanced users may consult the following website for a more in-depth discussion: `http://docs.opencv.org/doc/tutorials/calib3d/camera_calibration/camera_calibration.html`.

Also, the current registration process is purely based on the IMU, and it does not support translation (that is, the virtual object does not move exactly with the real world). To address this, we can apply various image-processing techniques such as mean shift tracking, feature-based tracking, and marker-based tracking to recover the full 6 DOF (degree of freedom) model of the camera. SLAM, for example, is a great candidate to recover the 6 DOF camera model, but its detailed implementation is beyond the scope of this chapter.

See also

Indeed, in this chapter, we have only covered the fundamentals of AR. The field of AR is becoming an increasingly hot topic in both academia and industry. If you are interested in implementing AR data visualization applications on the latest wearable computing platforms (such as the one provided by Meta that features 3D gesture input and 3D stereoscopic output), visit the following websites:

- `https://www.getameta.com/`
- `http://www.eyetap.org/publications/`

For further technical details on AR eyeglasses, please consult the following publications:

- Raymond Lo, Alexander Chen, Valmiki Rampersad, Jason Huang, Han Wu, Steve Mann (2013). "Augmediated reality system based on 3D camera selfgesture sensing," IEEE International Symposium on Technology and Society (ISTAS) 2013, pp. 20-31.
- Raymond Lo, Valmiki Rampersad, Jason Huang, Steve Mann (2013). "Three Dimensional High Dynamic Range Veillance for 3D Range-Sensing Cameras," IEEE International Symposium on Technology and Society (ISTAS) 2013, pp. 255-265.
- Raymond Chun Hing Lo, Steve Mann, Jason Huang, Valmiki Rampersad, and Tao Ai. 2012. "High Dynamic Range (HDR) Video Image Processing For Digital Glass." In Proceedings of the 20th ACM international conference on Multimedia (MM '12). ACM, New York, NY, USA, pp. 1477-1480.
- Steve Mann, Raymond Lo, Jason Huang, Valmiki Rampersad, Ryan Janzen, Tao Ai (2012). "HDRchitecture: Real-Time stereoscopic HDR Imaging for Extreme Dynamic Range," In ACM SIGGRAPH 2012 Emerging Technologies (SIGGRAPH '12).

Index

Symbols

A

B

C

D

E

F

G

I

J

L

M

O

Thank you for buying
OpenGL Data Visualization Cookbook

About Packt Publishing

Packt, pronounced 'packed', published its first book, *Mastering phpMyAdmin for Effective MySQL Management*, in April 2004, and subsequently continued to specialize in publishing highly focused books on specific technologies and solutions.

Our books and publications share the experiences of your fellow IT professionals in adapting and customizing today's systems, applications, and frameworks. Our solution-based books give you the knowledge and power to customize the software and technologies you're using to get the job done. Packt books are more specific and less general than the IT books you have seen in the past. Our unique business model allows us to bring you more focused information, giving you more of what you need to know, and less of what you don't.

Packt is a modern yet unique publishing company that focuses on producing quality, cutting-edge books for communities of developers, administrators, and newbies alike. For more information, please visit our website at `www.packtpub.com`.

About Packt Open Source

In 2010, Packt launched two new brands, Packt Open Source and Packt Enterprise, in order to continue its focus on specialization. This book is part of the Packt open source brand, home to books published on software built around open source licenses, and offering information to anybody from advanced developers to budding web designers. The Open Source brand also runs Packt's open source Royalty Scheme, by which Packt gives a royalty to each open source project about whose software a book is sold.

Writing for Packt

We welcome all inquiries from people who are interested in authoring. Book proposals should be sent to `author@packtpub.com`. If your book idea is still at an early stage and you would like to discuss it first before writing a formal book proposal, then please contact us; one of our commissioning editors will get in touch with you.

We're not just looking for published authors; if you have strong technical skills but no writing experience, our experienced editors can help you develop a writing career, or simply get some additional reward for your expertise.

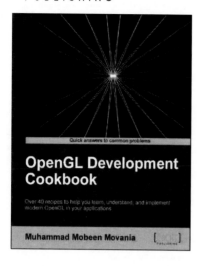

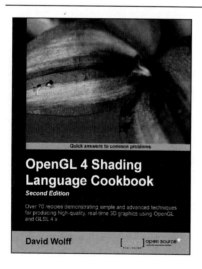

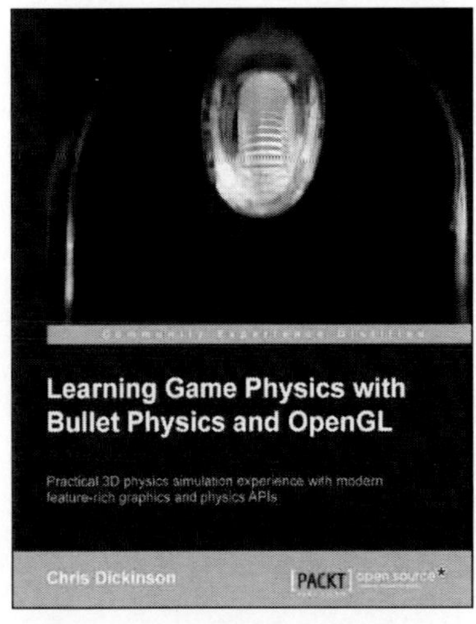

Learning Game Physics with Bullet Physics and OpenGL

ISBN: 978-1-78328-187-9 Paperback: 126 pages

Practical 3D physics simulation experience with modern feature-rich graphics and physics APIs

1. Create your own physics simulations and understand the various design concepts of modern games.
2. Build a real-time complete game application, implementing 3D graphics and physics entirely from scratch.
3. Learn the fundamental and advanced concepts of game programming using step-by-step instructions and examples.

MATLAB Graphics and Data Visualization Cookbook

ISBN: 978-1-84969-316-5 Paperback: 284 pages

Tell data stories with compelling graphics using this collection of data visualization recipes

1. Collection of data visualization recipes with functionalized versions of common tasks for easy integration into your data analysis workflow.
2. Recipes cross-referenced with MATLAB product pages and MATLAB Central File Exchange resources for improved coverage.
3. Includes hand created indices to find exactly what you need; such as application driven, or functionality driven solutions.

Please check **www.PacktPub.com** for information on our titles